INNER SPEECH AN
THE DIALOGICAL SELF

NORBERT WILEY

INNER SPEECH
AND THE DIALOGICAL SELF

TEMPLE UNIVERSITY PRESS
Philadelphia • *Rome* • *Tokyo*

TEMPLE UNIVERSITY PRESS
Philadelphia, Pennsylvania 19122
www.temple.edu/tempress

Copyright © 2016 by Temple University—Of The Commonwealth System
 of Higher Education
All rights reserved
Published 2016

Library of Congress Cataloging-in-Publication Data

Wiley, Norbert.
 Inner speech and the dialogical self : an unexplored continent /
Norbert Wiley.
   pages cm
 Includes bibliographical references and index.
  ISBN 978-1-4399-1327-7 (cloth : alk. paper) — ISBN 978-1-4399-1328-4
(pbk. : alk. paper) — ISBN 978-1-4399-1329-1 (e-book)   1. Self-talk.
2. Self.   3. Identity (Psychology)   I. Title.
  BF697.5.S47W55 2016
  155.2—dc23
                                                        2015022874

∞ The paper used in this publication meets the requirements of the
American National Standard for Information Sciences—Permanence of
Paper for Printed Library Materials, ANSI Z39.48-1992

Printed in the United States of America

9 8 7 6 5 4 3 2 1

To my student Mike Flaherty and my colleague Robert Perinbanayagam, both of whom helped me enormously in writing this book

CONTENTS

	Acknowledgments	ix
	Introduction	1
1	What Is Inner Speech? Structure and Functions	9
2	When Does Inner Speech Originate in the Child?	22
3	Is There a Self?	34
4	Identity	43
5	Inner Speech as a Language: Saussure and Chomsky	56
6	Inner Speech and Agency	75
7	Pragmatism and the Dialogical Self	91
8	The Pragmatist Theory of the Self	109
9	Bakhtin's Voices and Cooley's Looking-Glass Self	134
10	Inner Speech Theory	150
	Conclusion	175
	References	181
	Index	191

ACKNOWLEDGMENTS

For advising on the entire manuscript, I thank Margaret Archer, Hans Baker, Christine Chambers, Randall Collins, Robert Dunn, Michael Flaherty, Hubert Hermanns, Robert Perinbanayagam, Thomas Scheff, and Frederick Vandenberghe.

For advising on individual chapters, I thank Lonnie Athens, Derek Bickerton, Peter Carruthers, Ira J. Cohen, F.E.X. Dance, Tonya Kim Dewey, Caryl Emerson, Viktor Gecas, Eugene Halton, Linda Hecker, John Heil, James Hoopes, Glenn Jacobs, John R. Johnson, Marcel Kinsbourne, Rodney J. Korba, Alain Morin, Claude Panaccio, Anne Warfield Rawls, Dmitri Shalin, Leonard J. Shedletsky, and James Wertsch.

Thanks go to Ginny Horning for taking the author photo.

INNER SPEECH AND
THE DIALOGICAL SELF

INTRODUCTION

This book is a comprehensive treatment of inner speech—also called self-talk, internal conversation, and inner dialogue. By "comprehensive" I mean I try to cover all the important facets of this topic, providing an overview. In a few cases I go more deeply into a topic, hoping to add to it.

My approach is as a humanistic social theorist, leaning toward the classical pragmatism of Charles Sanders Peirce, John Dewey, William James, and George Herbert Mead. This means emphasizing the semiotic and dialogical features of the topic while skipping over many of the biological and neurological issues. In addition, I emphasize theory over empirical research. There are actually few empirical studies of inner speech, particularly within sociology, but there is a scattering of such studies in several fields. In other words, this field, at present, has only moderate visibility, but these publications and their visibility is increasing.

Given these limits, I try to hit all the important aspects of this topic. Inner speech is considerably more central to human life than is widely understood. As Oliver Sacks puts it:

> "We are our language," it is often said; but our real language, our real identity, lies in inner speech, in that ceaseless stream and generation of meaning that constitutes the individual mind. It is through inner speech that the child develops his own concepts and meanings; it is through inner speech that he achieves his own identity; it is through inner speech, finally, that he constructs his own world. (1989, 59)

The centrality Sacks attributes to inner speech is difficult to see because by its nature this form of speech has low visibility. It is silent; we are not always paying attention to it, particularly if it is a passive daydream; and we are usually busy doing something, such as driving a car, cooking, or talking to someone.

This inattention is probably due to its low visibility in our consciousness. However, its prevalence is much greater than people realize. As Noam Chomsky says:

> Language is not properly regarded as a system of communication. It is a system for expressing thought, something quite different. . . . [L]anguage use is largely to oneself: "inner speech" for adults, monologue for children. (2002, 76–77)

And in another place, he says:

> Now let us take language. What is its characteristic use? Well, probably 99.9% of its use is internal to the mind. You can't go a minute without talking to yourself. It takes an incredible act of will not to talk to yourself. (2012, 11)

This introduction positions the topic in its major contexts: intellectual history, the major academic disciplines, and other human faculties and capabilities that are affected by or make use of inner speech.

Introduction: The Nature of Inner Speech

Inner speech, as stated, is difficult to observe, since we cannot see it in other people. We get direct contact with it only in ourselves, and even here it usually goes on in the inner reaches of our consciousness. It is like dreams in that it is difficult to see and hard to explain. But dreams are passive experiences that happen *to* us, whereas inner speech is an active process, often quite deliberately used *by* us and aimed at important goals.

We do encounter some inner speech in novels and films, although these texts cannot be completely faithful to their topic. If they were structured exactly as we experience inner speech, the audience would be unable to understand them, as with some of James Joyce's extreme examples. L. S. Vygotsky points out that inner speech, if viewed as we actually experience it, is a private language that only the speaker can understand (1987b, 204, 278). Fiction writers have to find a balance between imitating inner speech, on the one hand, and making it understandable, on the other. People who reveal examples of their own inner speech also have to strike this balance.

Some Examples of Inner Speech

The following examples are somewhat long, but the best way to discuss inner speech is to have some texts in front of you. In the first example, a waitress reports on her thoughts going to work. Her inner speech is presented linguistically along with brief sketches of her imagery.

> "*Only eight minutes, takes five to change. I've got to book* [hurry]." Imagery: A disgustingly filthy locker room. Visions of me running from table to kitchen table. Sounds. Forks and knives scraping plates, customers yelling over each other. "*I have to make money. At least it's not as bad as last summer.*" Memory imagery: A tiny dumpy diner. Visions of me sweating. Sensations of being hot. Visions of thirty marines eating and drinking. Sounds: country music on a blaring juke box. "*I'll be right there, just a minute please.*" Sensations of burning my arm in a pizza oven. Visions of dropping glasses. Sounds: Glass breaking, manager yelling, marines cheering. "*Oh God, get me out of here.*" Sensation: Cringe, humiliation. "*I hate waitressing. Can't wait to graduate and get a decent job.*" Visions of a paneled, brightly carpeted office with scenic pictures and healthy plants. Visions of me fifteen pounds thinner in a new skirt suit from Lord and Taylor. A great-looking coworker is pouring us coffee. Sounds of a clock chiming five o'clock. "*Sure I'd love to go out Friday night.*" (Caughey 1984, 135; italics added)

A second example is of a girl, a little under two years old, overheard when she was in her bedroom. The researcher sees this as an example of imaginative play. This text is what is called private speech, but it has the same qualities as inner speech.

> Go Grandma and buy a pretty doll Grandma for me under the bed for me to play the piano . . . get up cling, cling-ling-ling. Grandma comes up the steps. Oh, oh, ah, ah, ah, lying on the floor tied up no cap on Theodosia (the doll) lie on the bed, bring yellow sheep to Theodosia, run tap, tap, tap, for Lena. Strawberries, Grandma, wolf lie on bed. Go to sleep darling Theodosia you are my dearest; everybody is fast asleep. . . . A cat came in here, Momma caught it, it had feet and black boots on—short cap, band on it. Poppa ran, the sky—Grandma gone—Grandpa resting. (Singer 1966, 134)

A third example is from the thoughts of the social theorist Randall Collins:

> Music is going through my head, an aria from Don Giovanni, which I had seen the previous weekend with my wife. "*What scene is that*

from?" Vague images of different scenes in the opera. I notice a woman, of professional age and dress, ahead of me amidst the crowd of students on the walkway. "*Is that the egregious Elizabeth Dougherty?*" On closer approach, it is not the woman professor I am thinking of. "*Damn economists.*" Vague imagery of economist on a university committee. "*Economists have bad values.*" Feeling pleased with myself for the lapidary formulation. (2004b, 201)

Another example is that of John Johnson, who is illustrating the condensed quality of inner speech. His is a to-do list with only three items: "car, dinner, kids." He explains the meaning of this string of words as follows: "Make sure to fill up the car's gas tank, stop by the store and pick up a gallon of 2% milk and a loaf of whole wheat bread, and be certain to pick up John and Kate from daycare before coming home" (1994, 177).

And a final example:

Sometimes the things you do with inner speech are so natural, habitual, and even kind of silly that it never occurs to you to share them with anyone else. One thing that comes to mind is using code words. One of mine is "Windsorize." Years ago I worked with several dozen doctors in Kaiser ER/Minor Injury Clinic. The fastest ones didn't always give the best care, but we liked them because they kept the patient flow moving right along. This meant far less nagging from patients who were sick of the long wait to be seen.

A super fast one was Dr. Windsor. I suspect he cut corners, but he had a way of just zeroing in and getting the job done with a high degree of efficiency. So "Windsorize" is now a routine expression in my inner speech. (Katie Wiley, e-mail, February 12, 2015)

Katie Wiley's example shows how condensed inner speech can become, into a single word in this case. This condensation is figurative, to be sure, but it does not seem to usually involve metaphor. Instead, metonymy, or the part for the whole, seems to be the main figurative device.

These examples show how inner speech violates the linguistic rules of ordinary language. Sentences are fragmentary, semantics is irregular, and nonlinguistic images abound. The waitress shows how inner speech can be full of imagery. Jerome Singer's childhood example shows how both vocabulary and grammar can be irregular and fluid. Collins shows how inner speech can veer from one theme to the next, including imagery. Johnson shows how inner speech can be squeezed into a small number of words. And Katie Wiley's code word shows how inner speech can gather a complex and wide-ranging meaning into a single word.

Historically, inner speech has been identified and named at least since Plato. He saw it as the medium of thought (1961, 189e, 190a, 263e), and he envisioned it as going on in ordinary language. For a long time after Plato, philosophers viewed inner speech in a more abstract manner. Augustine turned attention from inner speech in ordinary language to what he called mental language (Augustine [417] 2002, 34). This, for him, was the abstract language of pure thought. It did not entail words, at least not in any ordinary sense. For Augustine the thinking process used pure concepts or abstractions, even though they might be organized like sentences.

His mental language has a resemblance to the mentalese of contemporary cognitive science, identified especially with Jerry Fodor (1975). Fodor's medium, as he sees it, is an inborn or unlearned and unconscious stream of thought. Mentalese is like the Scholastics' mental language in being abstract, quasi-linguistic, and inborn, but it differs in being completely unconscious. The Scholastics' mental language was sometimes conscious and sometimes unconscious. Fodor (and also Noam Chomsky) thinks you need a preexisting language to learn a language—a point subject to scholarly debate. I am in the group that thinks children learn a language pretty much from scratch, without an inborn preexisting language. But that is a point that comes up later. Now I just identify inner speech and contrast it with closely related ideas about language.

Inner speech in my sense, then, is different both from Scholasticism's mental language and cognitive science's mentalese. It is in ordinary language rather than pure abstractions, and it is not unconscious or inborn. We speak it silently to ourselves, and we can observe ourselves doing this. Inner speech is also unlike ordinary, external language in that it has an abbreviated syntax and a self-styled semantics. These structural features are looked at more closely in Chapter 1. These qualities were noticed and explained by Vygotsky in fascinating detail (1987a). Vygotsky is discussed in Chapters 1 and 10.

Inner speech also is often chaotic in the sense that one theme (e.g., "What shall I make for dinner?") will appear, then it will be interrupted by a different theme (e.g., "What shall I wear when we go out tonight?"), and then, surprisingly, our first teenage kiss will appear as still another theme. At times we have to ride this shifting stream of consciousness like a wild horse, forcing ourselves back to whatever our main concern was. This clashing assortment of themes can be compared to a musical score (an idea suggested to me by Michael Nguyen).

Up to now I have given a rough idea of inner speech, showing the sort of thing we designate by this term. The distinctions I have made so far also give us four different media: inner speech, interpersonal speech, mental language, and mentalese. There is also a fifth linguistic medium, private speech, which is the thinking-out-loud that children do from around ages two to seven.

These are vocalizations, but they are aimed at oneself. At one time, private speech was thought by some scholars to be itself inner speech, but that usage has been abandoned. On the one hand, private speech is now considered a distinct form of discourse. On the other hand, private speech does have a lot in common with inner speech.

The study of the Scholastics' mental language deflected attention from inner speech for many centuries. Occam (1287–1347) had what was perhaps the most developed theory of mental language. But Occam's epistemology, his nominalism, was controversial, so most of the Scholastics opposed his views. In addition, soon after he lived, modern philosophy, with René Descartes and Thomas Hobbes, drew attention away from Scholasticism and mental language (Normore 2009).

Inner speech as such was not rediscovered until Charles Sanders Peirce began writing about it in the mid-nineteenth century. It is striking that such a powerful feature of human psychology could be ignored for so long. It *was* used in literature—for example, in Shakespeare's soliloquies—but it was ignored by scholars. In addition to Peirce, the other pragmatists also wrote about this topic, partly under his influence. Peirce's comments are mostly in his unpublished papers, and he did not do much analysis of this phenomenon even there.

Peirce's main interest is in looking at inner speech as a means of choice and self-control. We can regulate ourselves, he argues, by analyzing our personal problems, particularly bad habits, in our minds and using inner speech to map out and practice solutions. The actions that we take to cope are first taken in our minds. In that way inner speech guides our lives as we move from problem to problem and toward our overarching goals. This is typical Peirce, introducing a powerful if somewhat undeveloped idea that has just lain there, for many decades, in his unpublished papers.

Although Peirce rediscovered inner speech over 150 years ago, his views were not organized and made available until recently when Vincent Colapietro (1989), who mined Peirce's neglected unpublished papers, wrote his pathbreaking book, *Peirce's Approach to the Self*. Colapietro's research gave a push to the study of inner speech, especially in the social sciences. Colapietro's new material on Peirce helped me construct a systematic model of inner speech based on the combination of Mead's views and those of Peirce (Wiley 1994, 18–39). Subsequently, Margaret Archer wrote three influential books on inner speech, using the same pragmatist sources (Archer 2003, 2007, 2012).

The importance of Peirce for this book is not only in his rediscovery of inner speech; he thought the defining feature of human nature was inner speech. Humans, he says, are signs, words, or language (1934, para. 313). This language is largely in what we say to ourselves as we think our way through and regulate our lives. He argues that inner speech is a core feature of human nature.

Russian theorist Mikhail Bakhtin takes a similar position. Bakhtin's term is "dialogue," and he speaks about both interpersonal and intrapersonal dialogue. For him these two forms of dialogue tend to merge into each other, as they tend to do in real life. As Bakhtin puts it:

> The dialogic nature of consciousness [is] the dialogical nature of human life itself. The single adequate form for *verbally expressing* authentic human life is the *open-ended dialogue*. Life by its very nature is dialogic. To live means to participate in dialogue: to ask questions, to heed, to respond, to agree, and so forth. In this dialogue a person participates wholly and throughout his whole life: with his eyes, lips, hands, soul, spirit, with his whole body and deeds. He invests his entire self in discourse, and the discourse enters into the dialogic fabric of human life, into the world symposium. (1984, 293)

In another place he clarifies the two forms of dialogue:

> This external dialogue, expressed compositionally in the text, is inseparably connected with internal dialogue, that is, with micro-dialogue, and to a considerable extent depends on it. (1984, 265)

The idea that humans can be defined as language and internal dialogue has had important political implications in American thought. The notion that all human beings are equal, both morally and legally, has gradually become central to the American belief system. This did not happen without plenty of struggle, largely from the minority population. I show later how Peirce's definition of humans as linguistic, in particular his omitting the body from this definition, led to the idea that humans are fundamentally selves (and the psychological attributes that go along with selves). This definition contradicted racism and led to political egalitarianism.

Another introductory attribute of inner speech is its relation to the stream of consciousness. Consciousness is a disputed philosophical issue since its features grate against the dominant materialist view in contemporary philosophy. To explain consciousness you need a property dualism. This position holds that, although body and mind are both part of the same overall substance, the mind has different properties than the body. These properties allow for qualitative consciousness, experienced from the subjective, or first person, point of view.

Consciousness itself, both in its first person perspective and in its qualitative features, does not admit of explanation by purely material processes. So consciousness is generally set aside as an unsolved problem for materialism, the so-called hard problem, although some philosophers actually claim consciousness is a delusion and has no relevance to the way human life proceeds (Churchland 1981). Life itself, so it is claimed, proceeds on one, presumably unconscious, track; and consciousness, despite its claim to being a window into reality, is merely a dream or delusion. This version of materialism is the opposite of my view.

The experience of consciousness is widely admitted to have the stream-like quality that William James attributes to it (1950a, 224–290). This is a metaphor, but it is so persuasive that it is generally accepted as the way we experience reality. Within this stream, however, are several organizing principles. A major principle is time, which is a measure of the stream's passage. The stream passes down a riverbed constituted not primarily by space but by time.

Another organizing principle is inner speech, which gives consciousness a discursive, as opposed to a purely flowing, quality. This discursiveness enhances the precision of consciousness. Inner speech also gives coherence to the way we experience the flow. More importantly, inner speech gives thought and meaning to our stream. Instead of consciousness being merely something that happens to us, inner speech gives us an interior control such that we can give enhanced cognition and direction to consciousness. Within the relatively passive and uncontrolled stream, we impose inner speech. This linguistic process gives us something of a boat within the stream and allows us to navigate these waters. Or as Peirce says, "Life is a train of thought" (1934, para. 314). Along with attention itself, then, inner speech is a process by which we can control consciousness. It gives significance and narrativity to consciousness.

To put this another way, inner speech *interprets* the stream of consciousness, much as Boris Eikhenbaum, the Russian literary theorist, claims inner speech interprets silent movies ([1927] 1974). One's everyday flow of reality, like a silent film, may require some sense making. Sometimes the interpretation is routine and effortless, but when there are puzzles or "jumps," the interpretation may require thought work and insight. As Eikhenbaum puts it, "Internal speech . . . makes the connection between separate shots. . . . Film viewing is accompanied by a continual process of inner speech" ([1927] 1974, 14). And "each scene is presented to the viewer in pieces, segments. There is much that the viewer does not see at all; the intervals between segments are filled up by internal speech" (27). Life, then, is something of a silent movie, and inner speech makes it hang together.

A final comparison is between inner speech and the language of lovers, pillow talk. Two lovers often communicate effortlessly and in fragmentary form. The syntax may be abbreviated, the vocabulary may be condensed, and there may be lots of in-jokes and intimate slang, including gurgles and eye messages. Lover talk is a lot like inner speech, because it is so stylized and compressed into a small space. A little means a lot.

1

WHAT IS INNER SPEECH?

Structure and Functions

The Structural Features of Inner Speech

Perhaps the major structural quality of inner speech is that it is inherently dialogical, a term that can mean at least three things in linguistics.

It can designate a form of speaking that is flexible, open, and welcoming to questions. This usage is from Mikhail Bakhtin (1984, 253). The opposite form of language is called monological. For Bakhtin this is a closed variety of speech, carefully boundaried and unwelcoming to questions. A professor's standardized lecture is often of this nature. In contrast, the great teachers use a dialogical style, which enlivens the minds of students and makes them think.

The second meaning is simply that there is both a speaker and a listener, both of whom are independent human beings. It is interactive or conversational.

The third meaning is the one that characterizes inner speech. This mode of speaking is inherently and invariably conversational. It is the self speaking to another aspect of itself. George Herbert Mead calls this the conversation between the I and the me (the past self). Charles Sanders Peirce calls it the conversation between the I and the you (the future self). The synthesis of these two views is a triadic formation in which the I talks to the you about the me.

These three modes of inner speech can be diagrammed as shown in Figure 1.1. The I-you-me synthesis seems the most useful to me, so I work with this version, though both Mead's and Peirce's formulations bring out important aspects of internal conversation. My synthesis, then, combines Peirce and Mead.

Mead: I ↔ Me (past self)
Peirce: I ↔ You (future self)
Synthesis: I ↔ You
            ↓
            Me

Figure 1.1 *Three versions of the dialogical self*

Does Inner Speech Have a Circular Structure?

At least two thinkers, Edmund Husserl ([1913] 1982) and Chris Fields (2002), have questioned the validity of inner speech by suggesting it is circular and thereby redundant. In their opinion we already know what we say to ourselves, since the same person is at both ends of the conversation. So why say it?

For example, I might say to myself, "I think I need some exercise, but I'll swim in the pool rather than take a walk." To be able to say this to myself, don't I already have to know it? And if so, what is the point of saying it? It is like saying a thing twice: "Hello, Hello" or "A cup of coffee please. A cup of coffee please."

Husserl's discussion of inner speech seems to regard it as pointless. As he says:

> One of course speaks, in a certain sense, even in soliloquy, and it is certainly possible to think of oneself as speaking, and even as speaking to oneself, as, e.g., when someone says to himself: "You have gone wrong, you can't go on like that." But in the genuine sense of communication, there is no speech in such cases, nor does one tell oneself anything: One merely conceives of oneself as speaking and communicating. In a monologue words can perform no function of indicting the existence of mental acts, since such indication would there be purposeless. For the acts in question are themselves experienced by us at that very moment. ([1913] 1982, 279–280)

Husserl is not entirely clear here, but he does speak of soliloquy as "purposeless," and his last sentence suggests we already know what we are saying to ourselves.

Chris Fields, who is a cognitive scientist, is clearer in his evaluation of inner speech. As he puts it:

> When stripped of its everyday familiarity, the virtually constant inner dialogue experienced by virtually everyone presents a mystery: why do we use language to communicate to ourselves. When examined from a design perspective in light of currently plausible cognitive

neuroscience, language seems highly non-optimal as an internal communication medium. Other than its role in maintaining the privacy of thought, proposed functions for self-dialogue raise more questions than they answer. Therefore, it is appropriate to question the role played by the familiarity of self-dialogue in shaping our intuitions about consciousness. (2002, 255)

These writers are working with a view of the self that is oversimplified. The self is full of dark corners, nooks, and crannies, and it is anything but transparent to itself. There are several terminologies that suggest the obscurities within the self: consciousness versus unconsciousness, honesty versus self-deceit, backstage versus front stage, and id versus ego versus superego, to mention a few. The self is like those complicated buildings, such as old hospitals, that have had a variety of additions and modifications over the years. You need a map to get around in these monstrosities. The self also has parts that are rarely visited and more or less forgotten. The memory, for example, houses long-term storage units, often rarely accessed, if ever. The self is also a bit like a bewildering hall of mirrors since we can look both outward and inward, even doing both at the same time. At the movies, for example, we are watching the movie, but also, in a more inward way, we may be talking to ourselves about the movie.

More specifically, there are several advantages to be obtained from internal dialogue, and these explain why we do it. For one, internal discussion can clarify our thoughts. It is one thing to have a vague idea, such as what you will do if you break up your marriage (or other romantic relationship). But it is quite another to try out different scenarios and make detailed plans. We leave many life issues deliberately vague because it is too soon to get specific, and detailed plans would clog our minds. Inner speech often explains to us what we can do and should do. It is like a flashlight guiding our way through the semidarkness of life.

It is also often true that we already know something, but this knowledge is in the form of nonverbal thought, not articulate language. Nonverbal thoughts are usually less precise than linguistic thoughts, so to go from imprecision to precision we need to talk to ourselves. We talk ourselves through a problem.

Self-talk can also function as rehearsal, the kind that will make the later, actual performance better. Athletes and artists sometimes practice in their heads. Any complex sequence of acts is more under our control if we imagine ourselves slowly and carefully doing it before we set out to actually perform the actions.

We can also do a variety of self-regulating mental experiments by way of self-talk. The experts on attention deficit disorder with hyperactivity (ADDH) say that children with ADDH often lack the capacity to foresee dire consequences (Barkley 1997, 279). These children have a weak inner speech capacity, and because of that they often use trial and error in the real world instead of trial and error in the mental world of inner dialogue. Will stealing something be worth doing? Not if the evidence will immediately point to you, the only person who was in a position to steal the object. A moment's thought (or internal dialogue) will disclose this fact. But if you are unable to speak inwardly, you may find this out the hard way. Kids with ADDH suffer a lot because of this inability.

Another purpose of inner speech is inner ritual, the attainment of confidence, will power, and the achievement of internal solidarity. Husserl ([1913] 1982) and Fields (2002) think of inner speech in too cognitive a manner. This process is also emotional, and it is important for regulating our emotions. If what we need is self-confidence, we cannot say, "We already know this, so why dialogue it?" The dialogue, which in this case is a "performative" (Austin 1970), itself produces the confidence, much as "The Battle Hymn of the Republic" enlivened antislavery sentiment in nineteenth-century America or the New Left protest songs empowered dissent in the 1960s. Inner speech rituals enhance the—poorly understood, at present—religious or sacred aspects of the self and how these aspects do their work.

The self also has several parts, aspects, or windows, each somewhat different. David Hume (1978) refers to the self as a community. The ideas of Peirce and Mead produced the I-you-me triadic self. These distinct subselves can dialogue with each other, often with quite innovative results. These mini-selves do not fully know each other, despite what Husserl and Fields suggest, and when they engage in internal conversation, the results can be illuminating. When Socrates engaged in dialogue with his pupils, they often discovered new truths. Similarly, when the community of the self conducts internal dialogue, the results can be insightful.

The other structural features of inner speech mainly concern semantics and syntax and how they are minimized or condensed. Vygotsky discovered and explained these qualities, so this discussion will draw largely on him (1987b, 243–285). At this point, though, it should be noted that the highly condensed linguistic structure is largely caused by dialogicality. The dialogical feature brings about and requires the slender linguistics—the syntax and semantics—of these locutions. In this sense the structural features hang together and are of a piece.

If you were somehow attached to another person, as Robinson Crusoe living on a desert island was to Friday, there are only the two of you, so you do not have to identify yourself when you speak to him. He already knows it's you. It's the same way with the "I" and "you." That "other" knows it is you doing the speaking. Therefore, you can get by with a minimum of words, even skipping the ones the other already knows you might say. If you say to yourself, "Stop," there is an implicit subject ("I" must stop). There is also an implicit object of the verb (e.g., to stop smoking, drinking, bragging, or some other bad habit).

Having shown how dialogicality is a key structural feature of inner speech, let me go on to discuss the syntactical and semantic structural features in more detail. Syntactically, this form of speech, as noted, is often simplified and abbreviated. This practice is like the use of condensed language in a telegram (or an e-mail or an electronic text.) In the telegram, omitting the subject and sometimes other parts of speech saves money. With inner speech it saves time and effort. It also focuses the communication on the essentials.

For Vygotsky the syntax of inner speech is, in his words, "predicated" (1987b, 267). By this he does not mean the predicate of a sentence in the usual sense. He means the thought that answers a question and supplies only the needed information. If the question concerns a time of departure, the predicate might be "eight o'clock." That would be the whole sentence. If one said to oneself, "The best time to leave would be eight o'clock," the first seven words would be unnecessary.

If the question were "Why are we selling the house?" you might merely say, "Money," rather than "We are selling it to get the money (or because we need money)." A predicated utterance, then, might omit the subject and possibly also the verb, not to mention possible modifiers. Inner speech's syntax is stingy, and it does not, for example, follow the formal syntax of Chomsky's model. Inner speech, given its abbreviated form, almost looks like pidgin or Creole, but it is always possible to unfold and expand the sentence into grammatically formal language, should this be necessary. Still, people do not actually do this with inner speech, except when rehearsing a formal statement, such as asking the boss for a raise or one's girlfriend for her hand in marriage.

Condensation and abbreviation are found throughout the examples in the Introduction. The waitress begins by saying, "Only eight minutes. Takes five to change." Without abbreviation this sentence would read, "I have only eight minutes, and it takes five to change clothing." But the strength of the waitress's example is the way she shows the interpenetration of ordinary language and imagery. Her semantics is more imagistic than verbal.

Singer's childhood monologue shows a little girl imagining getting a new doll from her grandma. She is picturing how the toy will bring new life to her bedroom. Her syntax and semantics bend to her imaginative creativity.

Johnson's example is a case of a three-word utterance, tightly condensed and requiring forty-two words to unfold. Collins's example shows how his mind moves in a labile way from topic to topic and from imagery to language, and Katie Wiley's example shows how we can telescope large swatches of meaning into a single word, referred to by her as code words.

Turning to semantics, inner speech has unique ways of handling meaning, again well described by Vygotsky. He has a complex explanation of inner speech's semantics, usefully summarized by Johnson (1994). He sees two broad features in Vygotsky's explanation: semantic embeddedness and egocentricity.

Semantic embeddedness means a word can have a bigger variety of meanings than it has in ordinary, interpersonal speech. It is embedded in a wide range of meanings. Ordinarily, "dinner" simply means the evening meal. But in inner speech it can have overtones and specifications, such as a particular item for an entrée, a special guest, a celebration, this or that restaurant, who's cooking, whether it will be early or late, who's on a diet, and so on. Embeddedness means the vocabulary uses the principle of "a little can go a long way." With a small but highly flexible and stretchable collection of words, to mention another structural feature, we can say (to ourselves) almost anything we want. One's inner speech vocabulary is much smaller than one's outer speech vocabulary. This means the semantics of inner speech is different from the semantics of outer or interpersonal speech.

George Herbert Mead refers to inner speech's small vocabulary as follows:

> The mechanism that we use for this process is words, vocal gestures. And we need, of course, only a very few of these as compared to those we need when talking to others. A single symbol is enough to call out necessary responses. But it is just as real a conversation in terms of significant symbols of language as if the whole process were expressed. We sometimes do our thinking out loud, in fully organized sentences; and one's thought can always presumably be developed into a complete grammatical unit. This is what constitutes thinking. (1936, 381)

The egocentricity of inner speech's vocabulary, to turn to Johnson's (1994) second point, refers to the way words can be individualized and hooked to the speaker. The meaning has the speaker's self or ego at the center and is thus egocentric. As an example, I once knew a guy named Tom, and he had the most engaging, trust-inspiring smile. All he had to do was flash that smile, and I would believe anything he said. The smile was so powerful I had to be betrayed a half dozen times before I got the point. Then I realized the smile, sucker as I was for it, was a big lie and his major weapon for getting what he wanted. Now in my mental wanderings I sometimes hear myself saying, "He's another Tom," or simply the condensed and highly egocentric "Tom!"

A peculiarity of inner speech semantics that Vygotsky does not mention is that imagery can function linguistically and syntactically in inner speech.

It is well known that some people sometimes think not in words but in such media as sounds, numbers, visuals, colors, tastes and odors, tactile feelings, kinesthetics, and emotions. The waitress's text from the example in the Introduction is full of imagistic thinking.

These images can be placed into syntactical slots, such as subjects and objects, and function as though they were words (Bickerton 1995, 106). For example, I can say to myself, "I'd like a burger" by adding the visual image of a hamburger to the words "I'd like a." Or I could drop the subject and the article, just saying the word "like" and then adding the image of the burger. I could even drop "like" and just produce the feeling of wanting a burger. This would create the single-element sentence of "wannaburger," which combines the hunger impulse with a sizzling hamburger.

A moment's thought shows that there are an indefinite number of ways we can form inner speech utterances that combine imagery and words—or even work solely with imagery. When we do this in our minds, the discourse is often so complex, fast, noncognitive (so to speak), and semi-unconscious that it is difficult to catch. Still, this is how the human animal seems to work and it means that inner speech is, in some ways, more complicated than outer speech.

There is also a phonetic peculiarity to inner speech, to mention another structural quality. Obviously, imagery is nonverbal and therefore has no phonetic presence. This gives inner speech a phonetic contrast to outer speech. In addition, Vygotsky points out that we often "think" the words rather than pronouncing them in our minds. "We never have the need to pronounce the word fully in inner speech" (1987b, 275). This imagining instead of pronouncing the word is another phonetic idiosyncrasy of inner speech.

A Possible Objection

Interpersonal or outer speech is full of errors. The linguist abstracts from the errors and just uses the pure rules, as in Chomsky's competence. Aren't my examples of irregularities in inner speech also just errors? I think it makes more sense to call them linguistic innovations. Inner speech can be regarded as a language of its own. These innovations are a second set of rules, superimposed on the ordinary rules of outer language. Vygotsky's predication, for example, which results in an abbreviated syntax, is a linguistic rule.

When you have two sets of rules, one stacked on top of the other, it is difficult to identify nonconformity or error. You need a third set of rules or agreements that sort out the conflicts between the two existing sets. Since the two sets of rules contradict each other to some extent, it would be arbitrary to say which form of rule violation is an error. This would make it impossible to just abstract from the errors, however we define errors, and conclude that Chomsky's rules prevail.

While it is true that ordinary speech works within a network of rules, inner speech works within a more complicated set of controls. These controls might better be called a "field" (Fligstein and McAdam 2012) than a set of rules.

The most pressing control is what can merely be called efficiency. Inner speech works without an audience, except for the person doing the internal talking. This lack of audience weakens the interpersonal linguistic rules. The special rules, identified by Vygotsky, that operate to steer our inner speech, are all of an efficiency nature. So, this field has two sets of linguistic rules, the most distinctive and pressing being those that we form to speed up and economize in the inner theater.

In addition, there are at least two more controls in the inner speech field. One is our emotions. Inner speech is much more emotional than outer speech. In fact, when we rehearse outer speech by first saying something internally, we usually tone down and repress our emotions. But when we just speak to ourselves without any outer speech, our emotions run rampant. This theater is private, and no one but ourselves will witness our feelings.

Still another set of controls over inner speech is the unconscious, using this term for the classical emotional unconscious rather than the recently popularized cognitive unconscious (Hassin, Uleman, and Bargh 2005). The unconscious may have its own language, or at least it might code its feelings and meanings in linguistic media. Inner speech is often close to the unconscious, which makes it saturated with the emotions of the unconscious.

One clue to the language of the unconscious is sleep talk—that is, what people say to themselves as they sleep. Most people never hear sleep talk except from their spouse, their lover, or someone in their family, although a military barracks in the middle of the night is alive with sleep talk. Sleep researchers say that sleep talk is usually quite fragmentary, often limited to a single word, and frequently too mumbled to understand. The example I use is from a sleep laboratory, recorded while an experimental subject, a college English major, was sleeping. The experimenter whispered the subject's name ("David") into his ear, and, in his sleep, the subject uttered these words:

> David—I day David that you—that's you that day—dated—day—dravid—dave dravid about 25 or 30 noked naked day dreams—the second dream tie it all up—you kept bouncing them on—you kept bouncing them on and on as if you had a regular meter. (Arkin 1981, 413)

This text seems to follow no linguistic rules, neither interpersonal nor intrapersonal, although it does suggest Jacques Lacan's language of the unconscious. As we lie in bed approaching sleep, we can sometimes notice ourselves engaging in a highly innovative and uncontrolled kind of language. This inner speech is presumably influenced by the unconscious. And when completely unconscious, we may speak in the enigmatic manner of David's utterances.

Functions of Inner Speech

A defining feature of inner speech, in addition to its structure, is how we use it, what it does for us, what functions it performs. These are touched on in the discussion of Husserl and Fields, but now I look at three of them in more detail, including how we think and arrive at explanations, how we plan and regulate our lives, and how we pass the time in daydreaming. Three other important functions of inner speech, which I merely list and do not stop to discuss, are how we engage in creativity, how we use social intelligence, and how we use inner speech in memory searches. We also do more modest and mundane things with inner speech, such as making to-do lists, practicing our skills, and reviewing our recent activities to see what we did wrong. The functions of inner speech are almost like having another arm or leg. These functions assist us with almost any mental task we might choose to do.

Ordinary Thinking

The thinking process in which inner speech is most evident is seen in one of Abraham Kaplan's ideas (1964, 3–11). He makes the distinction between the way we use logic or reason in our lives and how logic professors describe the way we reason. The first he calls "logic in use," and the second he calls "reconstructed logic." Logic in use has an untidy character because it includes the details of our practical problems, such as who to invite to a party, what job offer to accept, or what outfit to buy. This logic operates in a loose manner, skipping steps and reaching conclusions as efficiently and rapidly as possible. Reconstructed logic has a formal, smoothed-over quality. It describes only the flow of reason itself, not the more practical, problem-solving work we do with reason.

Logic in use is usually guided by inner speech. The bedroom light won't work, so I say to myself, "Is it the bulb, the switch, or the power? Oops! I forgot to pay the bill." Or "Where are my good shoes? Not under the bed. How about the closet? Oh yes, I took them off in the bathroom, and here they are, under this dirty towel."

My point is in the "I say to myself." As Peirce puts it, "Meditation is dialogue. 'I says to myself, says I,' is the vernacular account of it; and the most minute and tireless study of logic only fortifies this conception" (1979, 258–259). The power of inquiry is largely the power of inner speech. In this medium we ask questions and give answers, often in a progressively more precise manner. This give and take resembles the conversational style Socrates used with his students. Socrates pursued truth, particularly definitions, with this method. Our inner speech can use the same method, although in an intrapersonal rather than in an interpersonal field. One facet of our self is our "Socrates" and another facet is his students.

Sometimes people say something aloud if it is central to their reasoning process. This may be their resolution of a problem that they have been working on for a long time. One might say, "Oh! Now I see it!" to make the point that this is a long-sought solution. We sometimes think aloud to emphasize an important conclusion, speaking audibly being similar to underlining or italicizing an important written statement.

Of course, researchers also ask more important questions, such as what causes a given disease, how to influence climate change, or how to purify a body of water. Logical questions range from the most abstract and general to the most concrete and immediate. But it is in our everyday, practical problems that we can most easily spot inner speech.

The other functions of inner speech, such as self-regulation and achieving identity, are more hidden than the thinking process. But certainly they are not more important. Thinking is perhaps the most powerful of human traits. It is this process that creates anthropology's "culture," perhaps the greatest of human achievements.

Notice that little of inner speech is devoted to purely causal, quasi-scientific ruminations. We are more likely to be thinking of practical means-ends issues, such as how to produce some kind of artifact. In Aristotle's (1984) famous discussion of the four causes, his example is the crafting of a bronze statue, not something abstract and world-shaking.

Another common purpose of our thought life is some kind of social goal, such as getting someone to think well of us. An example of this is Erving Goffman's "presentation of self" (1959). We are constantly monitoring how we appear to others, and much of this is done by inner talk (Stone 1981).

Our physical appearance is an important part of this self-monitoring. Are we dressed appropriately, maybe in an eye-catching way? Frankie Valli's "Walk Like a Man" evokes an intensive emotional concern for a masculine appearance—looking self-confident, physically attractive, and perhaps a bit formidable. Most men are more or less continuously concerned with their masculine identity, and the body language of walking like a man can be an important strand of this identity.

Self-Regulation

Self-regulation, in contrast to logic in use, refers to all the ways we control our actions or agency. Chapter 6 is devoted to agency, but at this point, agency is treated briefly as a function. Inner speech is a major way in which we self-regulate, and there are several ways in which inner speech shapes our activities. One is that we simply monitor or talk our way through actions. We give ourselves directions as we move from step to step. Children are already doing this audibly in the thinking-out-loud stage around ages two to seven. Vygotsky (1987a) discovered this process by observing the activities of children in Russian orphanages. Children tell themselves what to do next and, when making a mistake, correct themselves. This kind of audible self-talk is not quite the same as inaudible inner speech, but it is rather similar. Vygotsky thinks that the talking-out-loud stage is gradually transformed into inner speech.

Children sometimes seem unaware that the other people in the room can hear what they are saying; they treat these locutions as though they were inaudible. One of my children would plan minor crimes, like stealing cookies, with audible private speech, seemingly unaware that I could hear him. Sometimes I would simply hide the cookies, but at other times I would let him go ahead with the "crime."

Adults also talk themselves through the steps of a complex activity. For example, my wife and I are driving the 120 miles from our home on the Northern California coast to San Francisco. There are about eight route changes, each of which entails some inner speech as a self-reminder. Or we are grocery shopping, carrying a shopping list and self-talking our way through this list.

Another self-regulation is that we try to break bad habits or create good ones by mentally modeling the behavior we want. You are trying, let us say, to drink less alcohol—to follow medical advice and quit after the second drink. You imagine you have reached your limit but still want another drink. You then imagine yourself denying that impulse and drinking something nonalcoholic. If you do this in your mind, you have a greater chance of doing it in reality. This is not a foolproof method, but if you are persistent and pick yourself up after you fall, you have a chance of getting some control over the habit.

A third is that we can improve our skills, such as a tennis stroke or speaking in public, by imagining ourselves doing the activity. We perform the action mentally or imaginatively, perhaps over and over again, in the attempt to achieve a more perfect skill. This method is now used widely by athletes, and there is reason to believe that many nonathletic practices, such as courtroom arguing, driving a car, or playing the piano, would also be improved by purely imaginary practicing.

A fourth way we use inner speech to self-regulate, touched on earlier, is by engaging in internal rituals that will relax, focus, and give confidence to our selves. Mood control, such as alleviating depression, is a form of this. An example is the religious rituals that Émile Durkheim (1995) claims give solidarity and meaning to a society. He wrote about the small, aboriginal clans that existed in the Australian desert around the turn of the century. His theory of how the aborigines created their religious culture rests on his idea of reality construction. If a group assembles and is conscious of its being together, its members may introduce symbols that represent the meanings they want to embrace—or more likely the meanings they already embrace and that are stitched into their everyday culture. Mythical origins of the society would be an example of this. Durkheim does a brilliant job of showing how this social construction works. The process he describes has now been used to explain various other cases of social construction. Goffman (1967) shows how the self can be strengthened by ritual, and Collins (1982, 130–132) generalizes Goffman's interpretation of Durkheim to cover a variety of primary group situations.

Daydreaming

Daydreaming is a form of inner speech that is useful especially for its entertainment value. If we distinguish instrumental or task-oriented inner speech from the expressive or end-in-itself variety, we find daydreaming as the major expressive form. To a certain extent, inner speech *is* daydreaming. By that I mean when we let the mind go slack and withdraw all control, the mind by itself usually daydreams. There are also some unfortunate people who automatically worry when their mind goes into a slack state, but they are in the minority (Hazlett-Stevens 2005). For most people daydreaming is the way they let their inner self do what it wants—namely, engage in what Sigmund Freud calls "wish fulfillment," though he is talking mainly about night dreams.

Another interesting feature of daydreams is that we sometimes find our most effective creativity in these reveries. In my case, I am often stumped on finding the words for a slippery idea. I may have a vague but useful thought by the tail, but I cannot give it verbal expression. Then, to my surprise, the solution appears when I am daydreaming in the shower or in the swimming pool. For some reason water often opens my mind. Trying to think through an issue might be ineffective, but when you quit and turn to leisure, or sometimes to a night's sleep, the solution may surface unannounced.

Turning to an example of how imagery might work in daydreaming, take the "Walter Mitty" routines where we imagine ourselves as heroes and heroines. You are in a state of mental slack, perhaps in bed preparing to fall asleep, and you suddenly begin daydreaming about some exploit. There is a burning building and you enter it, risking your life to save a baby asleep in a crib. You leave the building with the babe in arms, and a crowd of onlookers cheers your heroic act.

Another example of many people's favorite daydream is the sexual adventure. Here the visual and tactile images are usually central, not to mention the sexual arousal itself, which is a kind of emotion or passion. These can begin spontaneously, such as when lying down or driving a car. It should be no surprise that these dreams are most common among teenagers, especially boys, and decline with age. They become almost nonexistent among the very old.

Daydreams have been studied by several careful scholars, and we know quite a bit about their overall traits. One scholar, Jerome Singer, says daydreams are "unfinished business" (1966, 8), probably including tasks that are on our to-do list. Accordingly, some daydreams are purposive and seem to be attempts to solve problems. If we are thinking about taking a vacation and, all of a sudden, we begin daydreaming about vacation spots, these dreams can be seen as "planning the vacation." In contrast, some daydreams are clearly ends in themselves rather than purposive. These are meant to fill in time and entertain us, especially when they lift our mood or give us vicarious pleasure.

When people are sampled about their thoughts, about half the time they say they are daydreaming (Klinger 1990, 83) so this form of discursiveness is a major way people spend their time. The themes are usually pretty ordinary and connected to one's everyday life. Such flashy topics as sex, violence, and heroic exploits occupy a small amount of people's time. Their frequency also diminishes with age. The teenage years are the peak time for highly imaginative daydreams.

Conclusion

This chapter sketches the structure and functions of inner speech. This is comparable to the biological distinction between anatomy (structure) and physiology (functions). My purpose is largely to make readers more conscious of their inner speech. Actually, everyone's use of inner speech is somewhat different, and I am assuming a typical or average use of inner speech in each person.

I do not pay much attention to the extremes—that is, either continuous inner speech or the absence thereof. A striking case of constant inner speech is seen in the biography of Charles Horton Cooley, an expert in child development and a famous sociologist in the 1920s and 1930s (Jacobs 2006). He was shy to the point where he could barely function socially, say, at dinner parties. But his inner speech was unusually rich and creative, and he was a pioneer in describing this process. He made a successful theoretical career, largely out of his understanding of his inner speech and how it organizes our inner worlds.

2

WHEN DOES INNER SPEECH ORIGINATE IN THE CHILD?

This chapter discusses the question of when inner speech begins in the life of a child. This issue is important not only for child development but also for telling us about the nature of inner speech. Vygotsky (1987a) thinks inner speech is the internalization of outer speech and that it comes after outer speech has already been reasonably mastered. In particular, he thinks that private speech (the talking-out-loud period) comes before inner speech. Children can, in doing a complex task, instruct themselves verbally and audibly about which steps to take. Private speech seems like a mapping or self-regulatory process for the most part. In this regulatory function it is similar to inner speech, except that it is out loud. Over the years that private speech runs its course, so argues Vygotsky, it becomes ever more abbreviated and gradually goes silent or underground into the inner speech venue.

Vygotsky may be right, that inner speech is the successor of private speech and that the one glides into the other, but this may be only part of the story. It is also possible that inner speech comes, albeit in a quite crude manner, in the first and second years of life. If inner speech, even in fragmentary form, starts this early, this makes inner speech a more important part of a human's life. These early years are when basic personality is being formed and values and culture are being assimilated. If inner speech starts at age one or two, rather than Vygotsky's age seven, then inner speech is instrumental in the crafting of one's early selfhood. We make ourselves, in part, with inner speech. This early dating of inner speech would also strengthen Peirce's idea that the core of human nature is language.

The early importance of inner speech is suggested in the Oliver Sacks quotation given previously:

> It is through inner speech that the child develops his own concepts and meanings; it is through inner speech that he achieves his own identity; it is through inner speech, finally, that he constructs his own world. (1989, 59)

The concepts and meanings Sacks refer to are being learned around age two, when language is first learned, not around age seven.

There are no technical concepts for explaining the origin of inner speech, but I think I can rough it out. I proceed with tentativeness and a kind of "maybe" assertiveness. If nothing else, I want this argument to be out there and available to scholars as something to think about.

If we remember that inner speech can be conducted in sensory imagery as well as in verbal language, it would seem that little children might not need much formal semantics, not much vocabulary, to begin inner speech. If they have approximate syntax or grammar, then maybe they can begin a variant of inner speech earlier than Vygotsky thinks.

Perhaps the main thing you need to initiate inner speech is not formal language but the dialogical pair (i.e., the two aspects of the self that talk to each other). An infant can get this second or reflexive self when he or she discovers that he or she has (or is) a self. This gives the duality of you and the self you have discovered. Once the pathway between two aspects of the self is established, it would seem the child could begin internal communication and cross the intrapersonal bridge with quite modest communication resources—less than the full-fledged language Vygotsky thinks is necessary.

Of course, you also need to have something to say, but this may not be difficult to find. All you really need is a verb or what amounts to a verb, such as "eat," "grab," or "move." These are linguistic elements, but these words describe our actions. If you can eat and you can remember eating, you can represent this process to yourself merely by imagining yourself eating. In other words, even without the word "eat" you have the sensory image for representing and communicating with yourself about eating. "Wanting" is the same. You can feel the wanting or remember it even if you do not have the word for it. This means you can say, "Want to eat" before you have any formal vocabulary at all.

Syntax, or the stringing out of a meaning, is merely the representation of action. When we act, we are a subject performing an action on an object. Subject, action, and object are syntactical elements. This makes them linguistic. But these three are also elements in one's behavioral routines. Syntax reflects and represents the ordinary activities we do, even well before we have any linguistic powers. In other words, to a certain extent, syntax comes to the child before semantics. Therefore, we can grasp meanings by imagining actions. It would seem we can think with these strings of action just as we can think, later, with linguistic strings. This action-thought would obviously be imprecise and poorly formed. But it would still be thought, and this thought could be a form of communication, if not formal speech.

The point I am moving toward is that, if you have some kind of inner duality, there are a lot of communication media that can cross that bridge (i.e., communicate from one part of the self to the other). Vygotsky has the child waiting until he or she has the full use of language, after about five years of being able to use language and engage in conversation and also after several years of talking to oneself aloud (private speech). In the meantime, the child has been thinking, planning, and solving problems. If the child has been talking to others for several years, is it reasonable to say the child has been unable, in any way, to talk silently to him- or herself all this time?

It may also be possible, as I suggest, for baby to think with the representation of actions. For example, Freud ([1920] 1961, 14–16) thought that when his year-and-a-half old grandson tossed a stringed toy from his chair and then gleefully pulled it back, this tossing represented the departure and return of the mother. If so, baby could merely recollect the tossing and thereby reexperience the catharsis of the returning mother. This might be a rather consoling daydream. And if remembered actions can stimulate a kind of early thought, along with some inner speech, other scenarios (e.g., food-related ones) could also be entertained.

A related matter is early reading. Many children begin reading around age four, and quite a few start earlier. It is generally believed that silent reading is accompanied by some kind of inner speech (Abramson and Goldinger 1997, 1059). If so, this is a case of pre-Vygotsky inner speech.

I think it is possible for children to be engaging in intrapersonal mental activity without much awareness, which would make it difficult to research this activity. Alison Gopnik's (2009) "philosophical baby" suggests that significant thinking, along with an early form of inner speech, is going on, even in quite young babies. If baby's behavior shows that he or she has thought through a problem, then it is reasonable to say the thinking process was in some kind of communication media, even if not formally linguistic. And this thinking process, along with whatever internal communication form it takes, looks like inner speech in the broad sense of the term, even if baby has only a dim awareness of his or her mental processes (Flavell et al. 1997).

I think what influenced Vygotsky (1987b, 54–66) on this matter was the importance of his debate with Jean Piaget. Piaget thought private speech was "egocentric" and meaningless. Anyone who has listened to children talk to themselves knows this is incorrect, but Piaget was a prestigious scientist and he held this opinion with complete confidence. Vygotsky did listen to and experiment with children, and he knew Piaget was wrong. So he concentrated on showing that private speech was rational and meaningful. Children say a lot of things in this medium that are obviously self-regulating, and Piaget's position was easy to disprove.

It is also easy to see why Vygotsky would not have considered the possibility that children were having an earlier, if probably much weaker and less effective, experience with inner speech. This might have gotten in the way of his anti-Piaget position, and it would not give him any ammunition for winning this argument. On the contrary, it would be a distraction and might even weaken his argument. So, given Vygotsky's position in intellectual history, it is understandable that he missed (what I think may be) the earlier and less dramatic occurrence of inner speech in children.

If you think the child has been engaging in some kind of inner speech throughout the years of private speech from ages two to seven, the meaning of the private speech becomes a more interesting issue. If the purpose of private speech is largely self-regulation, why conduct speech aloud when one is simultaneously engaging, according to my hypothesis, in silent (if crude) inner speech?

The child seems to be working with more than one "voice," during this time, and perhaps each one has a distinct strength. The child's self-styled language, which is the inner language of those years, is a pastiche of imagery, concepts, emotion, pidgin, gestures, minimal syntax, and perhaps action chunks or practices. The grammatical rules, like the semantic mix itself, would also be to some extent the personal construction of the child. It would therefore be at least a semi-private if not a fully private language. Vygotsky thinks the later inner speech is a private language, but if so, the earlier one would be even more private.

The two voices, internal and external, would also be aimed at two different audiences. The inner voice would be aimed exclusively and privately at the self. This voice controls the thinking process, organizes the stream of consciousness, and steers the dialogical self. The outer voice, in addition to being a variety of self-regulation, would be a rehearsal for communicating with others.

The context of the fight with Piaget led Vygotsky to think private speech was preparing the child to push speech underground and turn it into inner speech. The argument with Piaget, which Vygotsky had been staking his entire career on, required the cleanest and most convincing series of steps. Making inner speech wait until private speech had been perfected and was ready to be suspended was the most powerful way Vygotsky could defeat Piaget (which he did).

But perhaps Vygotsky overdid it. He could have refuted Piaget with just his experiments on private speech. He did not need to keep inner speech waiting in the wings for so long. He may not have won the argument so convincingly if he allowed for an earlier onset of inner speech, but the result is that he gave us what may be a misleadingly late start of inner speech.

My argument is that inner speech has two trajectories. One is the way baby's thinking process keeps developing a firmer and more effective symbology or representational system. The logic of this thinking has a quasi-linguistic form, as I have been arguing. The other trajectory is the growth of formal language itself. When language reaches a certain degree of ripeness, after several years of talking aloud to oneself, it is ready to go underground and become inner speech. Thought and language converge around age seven, and they become, in a running start, mature inner speech.

The Development of Inner Duality

To have inner speech there has to be an inner duality—that is, a speaker and a listener or a communicator and a communicatee. Theorists seem to arrive at an inner duality in various ways. René Descartes (1987, 101) thinks we can discover ourselves in a "cogito, ergo sum" (I think, therefore I am), although he does not state the age when this realization might appear. He reaches this argument after a long climb through various preliminaries, and he does not actually say we all reach this insight. But it would seem to be at least implicit in everyone's cognitive development. This insight would result in the duality of a knower and a known. Descartes does not explicitly discuss inner speech, but his concepts would allow it.

Immanuel Kant actually does speak of inner speech, but not in any detail ([1800] 1978, 85). His version of the inner duality is as follows:

> That I am conscious of myself is a thought that already contains a twofold self, the I as subject and the I as object. How it might be possible for the I that I think to be an object (of intuition) for me, is absolutely impossible to explain, even though it is an indubitable fact; it indicated however, a capacity so highly elevated above sensuous intuition that, as the basis for the possibility of understanding, it has the effect of separating us from all animals, to which we have no reason for ascribing the ability to say I to themselves, and results in an infinity of self-constituted representations and concepts. But a double personality is not meant by this double I. Only the I that I think and intuit is a person. The I that belongs to the object that is intuited by me is, similarly to other objects outside me, a thing. ([1804] 1983, 73)

With this double I, Kant is close to Mead's I-me distinction, though Mead never noticed this point in Kant (Mead 1934, 173–178). Kant does not connect the dual self with inner speech, but he obviously could have. All he had to do was to make the self-awareness more explicit and then start the conversation between the two aspects of the self. So, like Descartes, Kant had the inner duality, but he did not do much with it.

Peirce (1984), in contrast, does not think self-awareness is intuitive but rather a matter of reasoning. He thinks the discovery of the self comes when you first make a painful error that forces you to look for its cause. This search, in turn, brings you to the discovery of your self. Instead of Descartes's "cogito, ergo sum," Peirce has "fallor, ergo sum" (I err, therefore I am).

Peirce's example is a child impetuously touching a hot stove (1984, 202–203). When you feel the pain, as he reasoned, you back-trail and ask yourself why you performed the act, what caused you to do it. This leads you to realize there is a "self" behind your actions, bringing them about. Presumably there has been an implicit awareness of the self for some time, but this hot stove incident causes the child to search for the cause of his or her actions, and this search makes the awareness of the self explicit. It was that self that chose to perform the act. The discovery of one's self, for Peirce, explains the pain and the error. It also creates a loop, from the self to its actions to their consequences.

In other words, claims Peirce, baby has been choosing and engaging in actions right along but has been unaware of the choosing process. His actions have been unexamined and automatic. It isn't until baby encounters a bad outcome, getting burned, that baby gets interested in his activity or agentic process. Now, to avoid getting burned again, baby discovers the psychological "machinery" that directs and energizes his actions. This device is the will, or more generally, the decision-making process.

Whether Peirce is right or wrong in this bit of child development theory, I just want to use it as an example of how the duality of inner speech might originate. Baby can now visualize himself as a decision maker, and he can also talk to that decision maker, telling it, for example, not to burn him again. This inner speech "sentence" might be as simple as a painful feeling accompanied by a feeling of negation ("no more burning"). Peirce seems to be saying that this utterance is what originates the process of inner speech for the child. There seems to be no critical literature on Peirce's idea; that is, no one seems to have disagreed with him yet in print about how we first discover our selves as little children. But since I am only speculating about how inner duality and thereby inner speech might have originated in the infant in the first year or two, I do not need empirical evidence concerning my hunch. Peirce may be wrong here, but he is supplying a useful idea (inner duality).

This thought experiment of Peirce's also suggests that the burned finger and the search for its cause entails some form of inner speech. How might baby do this back-trailing? He could use memory to search for what preceded the burned finger and what might have brought it about. This would be an interrogation, and it would entail asking oneself questions. These questions would be addressed by the self to the self. We would be asking our self how this happened. Whatever the exact linguistic form, this interrogation would have to be some form of inner speech. Peirce does not explicitly make this point, but it would seem to be unavoidable. So this example not only leads to an internal duality but also seems to entail some form of early inner speech. It also seems clear that when baby realized that his "self" did the deed, there would be a powerful and emotionally overpowering understanding in baby, probably comparable to the mirror insight Lacan (2006) attributes to baby's self-development. Baby would now be the self and would also realize that this self was an enormously powerful resource for living his life.

Another way children can get inner duality is by their first recognition of themselves in a mirror. This puts them face to face with their self. In Mead's language, this discovery is that of the "I" first encountering the "me." Ordinarily, children seem to recognize themselves in a mirror as they approach two years of age. The resulting internal bipolarity gives children one of the essentials for inner speech. If this self-recognition is exciting and gives the child pleasure, it seems likely that the viewing child would communicate something friendly to the viewed child.

Lacan (2006) makes much of this enthusiasm. This could merely be a beaming smile, the meaning of which would be "I like you." This could be called the first act of inner speech. In a way it is "other," for the other self is outside one in the mirror reflection. But as soon as the now-recognized child leaves the mirror, the mirror child would be internalized into the child's psyche and available for subsequent, internal communication. This inner speech would be with the reflected child (which is Mead's me).

I have some familiarity with this mirror experience because I happen to recall my first self-recognition in a mirror as a child. I am sure I am not the only one for whom this experience was a powerful discovery. But so far, no one seems to have done the research necessary for finding these people and asking them what it was like. It was the intensity and the closeness-to-self that made it such a crisp and imprinted memory.

As a child, perhaps a little older than one year, I escaped from the kitchen, where my mother kept me, and crawled along the wall to the full-length mirror near the front door of our house. I stood at the mirror and saw the mirror child, as all the literature on this topic suggests, and I went through the classic search process, terminating in the "aha" of self-discovery. Most children do not know what they look like before this experience, because all they can see is the lower part of their body. The face itself is inaccessible. Lacan thinks this experience causes the child to identify not with himself but with the mirror image. He does not think the child could handle the cognitive insight of reflexivity at this early age, and as a result, he thinks the child would think the reflection was, in effect, some other entity, the "mirror child." He sees this as a kind of fallacy, this childhood identification with an alien entity, and he built an elaborate theoretical superstructure on this (alleged) erroneous mirror image.

In contrast, Maurice Merleau-Ponty also wrote about the mirror experience, although he thinks the child could accommodate to and understand the reflexivity (1964, 125–141). In his opinion, the child realizes that the mirror image is a reflection of himself as he actually looks. Perhaps Merleau-Ponty was drawing on his own personal experience in some way. When I raised my children, and they got the hang of the mirror, they seemed to fit the Merleau-Ponty interpretation. I once gave a short talk explaining my early mirror experience. This is posted, under my name, on YouTube. I might mention that there seems to be no literature, so far, comparing Merleau-Ponty and Lacan on the mirror question.

Now let me return to the inner duality question from the point of view of the self pronouns. Children's caretakers usually address them by name or as "you." It takes a while for a child to turn that "you" into a "me." This seems to be a halting, gradual process, but eventually the child can take the role of the parent and look at himself as the parents do. When children do this, they are treating themselves as a (linguistic) object and, via reflexivity, encountering their "me." The power of reflexivity, which is the same as finding your "me," comes from learning how to use the reflexive pronoun and also from learning how, in Mead's terms, to role-take your self. These processes give you a "me" and allow reflexivity. Notice the pronoun route to self-awareness is different from the mirror route, which is in turn different from Peirce's burned finger route. But they can be going on at about the same time, and obviously they can reinforce each other.

Role-taking and the use of the reflexive pronoun are social mirrors, but at the same time the child is probably discovering himself in the physical mirror. In other words, there are several routes to the duality within the self. Once that duality is established—that is, once you have both I and me (or whatever you want to call them)—you have the two poles of internal conversation. The machinery is there for inner speech. Your internal telephone, to use a ridiculous metaphor but nevertheless make a point, has been installed.

The Internal Dialogical Polarity

As a communication medium, inner speech goes on between two aspects of the self. These could be called a speaker and a listener. Some theorists have given formal names to these two poles, and some have not. George Herbert Mead refers to them as the "I" and the "me" (1934, 173–178, modifying these terms from their usage in William James (1950b, 371). In fact, this duality is a major way in which Mead approaches the structure of the self. The easiest way to define Mead's terms is to say that the I is the self-as-present and the me is the self-as-past. At other times, however, Mead speaks of the I as the subject and the me as the object, using these terms in a more or less grammatical sense. This latter distinction is not temporal but syntactical. In fact, Mead says so much about the I and me and does so in such a casual way at times that you have to interpret him to maintain any consistency. I do this by conceiving of these two concepts in temporal terms, even though this usage does not capture all of Mead's nuances.

Peirce also uses terms for the two poles of the dialogical self, but they are different from those of Mead. Peirce's speaker is I, just as with Mead. But his listener is the "you," defined as "that other self just coming into life in the flow of time" (1934, para. 421). The idea that thought and inner speech are directed to the immediately future self is part of Peirce's larger notion of "tuism." As Max Fisch puts it, "In 1891 Peirce defines *tuism* for the *Century Dictionary* as 'The doctrine that all thought is addressed to a second person, or to one's future self as to a second person'" (1982, xxix).

Peirce's tuism has at least two interesting implications. For one, he reverses Mead's idea of inner speech and has the I speaking to the future self, not the past self. Actually, Peirce probably did not know, in 1891, about Mead's I-me idea when he explained inner speech as directed to the you. But both Peirce and Mead seem to have something of the truth, as the self can address itself as either future or past.

The second implication of tuism is that a lot of inner speech is directed to someone other than the self, although this other person has to be given an imaginary interior presence. Take prayer, for example (Luhrmann 2012). People who pray address some kind of religious entity, often conceived of as inside themselves. I prayed a lot in early Catholic college, and it was as though God was in me at all times, available for communication. Actually, God could hear not only what I said to him but also everything else I thought, including the bad stuff. So the God of prayer was a two-edged sword, both as friend and as punitive judge. At the time, though, he was mostly a benign presence in me. More generally, prayer is a major form of inner speech for large numbers of people, and it is an example of Peirce's tuism.

Another kind of visitor to our theater of inner speech is any human person we might ensconce into our minds. Family members and friends can be more or less permanent visitors in many people's inner speech venue. These persons can be a consoling presence. We can also engage in the looking-glass self process with these visitors. Charles Horton Cooley ([1902] 1983, 184–185) says that what we imagine people think of us is sometimes internalized, particularly when we are young, and becomes a permanent aspect of the self-concept. Their opinion of us can, and often does, become our opinion of ourselves. This is his "looking-glass self" idea. But we can also conduct imaginary conversations with others and in that manner elicit approving comments from them. This resembles the "Walter Mitty" game in which we have self-flattering fantasies. These experiences can enhance the self-concept, and they are probably engaged in by many people.

People who tend toward emotional depression, however, may have disapproving visitors denouncing them and pulling their mood downward to an increasingly low level. Like God, then, these visitors can be a two-edged sword. One possible cure for depression is to conduct imaginary conversations in which you send your self-concept upward, toward a more positive view of the self. Psychologists who work with mood disorders report that this process often works (McKay, Davis, and Fanning 2011). If depression is caused partly by hormonal secretions, positive self-talk, it would seem, can "turn off" self-destructive hormones and turn on the good ones.

People in love might be in a permanent mental chatting relationship with their lover, talking to them in their minds throughout the day. On the one hand, this form of inner speech can be deeply gratifying and a major addition to one's mental health. On the other hand, lovers can also hurt each other deeply, both in words and deeds, including such seemingly minor actions as a disapproving glance. Here the looking-glass self operates like a weapon and can bring a traumatic blow to the self.

Returning to the two communicative poles of the internal self, there seem to be no other examples as crisp as those of Mead and Peirce. But inner speech itself is deeply analyzed by two Russian thinkers, Vygotsky and Bakhtin. These two clearly envision the internal dialogue as bipolar, just as Peirce and Mead do, but neither have a clear set of terms for the interior poles. To make my point, that inner speech is a dialogue between two aspects of the self, I have to find some way of finding bipolarity in the two Russians.

Bakhtin (1984, 255) is keenly aware of how the two dialogues—the interpersonal and the intrapersonal—often go on simultaneously. The inner one tends to control and direct the outer one. But Bakhtin tends to see the two as almost merging, and at times he seems to have trouble distinguishing the one from the other. This is partly because he pays such close attention to Raskolnikov, the antihero in Dostoyevsky's *Crime and Punishment*. Raskolnikov is so troubled that he himself often tends to talk to others as though he is talking to himself. He gives others hints of his crime in this way. There may be some of the schizophrenic's tendency to confuse the internal with the external dialogue here, Raskolnikov's particular psychopathology not being easy to diagnose. Bakhtin usually uses the term "other" for the second or listener pole of the conversation, whether interior or exterior. I therefore use the pair of terms "self" and "other" for the two poles of Bakhtin's internal conversation.

Vygotsky (1987a), too, lacks terminology at this point. It is possible that both he and Bakhtin dodged the analysis of the interior self to avoid potential conflicts with the (constantly varying) Marxist party line. It is also possible that this issue simply did not interest them. They both pursued other aspects of inner speech with intense enthusiasm. Nevertheless, both seem to implicitly regard the self as composed of two poles between which interior dialogue goes on. This is implied by their general approaches to inner speech. Using "self" and "other" for Bakhtin seems reasonably close to the way he spoke and thought. In the case of Vygotsky, there is also an implicit self-other dialogue, although in this case I use the terms "ego" and "alter." The pair of terms I use, then, for Bakhtin and Vygotsky are much like the pair of terms that Mead and Peirce use, although the Russians pursue inner speech in a way that is different and much more intense than that of the American pragmatists. This comes up again in Chapter 10's discussion of inner speech theory.

For now I merely present a table of interior dialogue terms as a presentational device or illustrative tool. In Table 2.1 I include several people other than Peirce, Mead, Vygotsky, and Bakhtin. Including these others provides a fuller picture of how one can conceptualize the internal duality.

Among the other thinkers in this table, James uses "I-me" in a way opposite to that of Mead, but James says little about inner speech, and his terminology is not of great importance. Martin Buber uses "I-thou" to introduce a reverential attitude toward the world and other people (2000, 19). He does not use these terms for the inner speech duality, but others do, particularly in a psychotherapy context (Cooper 2004). Cooley (1908) closely observes the onset of language in his third child, Mary Elizabeth. He wrote about her use of self-words. This child tended, when addressing herself, to use the term "you," reminiscent of Peirce's usage (which Cooley was probably unaware of).

Table 2.1 shows the bipolarity in seven thinkers. Mead and Peirce are the best examples, although James, Buber, and Cooley are helpful to make the larger point, that inner speech and dialogue presumes a bipolarity in the self.

TABLE 2.1 THE TWO POLES OF INTERNAL DIALOGUE

Thinker	Interior speaker	Internal listener
James	Me	I
Mead	I	Me
Peirce	I	You
Buber	I	Thou
Bakhtin	Self	Other
Cooley	I	You
Vygotsky	Ego	Alter

My discussion of how inner speech may have begun in the child during the first couple of years of life is related to Table 2.1. For baby to be able to talk to herself and to think in dialogical form, baby has to be divided into two parts. The means of communication—that is, the sense in which meanings are being communicated from one part of baby to another—is dependent on the framework of inner duality. There are several ways of conceptualizing this bipolarity, as Table 2.1 suggests, but this inner duality, in some form or another, is presumed by the idea of internal conversation.

I have been operating at the tentative, exploratory level in distinguishing the early (around age one or two) from the late (around Vygotsky's age seven) onset of inner speech. I am being similarly exploratory in analyzing the duality in the seven thinkers in Table 2.1. Still, this somewhat sketchy quality is fitting for an exploratory book, given how little research and systematic thought there has been on this topic. As this book proceeds I wrap up a number of issues that are left somewhat open in this chapter.

3

IS THERE A SELF?

I have now laid out a fairly extensive definition of inner speech, including how it fits into our lives. Since this speech process goes on in the self, it leads naturally to the question of what the self is. Unfortunately, there is no scholarly agreement on this matter, so no one has presented a clear and consensual definition. All the major disputes in philosophy cut across the self, and the best that can be offered is a list of contentious definitions. Nevertheless, in this chapter I discuss the idea of the self. In this discussion I emphasize the discipline of philosophy rather than psychology or the social sciences because philosophy is the heartland, both historically and contemporaneously, of disputes over human nature.

One of the first things you notice about the word "self" is that it is a wiggle word, or slider. By this I mean it has multiple meanings and therefore seems to require more than one definition. Most words, such as those representing physical objects, plants, animals, and even physical and cultural artifacts, have a single major definition. The definition may be imperfect and a bit ragged, but there is, at least for any given thinker, usually only one of them. In contrast, the self has a plurality of meanings, as I explain throughout this chapter, and it tends to resist unitary definition. The historical background helps explain why this is the case.

First, I give a brief review of the anti-self concepts—that is, ideas that argue there is no self. There are a large number of these, and they tend to dominate the discussion. To argue that there is, in any sense, a self, you have to confront the anti-self arguments. If you can disprove all of these, you are,

Is There a Self?

by process of elimination, proving that there is a self. That is the logic of this chapter.

Materialism is, by and large, anti-self, although the many facets of materialism produce a large number of anti-self ideas. But post-structuralism, which is not expressly materialist, can also lead to anti-self ideas. The great Parisian intellectuals of the 1960s (Claude Lévi-Strauss, Jacques Derrida, Michel Foucault, Roland Barthes, Jacques Lacan, and Louis Althusser) all hold some kind of upward reduction of the self, reducing or dissolving it into language and culture. I list each idea, of both the upward and downward reductionists, and give a brief response.

1. A political argument, meant to be a populist refutation of the self, is that the self is an elitist concept: white, male, heterosexual, young, rich, colonial, and so on. *Response:* This argument confuses the use with the abuse. My definition of the self is universal (i.e., it includes all minorities). It must be admitted, though, the concept of the self has sometimes been used in an elitist manner.

In contrast, the notion of identity, which is discussed in the next chapter, can be elitist. It can mean you have good mental health or an identity that serves you well. Rich people can, in a way, buy an effective identity. In fact, your social class, in Karl Marx's and Max Weber's economic sense, is usually central to your identity. But you cannot buy a self because to some extent you are born with it.

2. The self is a language effect (e.g., the word "I" is mistaken for the self). Or linguistic reflexivity is mistaken for psychological or ontological reflexivity. *Response:* There is a linguistic layer to the self, and it is possible to concentrate on this layer and ignore all others. But this is reductionist, for there are also psychological and ontological layers. The word "I" is, in a way, just a word. But it is also a word that refers to whomever is using the word. The word is reflexive, but its referent—the self—is also reflexive. In other words, the word "I" designates a double reflexivity. You need them both to capture the self's relation to language.

3. According to Foucault (1973), who I discuss in more detail later in this chapter, the Kantian episteme (or paradigm) creates both the birth and the death of the self. *Response:* This episteme is merely an epistemological device or a way of thinking about the self. The underlying self—that is, the ontological or real self—has remained the same throughout the historical periods during which Foucault's various epistemes have come and gone. To put it another way, the self has been the content and the epistemes have been the overlaid forms. Foucault, despite the elegant way in which he makes the argument, mistakes the form for the content.

4. Lacan ([1966] 1977) says the self is an illusion coming from seeing our reflection in a mirror. He also seems to think a child of about a year's age is not smart enough to figure out the doubling-back quality of a mirror and therefore would not know that the child in the mirror is him or her. *Response:* In contrast, Merleau-Ponty (1964, 125–141) says, as mentioned earlier, that we learn to adjust to the reflexive feature of the mirror, and in that way we perceive the reflexive nature of the self. I think Lacan, with no evidence, simply made a bad guess. He got it wrong, and Merleau-Ponty got it right.

5. The self is a trick by capitalism to "subject" people (Althusser 1971a). *Response:* True, the self, considered as a legal entity, can be saddled with rights and duties that are exploitive. Capitalism can and sometimes does do this. But the self can also be used, by some forms of socialism or communism, in a legally egalitarian manner. It is a flexible legal resource that can be used in more than one way.

Actually, Althusser borrows Lacan's mirror idea and applies it to capitalism, arguing that the idea of the self is a case of interpellation or false consciousness brought about by the mirror reflection. Capitalism has produced a lot of tricks, but I do not think Althusser's example is one of them.

6. Descartes was erroneous in stating his "cogito, ergo sum." *Response:* Descartes has become the bad guy in recent social theory, although few people seem to have actually read him. He believes that thinking implies the existence of the self (Descartes 1987, 101). Kant also thinks this (Kant [1781] 1965, 152), and Husserl argues against it at times and for it at other times (Husserl [1913] 1982, 549). I think the Descartes-Kant position is defensible, although there are also many other ways of reaching a self.

7. If you are given a tour of a university and you then ask, "But where is the university itself?" you are committing Gilbert Ryle's famous "category error" (Ryle 2009, 6). A thing does not have a separate existence over and above its constituents. *Response:* In the same way, the parts of the self—for example, the I-you-me or the ego-superego-id triads—*are* the self. If you look for some kind of self in addition to the constituents, you are committing Ryle's fallacy. If you think there is a self but that it is the same as its parts or constituents, you are not committing Ryle's category error.

8. Do some Asian religions (e.g., Buddhism) argue there is no self? *Response:* Robert Perinbanayagam (1991a, 24–25) argues persuasively against this idea. He quotes several texts that suggest all Asian societies have, in their own way, a sense of the individual self.

9. Jean-Paul Sartre (1957b) argues that the self exists only when we think of it; in between those thoughts, it does not exist (the refrigerator-light theory of the self). *Response:* Sartre thinks the self is a particular kind of nothingness. It becomes a something only when we address it. He does not really say there is no self but that it exists only at the second order of self-attendance.

I think this is an overzealous use of Occam's razor. True, we can conceive of there being no first order self, but then why would it exist at the second order? This is a lot like Althusser's idea that the self only exists when it is addressed or hailed. This idea gives too much power to the attending process. Another problem for both Sartre and Althusser (1971) is that there would have to be a preexisting self that did the hailing or addressing.

10. Postmodern electronic gadgets have destroyed the self by drowning it out. *Response:* This gives too much power to gadgets. Yes, people (especially the young) now spend a lot of time on cell phones, tablets, and so on, but these distractions are not powerful enough to replace the self. And who is doing all the gabbing if the self has been extinguished? This is the old, discredited idea of mass society now applied to electronics.

11. The self has only an "as if" existence—it exists only because we recognize it as existing. *Response:* This is a serious argument, but it applies to all sociocultural entities, not just to the self. The exact ontological status of the self, given that it is in the vague and highly disputed category of "relation," is certainly imprecise. And maybe it always will be. But sociocultural things *are* things, even if they do not have the conceptual crispness of material things.

12. Self is the teeny "homunculus" within the person, and within that entity there is a still teenier homunculus, and so on (infinite regress). *Response:* This argument simply misunderstands the nature of reflexivity. Agency is invisible to itself because it has the bipolar structure of reflexivity. If you think of the self as linear, you can stretch it, in the search for an autonomous actor, into infinity. But if you think of the self as a circle, which is the nature of reflexivity, the agent is dispersed or decentered into a bipolar field.

13. Some post-structuralists and postmodernists think culture and language completely absorb the self. This is upward reduction. *Response:* This is a more general version of the alleged linguistic fallacy, discussed previously. The self not only has a linguistic component; it is also an autonomous element in the culture. The self is a symbol, and culture is also a system of symbols. In fact, Franz Boas's (1911) discovery of culture also explains the autonomous self.

14. The self is a computer and therefore only a machine. *Response:* The computer, in addition to lacking true reflexivity, lacks a sense of meaning or understanding. In other words, it has syntax without semantics. More reductionism. This book hits this theme repeatedly.

15. The self is a story about "itself" and nothing else. *Response:* When we know the whole story, we know the whole self; otherwise we will be asking, as Ryle ridiculed, "Now that I have seen all the parts of the story, where is the story itself?" The self certainly is a story—in fact a lot of stories—but these stories are about something. A novel is complete in itself, and we cannot ask where the characters can be found. It exists in one of James's "special worlds" (1950a, 291–293). But the self exists in James's "main world," and a story about the self is nonfiction. It is about something—namely, the self. In other words, this fallacy needs to distinguish fiction from nonfiction.

These are the various arguments against the existence of a self. I am aware that these arguments and my counterarguments are inconclusive and that the discussion could and probably will go on indefinitely, but I want to make my position explicit. I think humans are selves, even though the nature of this self is quite complex and not easy to specify. The self is to a great extent inner speech and the agencies that engage in inner speech. Now I return to the history of the self idea in European thought.

When Europe was overwhelmingly Christian, before the Reformation, it was believed that the self was the immortal soul. The definition of the soul had a theological component, but given the religiosity of the times, it was accepted as the legitimate definition of what we now call the self. After Descartes (1987) and his "cogito, ergo sum" inaugurated modern philosophy, there was widespread disagreement over human nature. Descartes's explanation was unconvincing. His ideas of the body and soul were so at odds that they contradicted each other. He had trouble explaining the unity of the human being.

In addition, what had been called the soul gradually declined in interest and was increasingly ignored. Instead, the self, based on reflexivity rather than immortality, became the center of the human being. This disagreement came after Descartes's philosophy tended to split into two distinct and rival alternatives: materialism and idealism.

Over time, idealism and the other nonmaterialist philosophies diminished in importance, and the various forms of materialism, despite disagreements among the materialists themselves, held most of the field. At present the leading issue in philosophy continues to be the mind-body problem; how to explain the seemingly unbridgeable difference between the two. In this discussion the self is an aspect of the mind, so the mind-body problem is, to some extent, the self-body problem. Committed materialists, of course, explain the mind materialistically, in terms of the body and physical elements.

Still, there is a persistent school of philosophers and other thinkers who insist that the mind is different from the body and must be explained with nonmaterialistic concepts. Many of these thinkers are materialists who are open to explaining the mind with nonmaterialistic properties. John Heil goes so far as to say, "It would not be much of an exaggeration to describe non-reductionist physicalism as today's orthodoxy in the philosophy of mind" (2013, 183). In other words, although materialists rule in today's philosophy of mind, a significant number of them are in effect dualists. They admit that the mind cannot be explained with materialistic concepts. It is true that the mind is not a substance, but it is a "property bundle" that has some of the qualities of a substance.

To put it another way, science and scientists tend, for the most part, toward materialism and a view of the mind that reduces it to the body. In contrast, other social institutions such as law, the family, politics, high culture, ethics, religion, and even economics, tend to see the world dualistically as partly material and partly nonmaterial. This dualism can be a dualism of substances, which envisions both material and nonmaterial things, or more commonly it can be a property-dualism, which regards things as having both material and nonmaterial features. Either way, the natural attitude and the ordinary beliefs of ordinary people seem to be non-, if not actually, antimaterialistic.

This situation is somewhat like what Arthur Eddington in the 1920s referred to as the "two tables" (1928, ix–x). For science, the ordinary dining room table is composed mostly of air, with electrons filling only about a billionth of the space. But to common sense, the table is solid and continuous, composed entirely of wood, with no air whatsoever. We accept the table of physics as correct for physics, but the table of ordinary life is the one we use for everything else.

The contemporary equivalent of Eddington's table is the idea that people are computers, although the current comparison goes well beyond that of Eddington. The two tables are starkly different, and the point of the comparison is to show how dramatically distinct science is from everyday life. No one says the physics table is the real table. But with the computer analogy, some scientists say the computer is the same as the real person. In other words, it is not the differences but the similarities that are being emphasized. It is the claim that people have the same computational properties as computers. What happens, then, to the ways people differ from computers? How about their minds, feelings, imagination, meanings, and self-awareness? Although there are attempts to argue these properties away or to say computers have versions of these personal qualities, there is continuing disagreement over these issues.

The computer analogy is represented by a combination of disciplines called cognitive science. This interdisciplinary field draws mainly on psychology, philosophy, and linguistics, but it has an influence on all the social sciences. At first glance, this analogy seems far-fetched, for computers do not really have human qualities. They are machines, and they do what we make them do. But if you pose enough assumptions and lay down enough conditions, even some that may be contrary to fact, you can stretch the comparison enough to have a "computer person."

The most striking thing that people have and computers lack is understanding. This can also be construed as the ability to apprehend meaning, or Husserl's intentionality. We understand the meanings of things in the world around us and we know the meanings of language. This semantic capability is what has made humans the dominant species on earth, and it is the basis of culture. In contrast, the computer bears a resemblance to the simple adding machine. Just as the adding machine does not really understand numbers, even though it can go through the mechanical processes of arithmetic, computers do not really have an understanding of what anything is. They do not know any more than Eddington's tables know, although in some circles it is believed that computers have the same kind of understanding as people have.

One way to make the computer comparison look good is to deny that people have understanding at all. If you can convince yourself that people merely go through the motions of understanding and actually do not know their world any more than rocks or trees do, you can make the computer look like a human being. But you do this not by raising computers to the level of humans but by lowering humans to the level of mechanical computers. You have to deny many of what are ordinarily admitted as the qualities of human beings.

The other way to make the computer comparison is to elevate the computer and say it has all the powers that humans have. The main way this is done is to take syntax for semantics—that is, linguistic rules for meanings. If you program a computer to treat different parts of speech in different ways (i.e., with different rules), you have a computer that can handle syntax. Let's say you program the computer to be able to parse the sentence "I am hungry." This is syntax. But you cannot program or teach the computer to actually be hungry or experience the physiological feeling of hunger. Nor can you give it self-awareness or the sense of being an "I." But if you kid yourself somehow into thinking the computer has meanings and semantics, you have a computer person.

Let us say you program the computer to refer to itself. This, on the surface, is self-awareness or reflexivity. But it is mechanical or partial reflexivity, not true psychological reflexivity, which is total (Hanson 1986, 66–76). Humans can reflect on their entire selves, but computers can only reflect on part of themselves. The person can reach out to an outer or "meta" position and look at its whole self. But a computer is always in two parts: the reflecting language or program and the rest of the computer. So if you take mechanical for psychological reflexivity, you can claim computers are people. But this is a fallacy, given that the reflexivity is the mechanical variety.

Now that I have sketched the computer analogy, it should be no surprise that there is fierce disagreement over what a human being or self is. For cognitive science, a human is an animal that operates with what are, in effect, computer programs. These programs are sets of rules, similar in principle to the rules of arithmetic. If we were able to perform arithmetic operations but had no idea what quantity or number was, we would have computerized knowledge. It would be as though we were the cook in the kitchen, perfectly capable to putting together the most elaborate of meals, but lacking any capacity to taste the food and no ability to eat it.

Now that I have shown what controversy exists in the scholarly world over the definition of the self, I set this controversy aside and proceed with the process of definition. I mentioned that the human self is so multiple and has so many important facets that it may be necessary to use more than one definition to cover this multiplicity.

I have already pointed out that the self has a different face, if not outright definition, at different temporal locations. In particular, the self of the present is referred to by the pragmatists as the "I," the self of the immediate future is referred to as the "you," and the self of the past is called the "me." These selves all have the same basic properties, but they have different dialogical roles. Several of the great philosophers, including William James, Edmund Husserl, and Martin Heidegger, claim that *the self is time*. At various places in this book, I look at how the self has time as a major characteristic (Flaherty 2000). At this point I merely indicate that the self's different relations to time make it difficult to work with a single definition of the self.

The semiotician Robert Perinbanayagam thinks the multiplicity of the self requires a "maxisign" (1991a, 11). By this he means it takes several signs or symbols to define a human being. Perinbanayagam is an expert on the semiotic nature of the self. He is also one of the few who are equally at home with the American semioticians Peirce and Mead and the Russian semioticians Vygotsky and Bakhtin. In addition, he knows Asian religions, which have their own understandings of the self. This widespread knowledge, drawing on different cultural repertoires, makes Perinbanayagam's writings on the self of singular importance (1985, 1991b, 2000, 2006, 2012).

The American and Russian theories of the self have not yet been integrated effectively, although I attempt to do some of this in Chapter 10. The lengthy Cold War between the United States and what was then called the Soviet Union made scholarly connections between the intellectuals of the two countries quite difficult. In addition, both countries engaged in some censorship, the Soviet Union more so than the United States, and this censorship has had a pejorative effect on scholarship. Also, the Cold War seems to have been an important factor in rapidly boosting the importance of cognitive science in academia. The U.S. government thought—erroneously, I believe—that cognitive science would help it beat the Soviets, so the government provided much of the money for the various strands of cognitive science (Solovey and Cravens 2012). Money does not explain everything, but it does seem to have been a significant factor in which ideas about human nature have been deemed most important.

Returning to the problem of defining the self, Perinbanayagam draws on three major sources for his definition. These are Bakhtin, for whom the key human trait is dialogism; Mead, for whom the major human trait is internal self-awareness or reflexivity; and Peirce, for whom the human is language, signs, and symbols. These three traits of dialogism, reflexivity, and semiosis are closely related and even, to some extent, imply each other. Nevertheless, each captures one of the most defining attributes of the self.

Peirce's linguistic definition of the self implies Mead's reflexivity, for the major feature of linguistic meaning is reflexivity. Bakhtin's idea that the self is dialogue is also close to the thoughts of Mead and Peirce, for when we address ourselves (Bakhtin), we do it with language (Peirce), and our meaning is delivered in a reflexive rather than a linear manner (Mead).

4
IDENTITY

Having given an idea of how to define the self, I turn to the slightly less abstract idea of an identity. This term has been used in a variety of ways in philosophy and the social sciences. John Locke's definition of the self as our "sameness," or similarity over time, is perhaps the most famous of these definitions ([1689] 1979, 335–338). This definition, which hinges on human memory, is not universally accepted, but it seems to be a reasonable notion as to *who* we are. We are the same person we have always been, and our proof of this is that we remember ourselves as always having been this person. The "thisness" remains the same.

Another way of looking at identity is *what*, rather than who, we are. The question is not *who* has these characteristics but *what* are the distinguishing characteristics? Obviously, the defining traits of human nature itself, what used to be termed the "essence" of humanity, cannot be the answer to this question, for we want to know what distinguishes *this* person, not *all* persons. And although this is not the question that Locke asked, it is the question that seems to be something of an obsession for contemporary human beings.

In the first section I give a sense of what these terms might mean. In the second section I show how we use inner speech to construct, develop, protect, and revere our identity. By "revere" I mean we treat the identity as a sacred object, doing what we can to enhance this sacredness.

If we attempt to clarify the notion of identity, though, we soon realize it is among the most difficult ideas in social psychology. People keep coming back to identity issues partly because the definition of identity is itself an issue. A major reason for this slipperiness, I think, is that the relation between identity and the self is unclear. For some scholars, notably Goffman (1959, 252), identity is the same as self, but for many others identity is only part of the self. I present my idea of what an identity is, and then I confront several identity problems, including the relation between the self and identity, and show how my approach can help clarify them.

For me the self has three levels or parts. The most defining of the three is the generic level. This level includes the traits that all selves have, beginning when we split off from the chimpanzees. Second is the level of identity. This has important traits or chunks of meaning, but they are subject to change, even if only slowly. The least important of the three levels, at least definitionally, is that of minor habits and everyday affairs. I call this the quotidian level. Figure 4.1 illustrates the three-level self.

In dividing the self into three parts, I attempt to follow Socrates's advice and cut nature at the joints (Plato 1961, 511). The joints articulate different parts of an organism—parts that differ in their makeup or composition. The

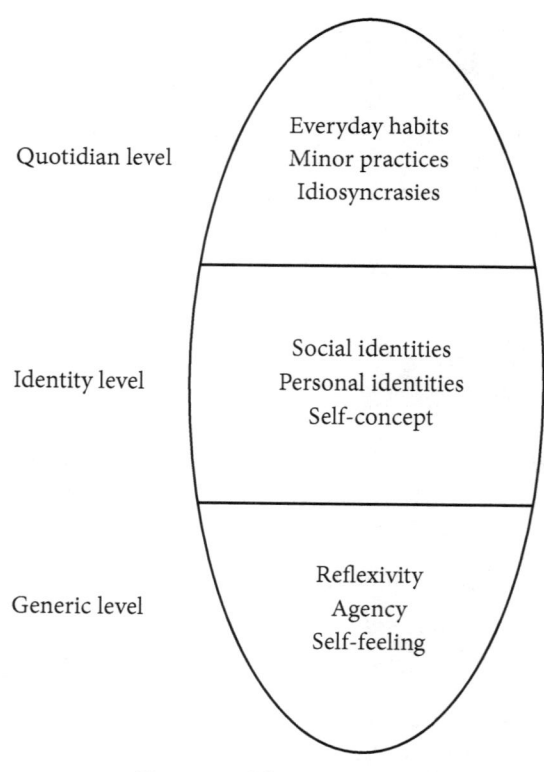

Quotidian level	Everyday habits / Minor practices / Idiosyncrasies
Identity level	Social identities / Personal identities / Self-concept
Generic level	Reflexivity / Agency / Self-feeling

Figure 4.1 *The tripartite self*

generic self differs noticeably from the identity and the identity differs from the quotidian self.

Among these generic traits on the first level are thinking, wanting, and acting. I would also include the James-Cooley notion of "self-feeling," which is the bridge to emotion. The first three qualities are the grounds for reflexivity, internal dialogue, and agency, and they underlie the definitions of Bakhtin, Peirce, and Mead mentioned earlier. These properties vary in nuance from culture to culture and from era to era, but they do not actually come and go. They are always present, and they are so in a way that defines the human being.

Boas (1911), the founder of cultural anthropology, shows that primitives think with the same logic as everyone else. In making this argument he disproved a widespread opinion in anthropology, especially evolutionary anthropology, that the mind of primitives was inferior to the mind of moderns. Wherever humans are, so goes my argument, the generic traits are present and in more or less the same way. If the universal generic traits ever disappear, it will be because we ruined our brains and our world in such a way that our species has become extinct.

The core traits of the first level are not fully present at birth. There has to be an ontogenetic process in which baby learns reflexivity from caretakers, as Mead is famous for explaining. What we are born with is the *capacity* for generic selfhood. Assuming normal parental care and social support, baby will learn the practices of thinking and acting from solicitous caretakers. Unfortunately, not all babies receive these gifts. Some are not appropriately brought into humanity—for example, they are poisoned by toxic drugs during pregnancy—and they do not attain the first level. But these examples of failed basic socialization are not a major concern of this chapter. I only want to point out that the generic human traits, which come through successful primary socialization, are at a level distinct from and more fundamental than the level of identity.

The second level is that of identity itself. Identities can vary from one person to the next and, for a given person, from one period in his or her life to another. Also groups such as families, communities, and even nations have identities. But these are not relevant to the present discussion, so I ignore them.

An important distinction for the identity of the person is between social and individual identities. Examples of the former are the demographic attributes, such as ethnicity, gender, and sexual orientation, although these traits are more profound than mere demography would suggest. We also have qualities that we obtain or form on our own, which are the individual or personal identities. Some people are patient, ambitious, kind, empathetic, or cold. Personal identities are what we usually think of as distinctive of a person, although they are often connected to social identities. For example, I am (according to my wife) kind, smart, and loyal, but I think I am also emotionally reserved, slightly depressed, and a slow learner. These traits coalesce in some way and form a personal style. The style is, in a way, the identity.

There is also a kind of self-awareness by which we think of ourselves as having these identities. This can be called a self-concept. Cooley's looking-glass self, which I discuss in Chapter 9, includes the self-concept. If the identities are coherent and comfortable, the self-concept will be robust and healthy. If the identities are strained, contradictory, or ineffective, the self-concept will be similarly in disarray. For many people the most difficult problem in life is attaining a well-fitting identity and a gratifying self-concept. In these cases much of their inner speech is spent trying to achieve an acceptable identity.

In contrast to the generic self, the level of identity gives us our individuation and self-definition. We are the person we are mainly because of our identity. Minor or quotidian traits can come and go. And generic traits are the same for everyone. It is the identities that give us our distinguishing qualities. And it is these that make or break us as satisfied human beings.

In other words, it is our identity that gives us a life. Some people have no distinct identity, some have a weak and ineffective one, and some have masterful and highly gratifying identities. As I use the term, your identity is a powerful influence on your mental health. A good identity makes you a happy person and a faulty identity can make you miserable.

I also define identity both as a process and as a set of traits (a "product"). Certainly, all the identity work and self-formation that we do is a continuing process. But these processes usually jell into some qualities that may abide and thereby define us.

I also refer to identity as both singular and plural, depending on whether we are looking at a single trait or several at once. When all the traits are looked at together, as a totality or gestalt, we can again use the singular term "identity." These terminological distinctions are matters of convenience.

The third level, which is that of the quotidian self, is, in some ways, the most superficial of the three. It includes ordinary practices and everyday life. Compared with the other two levels, these traits are of less importance. But that is not to say they are of no importance whatsoever. In close relationships such as the primary group or the romantic couple, it is often the little things that count the most. Sloppy bathroom or kitchen habits, or what one person deems sloppy, can become the dominating issue. And although the state of a relationship may depend heavily on the two identities, the quotidian traits can also exert an influential presence.

When we first meet people, we might quickly establish their identities, at least the social component. But having done that, and assuming a continuing interest, it is the quotidian traits we start observing. This is what we see, and these features may form our first impressions. The quotidian qualities are the details of the lifestyle, and if our two lifestyles do not mesh well, the possible relationship may not look worth pursuing. Each of the three levels of the self, then, has its own importance, and the making of a good life, especially in close relationships, requires attention to all features of the self.

As indicated, the identity itself has two aspects: social and personal. The social identity is the quasi-demographic traits mentioned earlier. The individual identity traits are those attributes that we build into ourselves as our lives go on. These traits are, to a great extent, a matter of our choosing, unlike some of the social traits we are born with. The social-demographic traits, however, can also be a matter of how we define them. For example, our ethnicity is how we emphasize and practice it, our gender is how we design it, and our sexual orientation can be a lifetime of experimentation. But for now I only show the differences among the three levels, especially how identity is different both from the invariant, universal traits of the self and also, in a less sharply differentiated way, from the less important quotidian traits of the self.

Review of Identity Issues

Self versus Identity

It should be obvious that I distinguish between identity and the self, the identity being only part of the self. The self includes all three of the levels outlined in Figure 4.1; the identity is only one of the three. The identity can be poorly formed and badly troubled, even though the generic self is just fine. We can have our full powers of thinking and acting, even though we might be paralyzed with indecision concerning what we value and what we want to be.

There can also be problems with the generic level of thinking and acting, and these are likely to be much more serious than problems of identity. Generic problems are usually caused by psychosis, brain damage, or genetic abnormalities. If your thinking is not proceeding in a normal way or if you cannot act, you may have a severe mental illness. Thought disorder is associated with schizophrenia, and problems with acting are associated with serious depression. In contrast, problems with identity are, in psychiatric terms, usually of a less severe nature. These are likely to be nonpsychotic, but they can still seriously diminish a life.

The sociologist most known for equating the self with our identity is Goffman. In his first but highly influential book, *The Presentation of Self in Everyday Life* (1959), as well as elsewhere, he consistently talks as though the self is only a social product, and that it never really attains any autonomy. For him there is no core self (i.e., my generic level) that we are born with—or rather that we form soon after birth. We construct the self, according to Goffman, with our self-presentations, and society also forms our self as it responds to our presentation. Goffman never says this in plain English, but he makes comments that unmistakably imply this derivative view of the self:

> This self... is a *product* of a scene that comes off, and it is not a *cause* of it. The self, then, as a performed character, is not an organic thing that has a specific location, whose fundamental fate is to be born, to mature, and to die; it is a dramatic effect, arising diffusely from a scene that is presented. (1959, 252–253)

> Universal human nature is not a very human thing. By acquiring it, the person becomes a kind of construct, built up not from inner psychic propensities but from moral rules that are impressed upon him from without. (1967, 45)

What seems to explain Goffman's approach to the self is that he draws on a version of James's self-feeling as a definition of the self, rather than the more cognitive Mead-Peirce view. Arguing against James and Cooley, Mead (1934, 173) thinks self-feeling cannot explain the origin of the self in the infant, and therefore he rejects this approach. But James and Cooley define the self not in the cognitive terms of Mead's reflexivity or Peirce's symbolism but in the emotional terms of self-feeling (James 1950a, 305–307; Cooley [1902] 1983, 169–170). The latter is a kind of proto-emotion, which can be seen as a bridge to the entire emotional side of humans.

In my own approach to the self, I combine the cognitive and self-feeling approaches (Wiley 1994, 131), since both are important and also conceptually compatible. If you use self-feeling without cognitive reflexivity, as Goffman seems to do, you have a thinner, more self-constructed self, and you lack the cross-cultural foundation in my generic level. Goffman makes a trade-off, downplaying the cognitive self to better explain human feelings and self-construction. But my tri-level model, which draws on both the cognitive and emotional approaches to the self, combines Goffman's strengths with Mead's explanatory reach.

Foucault and Subjectivity

Foucault (1973, 387) is known for his "death of the subject" statement, although all the French post-structuralists (Derrida, Lacan, Althussar, and Barthes) hold some similar idea. The "death of man" is presumably parallel to Nietzsche's "death of God" (2001, 94). Nietzsche's proclamation is an overstatement; for, despite the existence of many atheists, most people in any given country still believe in God. Similarly, Foucault's death of man or, as he also puts it, erasure of subjectivity, might also be interpreted as a matter of degree.

Certainly, Foucault is not referring to the generic powers of thinking and acting. If thinking had died, Foucault would not have been able to write his books. Nor could civilization have been able to continue. What Foucault says is that the humanistic epistemology of Kant, which claims that humans construct rather than discover meaning, has declined. But Kant's influence has been pretty much confined to professional philosophers, not to the world—or even the European—population. Epistemology, or how people find and make meaning, is very homegrown and stitched into common sense. People do not consult philosophers and then live their cognitive lives in conformity with someone's philosophy.

The prominence and intensity of individualism, and the corresponding importance of subjectivity, does vary across time and space, but it is not an all-or-nothing proposition. The relation between communalism and individualism changes at various times in history and in the cultures anthropologists have studied, but individualism itself is never wiped out; nor is communalism. Foucault's actual writings on this topic are so complex that at least one respectable scholar thinks Foucault is trying to explain and promote the rise of subjectivity rather than its death (Allen 2000).

In terms of my model, Foucault seems to be talking about a change in identities, not a change in the generic self. Not only individuals but also groups of all sizes have identities. The group Foucault seems to be talking about is the educated, philosophically attentive people in the world, especially in Europe and the industrial countries. These people work with a theory of knowledge, something like a Kuhnian paradigm, which is the idea closest to Foucault's episteme. This theory of knowledge is part of a group's cultural identity just as various other cultural systems, such as law or morality, are. These cultural schemes are in constant change, sometimes to the extent that they seem to require a new name. But these changes are not generic changes in my sense of the word. Perhaps one might say Foucault is talking about a change in subjectivity (how we think of ourselves) but not a change in the self or human nature as such. That latter alteration would be a change in species, and it would mean thinkers like Foucault would no longer be able to engage in creative thinking.

Social versus Individual Identity

For some lucky people identity comes easily. Their social identities are inherited from rich and powerful parents, and their psychological identities are developed in protected families and private schools. Their main social identity is that "we are better," meaning their family is better. The main psychological identity is that "we *deserve* to be superior" or "our superiority is *inherent* in us." As Weber says, the higher strata tend to justify themselves by "blood" (1946, 276). This means breeding, and it has strong racist overtones.

Other people have to fight for their identities, often being held back by their social identities. The U.S. Constitution, before the later amendments, defined Native Americans, African Americans, and women as inherently inferior. This is the opposite of the way rich parents usually define their children as inherently superior. Just as this equation gives rich people an easy ride to their mature identities, the minorities' horse gives them a hard ride to their identities.

Minority status hampers identity in two ways. Materially, it holds minorities back in climbing the economic ladder, lessening their chances in the class, status, and power spheres. And psychologically, minority status labels or saddles them with a set of ineffective personal qualities. Minorities have at times been regarded as less talented cognitively, less gifted physically, and sometimes even tied to deviant and criminal tendencies. At present minorities are heavily overrepresented in U.S. prisons.

In Chapter 9 I discuss Cooley's looking-glass self, which is a process that also hurts minorities. If people in the majority impute unattractive qualities to everyone in a minority, this force creates constant tension in the minds of minorities. If some individual thinks we are stupid or ugly, we just have to resist this once. Fight it out, and it's over. But if the opinion is constant over time and more or less universal in the majority group, it's a never-ending battle. And if the means of communicating these insults are indirect and embedded in institutions, it is that much harder to resist. So the looking-glass self can be quite the enemy of a healthy identity for minorities.

A special identity problem minorities have is what W.E.B. Du Bois calls "double consciousness" ([1903] 1994, 2–3). Minorities have a commitment to, or at least membership in, the country in which they live. But they also have membership in, and usually a commitment to, their minority. Minorities usually do not have the opportunity of leaving their minority groups, so for most of them this membership is a permanent trait. They have two cultures or consciousnesses: citizenship in their country and membership in the minority. These two cultures are in conflict, and the result is cognitive dissonance for the persons in question.

This double consciousness is a thorn in these identities, a trait that creates permanent discomfort. But if people in the minority ignore prejudices of the majority culture and pretend they are in a welcoming social environment, they will not see the punch coming, and they will have a more troubled life. Therefore, minority consciousness is inevitably based on a more or less subordinated, colonial identity (Blauner 1969), although this can be lessened to some extent if the minorities can move up the ladder.

Throughout U.S. history minorities have consistently fought for equality (i.e., for nonminority status). And it must be admitted that women, African Americans, Native Americans, and more recently, Latinos and gays and lesbians have done a remarkable job of alleviating their minority status. They now have many of the civil liberties and life chances they deserve. Unfortunately, however, in the last few decades economic inequality has become so extreme in the United States that minorities have merely exchanged one kind of minority status for another. Increasing economic weakness has replaced the cultural weakness of traditional minority status (Wilson 1980). This has led to the *re-minoritization* of U.S. society, losing much of the cultural minority but getting trapped into the new economic minority.

I do not speculate on whether the United States has the political will to restore significant economic equality and social mobility. Even though all Americans may have the same generic attributes of selfhood, and the minority system itself has been weakened, the economic class system is acting as an obstacle to the attainment of satisfactory identities. In other words, social identities are continuing to hold back personal identities. Formerly, the problem was the cultural weight of minority status, but more recently it has been transformed by the weight of economic inequality itself. Or to put it in Weber's terms, the status system of unequal lifestyles is being replaced by the class system of unequal life chances.

I have taken a look at the nature and problems of identity. My purpose is to present some new conceptual tools for analyzing this problem. The identity is in some respect the core of the self. Self-talk and inner speech are central to the ways we form and maintain our identities. It is now time to look further at how we use self-talk to maintain our psychological well-being.

Durkheim's Sacred Self

I mentioned earlier that we are, in a way, little gods and that our inner speech is central to this religion of the self. It was Durkheim who originated this idea. In his essay "Individualism and the Intellectuals" (1973), originally published in 1898, he points out how religion has declined, God is of diminishing importance, and very little remains as sacred. But as he points out, there is a striking exception. The human being, the individual, the self, has actually become more important and sacred as officially religious entities have become less so. Nowadays it is not religion but the system of law—criminal, civil, and administrative—that holds together industrial societies. Law is centered not on God but on the person. The rights of the self are, to a great extent, what integrate law. The strength of the "sacred self" idea is that it allows societies with disparate and conflicting religions to find something that unites them. This unifying element, expanding on an idea introduced by

Robert Bellah (1970), is the secular or civil religion. This religion centers on the sacred self.

An earlier religious idea, Auguste Comte's Religion of Humanity, bears some resemblance to Durkheim's sacred individual. Comte thought science was destroying traditional religion, so he invented an atheist religion of humanity to fill the gap, although it had only quite modest success. Durkheim instead thought that mechanical solidarity or the division of labor, which was roughly equivalent to Weber's rationalization, was destroying religion. For Weber the genius of bureaucratic rationality is a fusion of science and administrative law. Science presents rationality based on quantification and causal logic. Law presents rationality based on normativization and the corresponding regulation of human behavior. Causes and rules are distinctly different social influences, and it is Weber's insight that shows how the two combine to form the bureaucratic world.

Comte, as mentioned, was an atheist and formed an unimportant atheistic religion. Durkheim was also an atheist, but his highly successful theory of religion is based on the emotion of the "sacred," which functions like a god. Weber was also an atheist, but he was obsessed by questions about the meaning of life. One might say that he compensated for his atheism by acting like he was God, explaining as best he could (and possibly better than anyone else) the meaning of life. So atheism, interestingly enough, can have powerful religious consequences.

As bureaucracies grow, they draw on a hybrid structure of science and law that tends to erode all tradition. Weber has no secular religion to fill the gap. But his notion of substantive rationality, which is the inherent value underlying bureaucracy and giving it direction, is similar to Durkheim's sacred self.

Durkheim's sacred individual, then, which he offered to fill the disenchantment gap, is less grand than Comte's idea, and it was also never followed up on or developed by Durkheim. Nor has social theory done much with Durkheim's insight (Marske 1987). The vacuum in social charisma that Durkheim identified remains. But the possible ritualization of the self still possesses important possibilities, and it is an issue for inner speech. Self-talk is an obvious medium for the ceremonialization of the self.

It should be pointed out that when we care for our self as a sacred entity, we are not doing something bizarre or selfish. On the contrary, we are merely going along with the direction in which society is tending, as Durkheim and Weber explain. In other words, despite the secularizing trend, we all have one, highly valuable thing: our personhood and selves. And it makes sense to treat the self as highly valuable. Foucault may have been making a point concerning the technical history of philosophy in his "death of the subject" idea. But in ordinary affairs, if not in philosophy, he got things backward. The self has been becoming *more important not less* in the last couple of centuries.

To understand Durkheim's sacred individual or self, it is helpful to draw on James's concept of "worlds" (James 1950a; Schütz 1962). In talking about experience, James originated the idea of multiple realities, which he also refers to as universes or worlds. We live primarily in the main everyday world. This is the one we return to when we awaken from sleep. There are also other spheres of reality, less central than the main world. Sleep itself, along with dreams, is one of these. When we are asleep, we are not in the main world or even conscious. We are in another psychological universe, and this alternative world has its own dimensions and ontology. Other non-everyday or special worlds are science, the fine arts, sex and love, creativity, religious ecstasy, and chemical highs. Durkheim's idea that the self is a quasi-religious entity and can be rendered sacred fits James's idea of multiple realities, for the sacredness of the self is found in the special world of religious feelings.

Enhancing the Self

The ritualization of the self sharpens and enhances the self. It does this by increasing the solidarity of the "community" that constitutes the self. Group actions, such as family holidays, birthday parties, and intimacy rituals can strengthen the self, but much of this ritualization is also done when we are alone, in communication with ourselves. Throughout this book I use "inner speech" in a broad sense to include not only ordinary language but also various nonverbal forms of self-talk. If you look at yourself in the mirror and smile—by which I mean a supportive, encouraging smile—you are using the language of gesture and engaging in self-talk in the broad sense. Much of the ritualization of the self, which we do by ourselves and privately, is this broadened kind of self-talk.

Durkheim thinks a thing can become sacred if the community wants it to be sacred and acts toward it in the appropriate way. Among the Australian aborigines, anything could become a sacred totem if the community ritualized the object. This process, as previously stated, required an assembly of the people, a focusing of their attention on the object, and the expression of symbols that defined the object as sacred (Collins 2004a, 48). For Durkheim all ritualization, both toward extra-empirical entities such as the gods, and toward elevated empirical entities, such as a nation's flag or some dignitary's grave, has these three features.

A ritual is a performative utterance in J. L. Austin's (1970) sense of the word, meaning it brings something into existence merely by symbolizing it. It does not do this in the main everyday world but in one of the special worlds, the religious one in this case. For Durkheim ritualization brings the sacred into existence merely by acting with respect and awe toward the object to be made sacred. For him the community could make a thing sacred by drawing on the community's solidarity. This solidarity, as he sees it, is the source of all sacredness. If you believe in God, this function of solidarity is how God works. If you do not believe in God, solidarity is itself the most sacred thing in reality. But Durkheim constructed his religious theory so that it would work both for believers and nonbelievers. His theory of religion is a notch above or "meta" to the question of God's existence.

In the case of the sacred self, the community constructs this quality in ceremonies that ritualize the self. These include such ordinary events as child birth, rites of passage, anniversaries, birthdays, and deaths. The ceremonialization of important deaths, such as the war deaths that Abraham Lincoln immortalized in his Gettysburg Address, are especially powerful for sanctifying the self.

But the self can also be made holy by actions that we perform alone. Durkheim thinks that it is only social action that constructs the sacred, but some of the things we do by ourselves are also social. In some respects, the self is a community. There are many parts, aspects, and even "selves" in the self. The I-you-me triad is an example of the plural self approach. Hubert Hermans and Harry Kempen's theory (1993), which allows for several core selves or "I's," is another. Freud's ego-superego-id is still another. Any view of the self that recognizes its plurality of roles or life stages invites ritual. If you assemble, so to speak, all the parts of yourself, you can initiate a self-ritual in the manner than Durkheim describes. If what you want is to soothe, enhance, or strengthen your self, you can utter to yourself an Austinian performative that is formed for that purpose.

One advantage of using Mead's me and Peirce's you at the same time is that you can explain self-encouragement better. When we are faced with a difficult task and we want to boost our self-confidence, we are likely to say something like "You've done it before, and you can do it again." In saying this, the I is talking to both the me (Mead's past self) and the you (Peirce's future self). Encouragement falls naturally into these grooves. We boost confidence in the future by complimenting the past. At halftime the coach tells the football team, "You've been here before, you've kicked butt and stopped the other guys, and you can—I mean *you will*—do it again." This is how we talk to ourselves when in a tough spot, and it draws on a comprehensive I-you-me theory of inner speech.

The way inner speech relates, then, to Durkheim's sacred self is to use Durkheim's three-part ritualization formula. We can soothe, grieve, encourage, embolden, and strengthen the self in this manner. In addition, more intimate relations with the self, such as meditation, can have substantial effects. Durkheim often referred to social solidarity by using the term "mana," which was used in religions of aboriginal Australia. This term was not defined with precision, and there is some historical dispute as to how it was actually used by the natives, but I simply adopt Durkheim's usage, regardless of its exact historicity. For him mana is a kind of psychological strength, not totally unlike the idea of divine grace in Christianity. This idea is also related to the leadership idea of charisma. If you or your community has mana, you are more effective and more confident, and you feel good about yourself. Similarly, if your internal self has mana, you are a better and stronger person.

5

INNER SPEECH AS A LANGUAGE

Saussure and Chomsky

Inner speech appears to be a language of some kind, but it is not clear what kind. The usual view is that inner speech is merely a minor modification of ordinary language. But inner speech has several qualities that make it quite distinct from ordinary, interpersonal language. I present these differences in this chapter and also ask whether these differences are enough to suggest that inner speech is a language of its own, distinct from ordinary language. In doing this I use Ferdinand de Saussure's (1959) notion of language as an analytical device or perhaps a foil.

Saussure made some distinct contributions to linguistics, but he now seems to have only a small following in that discipline, particularly in the United States. However, he has a commanding presence in the discipline of cultural studies, and in that sense his ideas have enormous intellectual power. His model of linguistics has been extremely useful for analyzing nonlinguistic aspects of culture. Since inner speech seems at least as relevant to cultural studies as to linguistics as such, I use Saussure in this chapter as my model of linguistics. It will be apparent that I am in only limited agreement with his thought, and I am not writing as a Saussurean. Rather, I am writing as someone who finds Saussure's concepts quite useful for bringing out the internal dynamics of inner speech.

At the end of this chapter, I briefly discuss Chomsky in relation to inner speech. Chomsky's linguistics, unlike that of Saussure, has had only slight impact on the social sciences, the humanities, and cultural studies. Chomsky's notion of grammatical theory, in constructing a model that he hopes will apply to all languages, is too abstract to have much influence outside of linguistics. So whereas Saussure has only moderate influence in linguistics but a commanding influence in other disciplines, Chomsky has enormous influence in linguistics but almost no influence in other disciplines. This is a paradox, but its explanation will be clearer at the end of this chapter.

I am an ardent fan of Chomsky's political books, which have made a significant contribution to American values. But even though Chomsky thinks these books are implied by his formal linguistics, they seem to have very little, if any, relation to his theory of language.

Turning back to the linguistic description of our topic, inner speech is a condensed version of outer speech, characterized by shortcuts and speaker peculiarities. As previously stated, one scholar, building on Vygotsky, distinguishes four features: (1) silence, (2) syntactical ellipses or shortcuts, (3) semantic embeddedness (i.e., highly condensed word meanings), and (4) egocentricity, or highly personal word meanings (Johnson 1994, 177–179). Even though all people seem to practice inner speech, there is little known about it as a language, other than the broadly defining characteristics. There are no systematic studies of vocabulary or syntax. In this respect it is like dreams. We all have them, but they are so private and vague they resist analysis. In fact, as people are approaching sleep, many find that their inner speech and daydreams get transformed into night dreams.

Despite the fuzziness of inner speech, I attempt to look at it as though it were an actual language, bearing similarities to ordinary or "outer" language. And I use ideas from Saussure to see the extent to which it can be treated as a language from his point of view. To do this I have to make several compromises and adjustments, but this seems unavoidable.

In this chapter, then, I draw on Saussure's (1959) major theses concerning language, among which are the following: (1) Language has two axes: a syntagmatic one on which linguistic syntax unfolds and a paradigmatic one on which we choose words from among their similars and opposites. (2) There are two ways of approaching language temporally. We can study it diachronically, as it originates and changes over time, or, as he prefers, synchronically, as it exists in the present moment. (3) We can define word meanings referentially, by their relation to some extralinguistic object, or, as he chooses, differentially, by their relation to the other words in the language. (4) We can distinguish between empirical speech ("parole") and formal language ("langue"), the latter being a smoothed-over version of the way people actually speak. Linguistics, he says, should study language, not speech.

I show that inner speech does not fit well into Saussure's notion of a public language. It is too personalized, self-styled, and privatized. But when one asks if this is a "private language," in the sense that Ludwig Wittgenstein (1958, para. 244–291) suggests is a contradiction in terms, it is a reasonable fit.

The Consequences of Being a "Silent" Language

When we switch back and forth from outer to inner speech, we certainly do make a lot of linguistic changes. Just going from audible to silent changes the physical layer of language—that is, the phonology and what Saussure calls the signifier. Instead of audibly spoken or written language, it is now all in our head. I do not pay much attention to this silence, but the absence of a phonetic level obviously makes inner speech quite different from ordinary language—in any definition of language.

Another effect of inner speech's silence is that it gives the speaker privacy. If you are having difficulty with a loved one, you can criticize him or her as harshly and bluntly as you want in this medium without arousing anger. This is a way of blowing off steam while maintaining the integrity of the relationship. This device is comparable to writing an angry letter to someone who has offended you but never actually mailing it. The letter can serve as a safety valve, relieving you of your uncomfortable feelings without actually offending the other person. An important part of our inner speech is those cathartic but unmailed mental letters.

The Two Axes: Syntagmatic and Paradigmatic

Saussure distinguishes two principles or axes along which the flow of language proceeds. The syntagmatic, which had long been discussed in linguistics, is that of sentence formation or syntax. The paradigmatic, which had not been singled out before Saussure, is that of word selection. The speaker must choose each word from among a batch of words, all somewhat similar in meaning. And the speaker must also pay attention to words that contrast, particularly binary opposites.

These two axes are structures that inform meaning. On the syntagmatic axis, ideas cannot be elaborated without syntax, otherwise they will be in the much weaker and less flexible form of pidgin language (Bickerton 1990, 118–122). On the paradigmatic axis, words get much of their meaning from their partners or associates (i.e., similars and opposites). These latter are unspoken in a sentence, so they function as an implicit verbal context.

Inner speech, too, has both axes, but their function is more relaxed and less controlling than in outer language. On the syntagmatic axis, the syntax of inner speech, as mentioned earlier, is abbreviated and simplified. Like the language people use in a telegram, this seems to be a simple matter of economy. Why keep saying "I" when you know the subject is always "I"? Just omit the subject, or as Vygotsky (1987b) says, "predicate" the sentence.

Nonlinguistic imagery may also substitute for parts of a sentence. If you are getting hungry, thinking about meeting your spouse at the end of a workday, planning your route home, or thinking about cooking, you might get the imagery of your favorite store, perhaps even of the produce sections and meat counter. If this visual (and olfactory) imagery enters your head, you already have a stimulus that can function syntactically. At this point you can think the simple, one-word sentence "Shop!" and say the whole thing. You don't need the subject, since it's the usual "I." And you do not need modifiers or clauses, since the store imagery is already supplying this information. With all the clues and visual context, the word "shop" is all you need to remind yourself to (a) stop at Whole Foods Market on the way home, (b) pick up a green vegetable, and (c) buy two cuts of fish, (d) some milk, (e) maybe some wine, and (f) possibly a low-calorie dessert.

The abbreviated syntax of inner speech seems to resemble pidgin language in its lack of crucial parts of speech. If it were actually pidgin, it could not handle complex ideas. But the syntax of inner speech is just as involved, if not more so, as ordinary speech. The difference is that inner speech is condensed and folded into itself. Still, all the parts of speech are there, and they could be produced in all their complexity merely by unfolding the internal utterance.

Writers do this all the time when their thought process gets to a highly illuminating insight. They stop the stream of thought, rerun the idea (and the internal language) that contained the insight, and sometimes utter the insightful sentence aloud to themselves. But when they speak it out, they do not use the elliptical syntax of inner speech. They switch to the syntax of outer speech, which is not abbreviated. In doing this they stretch out or unfold the syntax that was implicit in the insightful thought in the first place. The thought was so oversimplified that it looked like pidgin or infantile language. But when the writer replayed the thought to capture the fullness of its meaning, it became clear that the elaborate syntax was there all the time. It got folded into itself for economy, not because of the thinker's deficiency (see the "thinking aloud" research by, e.g., Ericsson 2001).

Inner speech also seems to resemble Basil Bernstein's "restricted code" (Bernstein 1971, 76–94; Tomlinson 2000, 125). Bernstein, who studied the speech patterns of different social classes in England, distinguishes the relatively concrete, local, and syntactically thin code of the less educated from the more abstract, universal, and syntactically rich code of the more educated classes, although both seem to be able to use each other's codes at times. He calls the former "restricted" and the latter "elaborated." But the resemblance of inner speech to the restricted code is misleading. Inner speech seems restricted because it is efficient to speak to oneself in this way. But this is merely the way the crushed or condensed feature of inner speech looks—not the way it has to be.

The uneducated, at least in Bernstein's theory, speak in a simplified code because this fits their local lives and modest educations. Perhaps some cannot speak in the elaborated code. Or, more likely, they use the restricted code as a mask of distrust in speaking to middle-class people. Many people using inner speech in this way do so out of simple convenience, and they could easily translate inner speech into a more elaborate code. In fact, if someone said, "A penny for your thoughts," you would automatically translate them from the abbreviated to a more elaborate code.

All these shortcuts speed up inner speech, making it a more efficient cognitive resource. The best scholarly estimate of this speed at present is ten times as fast as outer speech (Korba 1986, 1990). This speed may vary somewhat depending on the topic of internal conversation, but its rapidity explains how inner speech can keep up with rapidly changing problems. If you wake up to a burning house in the middle of the night, you can plan your escape route, using high-speed inner speech, just as fast as you need to. There are also probably times when one reacts by habit or by some even more physiological response. Then inner speech may be bypassed entirely. But for most problems, inner speech is fast enough to keep up with the demands of the situation.

The elliptical syntax of inner speech, then, is one of its strengths. Its speed creates a powerful intellectual resource, making it in some ways more useful than outer speech. Not that the two are completely distinct. During outer speech or interaction, all parties are simultaneously engaged in inner speech. This process interprets what has been said and rehearses what might be said. At these times inner speech probably runs the usual ten-to-one ratio, allowing it enough temporal play to digest and direct one's contribution to the conversation. But inner speech goes on privately, too, even when there is no conversation with others. At these times it can be seen most dramatically how this speech is useful for fast action.

The paradigmatic axis, too, has its peculiarities, including condensed and egocentric semantic principles. Along with abbreviated syntax, this semantics, as stated earlier, allows us to use fewer words. One is not trying to impress others or, for that matter, trying to capture precise nuances of language. This precision can be obtained later with ordinary language, assuming one needs it.

And if one repeats or overuses key words, even though this might be a deficiency in writing or in conversation, it can work just fine in the internal conversation. Again, you want the job done, and the appropriate language is whatever works best. This means the vocabulary can be quite small, and the same words can be used over and over again. Also adjectives and other modifiers can usually be dispensed with. If you say "girl" (or "guy") you need not add the word "cute," assuming you might want to. This can be handled by visual imagery. You picture a cute girl or guy or even turn on the feeling of "cuteness," making it an emotion rather than a visual image or word.

In this way key words can become condensed, allowing them to carry large numbers of other words or their many possible meanings. If someone makes me angry and I say to myself, "bastard," this can cover a variety of reasons for the anger. The person might have flagrantly wronged me (e.g., more or less stolen something of mine), he might have violated exchange rules by not taking his turn in doing me a favor, he might have insulted me in word or deed, or he may have harmed someone dear to me.

To specify a particular grievance, all you need is the word "bastard" along with a specifier. This specifier can be a visual image of the look on his face, an auditory image of what he said, the emotion of wrongness that we attribute to his action, or even some fringe words (e.g., "lying bastard") that are implicit in the shadow of the main word. The actual condensational processes are usually too complex to dissect, but we can see how one or a few words can be used for many, and how this helps makes inner speech both lean and fast.

Egocentricity also pervades these verbal peculiarities. One is one's own dictionary—that is, one can use words in ways that are peculiar to one's own emotional habits, desires, or personal slang. Each person has his or her own biography, and along this road there are lots of major, sometimes life-changing, events. These events are the stuff of one's personal mythology.

My inner vocabulary is full of these close-to-the-bone words. They are pervaded with what James and Cooley call self-feeling. This is a glow or mana or charisma, usually positive but sometimes negative, that attaches itself to the things closest to us: our persons, our bodies, our prized possessions, and the people who mean the most to us.

When words get their meaning from events peculiar to us, circumscribed by our own intra-subjectivity and completely meaningless in interpersonal conversation, we are in the house of egocentric vocabulary. These packed-with-meaning expressions give our inner speech its emotional flexibility and contribute to its lightning speed. They also show that some things, which are easily said in inner speech, cannot be introduced in outer speech at all. This is our own private little world. It is nobody else's business, and it does tasks for us that could not be accomplished in any other way.

In sum, Saussure's two axes certainly do exist in inner speech. But not as he describes them in outer speech. His syntagmatic and paradigmatic axes are heaped with meaning and complexity. In contrast, those of inner speech are both simpler and more complex. On the one hand, they are simpler in both semantics and syntax, using fewer words and fewer parts of speech. On the other hand, they incorporate so many extralinguistic elements—

visual imagery, tactile sensations, emotion, kinesthetics, smells, tastes, and sounds—that they are far more complex than Saussure's two axes.

So far, then, inner speech is partly responsive to linguistic concepts and partly not. This set of mixed effects will continue as I look at the other Saussurean ideas. I conclude by showing that inner speech both *is* a language (generically) and *is not* a language (specifically)—because its linguistic species has so many peculiarities unshared by outer language.

History versus Systematics

When Saussure compared the history and systematics of language, he framed the problem in terms of outer language. In that medium linguistic change is cultural change. But for inner language, change is not cultural, since this language is ensconced in someone's psychology. Rather, this change is an aspect of human development or the life cycle. And since each person's inner speech is something of a unique tongue, each would have a unique history—though there might also be a shared history based on physical and cultural evolution. In any case, it is clear that the history versus systematics issue would have to be redefined to apply to inner speech.

There are two ways of looking at the shared history of inner speech: phylogenetically in the species and ontogenetically in the life of the infant. The two approaches converge in suggesting that inner speech may have come gradually or in stages. The stages, then, and what they mean, are a major feature of the history.

I just touch on the phylogenesis of inner speech, since this process is known only in broad contours. Still, it is almost certainly a case of the "me" coming at an earlier time period than the "I." Early human communities, to speak very generally, had a highly corporate or integrated character, with little emphasis on the individual or the individual point of view. This social absorption of individuals would seem to encourage the me, the passive self, and virtually disallow the I, the originating or agentic self. The community, which is all-important in early prehistorical periods, would dominate the mind, including inner speech.

The "I" would be quite indistinct and undeveloped until the rise of the individual in urbanized societies. An early example is classical Greece from Homeric to Periclean times. In the *Iliad* and the *Odyssey*, early Homer has no references to psychological processes or elements of the self—no thinking, remembering, deciding, or anticipating, and so on. When these processes come up, they are explained either as physical workings or as the voices of the gods. The later interpellations of Homer, however (i.e., passages obviously written by later writers), do begin to talk about the mind, supplying terms for the major internal processes as well as for the self (Snell [1953] 1982; Onians [1951] 1988).

The more recent urban civilizations of the capitalist industrialization period seem to sharpen individuality even more and thus give more edge to the "I" component of inner speech. In broad strokes, then, it seems clear that humans became more self-conscious and individualized as societies moved toward the urban industrial model. The history of inner speech is one in which the "me" preceded the "I."

Turning to ontogenesis, children develop listening skills before speaking skills, suggesting that they are objects before becoming subjects. They decode before they can encode language. In a similar vein, they learn the word "me" before the word "I." They refer to themselves in the objective case as "me" or by using their given name, examples being "me hungry" or "Janey want cookie." "I" comes, somewhat laboriously, after the word "me."

I argue that this is more than just words. The pre-I infant not only thinks of him- or herself as me; this person is also confined to the me niche of inner speech. The person functions as a me in the thought process, with the other pole of the conversation being somewhat out of reach, though not out of earshot. When children think out loud, which child development specialists refer to as "private speech" (Diaz and Berk 1992), they create a similar externalization of inner speech. They are speaking to themselves as though taking the role of another, often that of the mother.

The staging of inner speech, such that some capacities come before others, explains these developmental oddities. Perhaps the infant discovers the "I" in something akin to Lacan's "mirror stage" ([1966] 1977). For Lacan this stage is from about twelve to eighteen months, and during this period the infant usually discovers his or her self. This discovery can occur in an actual mirror, or it can occur in a more diffuse experiential setting that Lacan seems to think of as a social mirror. As he puts it, "The idea of the mirror should be understood as an object which reflects—not just the visible, but also what is heard, touched and willed by the child" (Lacan 1949, 567; see also Rose 1982, 30). Lacan does not explain how what is heard, touched, or willed might act as a mirror or reflective device. But he opens the door to hearing the voice of others, especially close caretakers.

Lacan's reference to the child's will is reminiscent of Peirce's idea, mentioned earlier, that the child first discovers his or her self by making errors of desire (Peirce 1984, 202–203). What is discovered is an activity that the child was not quite conscious of before. The infant discovers that he or she has an inner energy that can want and seek after given goals, such as the enticing flame. This discovery could be attributed to something or someone else living in the child and controlling him or her. But Peirce thinks the discovery leads directly to a now visible, internal principle that is an actor or agent, or more simply a self.

To discover that you are a self must clear up all sorts of problems. You half knew it before, because you were using the self. You were making things happen, even though they seemed to be happening to you. You had a visceral if indistinct sense of your self all along. In fact, you had been listening to that, sometimes bewildering, self in internal conversations for quite a while. This self is the other end of the ongoing inner dialogue. That dialogical partner is not your mother or some outside authority; it is another part of you. And the conversation is private, no one can hear it, and you can talk about anything you want.

This discovery of self is a crucial step in the fleshing out of inner speech, for now the person has control of both ends of the conversation and can use it to its full potential. The "I" has been added to the "me." The child has moved grammatically from third to first person. And the old "me cookie" and "Janey wants" locutions are replaced by the more assertive "*I want cookie!*"

Presumably, the child will take a while getting used to this new faculty, but this power will soon become the clearinghouse for all aspects of the child. Desires, fears, habits, and understandings will now come together in the newly cleared field of consciousness. This field will be organized by what is now the fully formed dialogical self.

A second ontogenetic progression in the use of inner speech is the transition from nonlinguistic to linguistic elements of speech. I refer to this whole, nonlinguistic bundle simply as images or imagery. Linguistic elements, in contrast, are words and word combinations of language. These latter have full semanticity or meaning, and they are easily amenable to incorporation into syntactical formations.

It seems, as pointed out earlier, that imagery can be used in sentences once syntax has been learned and mastered. You have the empty forms and you can fill them with words or with other kinds of representations. We do this all the time in our inner speech. We can *say* "tree" or picture a tree, and the image can function, just like a word, as a part of speech. But it is not clear that imagery can be used in sentences before syntax has been learned—that is, as a pre-linguistic infant. Maybe there are precursors to syntax, such as a crude sense of the stages or structure of action. If the child has a mental picture of how "grabbing" can be used to get "food," that child may have enough syntax to entertain fantasies or daydreams about eating. This would be early inner speech.

It is known, however, that young children, especially those whose parents are deaf, can learn sign language before they learn ordinary language. This common practice is referred to as "baby sign." No doubt the syntax for these communications is simple and rudimentary, but it is still a case of syntax coming before semantics. Syntax is a set of practices for structuring action. We think of this action as linguistic, but it can also be in other media such as music, mathematics, dance, and painting.

I hypothesize, then, as suggested in Chapter 2, that before we have inner speech in natural language we have a weaker version in nonlinguistic, imagistic language. I now use the term "language" rather loosely, for I am applying it to any media, "linguistic" or otherwise, that can fit into the syntactical framework. I am also loosening up, or trying to loosen up, the notion of syntax. It is clear that images can be used as parts of speech after natural language has been mastered, but I extend this argument to say images can also be used as parts of speech before natural language has been mastered.

I have now shown two pairs of stages in the ontogenesis of inner speech. One is the movement from me to I, or rather to the I-me dialogue, a movement that is also enormously empowering. The second is the movement from imagistic syntax to fully linguistic syntax. This step also gives a great deal more power to inner speech as a device for self-steering. This second move may be the one Vygotsky places at age seven, although maybe it starts somewhat earlier.

My purpose in this section has been to show that the history of inner speech is important and should be studied along with systematics. In other words, Saussure's exclusion of history in favor of systematics does not seem like a good strategy for understanding inner speech.

Differential versus Referential Theories of Meaning

The traditional linguistic theory of word meaning is referential; that is, words are thought to refer to external objects or things, along with the ideas that represent those things. Thus "cow" refers to actual cows along with a list of properties that characterize cows. Within this tradition there has always been controversy over the nature of universal ideas—for example, nominalism versus realism—but this is a sub-issue against the more consensual background of referential theory.

One of Saussure's most revolutionary innovations is to argue that words are defined not in relation to external objects or ideas about those objects but to the other words in the language. He still works with both words and ideas, referring to them as signifiers and signifieds. But the signifieds or ideas are not generated by external objects. These ideational signifieds, too, as with words or signifiers, are defined in relation to each other, with no reference to extralinguistic entities. The cultural studies people just love this innovation, for it gives them a powerful resource for developing their analyses.

This is the differential as opposed to the referential theory of meaning. Previously, it had been thought that words were initially defined referentially, and then the differential component—that is, the relation to other words—operated as a supplementary, contextual factor. Reference gave basic meaning, and context gave additional and more precise meaning. Saussure completely removes the referential component and explains the definition as entirely a matter of relations among words. Thus language is pictured as a self-enclosed system, explainable on its own, with no need to refer to the external world. This is perhaps the single most defining feature of Saussurean linguistics as well as of the larger "structural" movement that it spawned.

The critics of structuralism, many of whom came from older versions of literary criticism, argued that the differential approach had fatal problems. It was unable to explain language acquisition, change, translation, or ostensive definition (by pointing). In addition, it was circular and philosophically idealistic. But the structuralists, despite the objections, stuck to their guns, and their theory was adopted by the post-structuralists and deconstructionists. Such arguments as the death of the subject and of the author are spin-offs from the differential approach.

I think the differential approach is an overstatement, although context certainly does add to meaning. As Dell Hymes puts it, the question of meaning "recalls De Saussure's famous thesis that in language there are only differences. In point of fact, De Saussure probably did not hold that purely negative conception of structure, but rather a view like that of [Kenneth] Pike, for whom features are jointly contrastive and identificational" (1964, 45). Hymes's "contrastive and identificational" are the same as my "differential and referential."

The two sources of meaning, then, seem to work together. When a previously defined word is used in a sentence, the syntagmatic and paradigmatic axes, which are the immediate context, impose additional meaning. In this view, the context can provide indispensible information about a word's meaning, but it does so in addition to, not instead of, a referentially defined meaning. The contributions of the two flows of meaning are each substantial and important.

It may also be true that the relative contribution of the two sources of meaning varies from one type of word to another. "Relations" would seem to be more differentially defined than non-relations. And terms drawn from relationship clusters, such as kinship systems or pieces in a chess game, on the one hand, would seem to be largely differential in definition. On the other hand, classifications of ordinary biological species, such as apples or frogs, would seem much more referential.

Given the two sources of meaning, one might still ask if the referential-differential balance of outer speech is about the same in inner speech. Whatever the relation between the two semantic streams, is there any reason why this relation would be different when we shift to inner language? I argue that inner speech is even more referential than outer speech in some respects but also even more differential in other respects. In other words, its semantic system is polarized between the differential and the referential.

Considering the peculiarities of inner speech, I think its vocabulary would be more differentially defined—that is, more "structural"—than outer speech. First, let me recall the special qualities of inner speech as silent, elliptical, embedded, and egocentric. These qualities make it relatively private, both in the words and their meanings. And these privacy walls push things together, creating links and dependencies among the words.

Let us take the analogy of an intimate relationship, one that has some degree of deviance, with consequent secrecy—in other words, a sexual affair. The mini culture of the relationship tends, because of secrecy, to be cut off from society at large. This culture gets isolated. There is the relationship time, the place, the transportation, the talk, the rituals, and so on. The relationship elements are cut off from the outside world, and they inevitably share in that "relationship" feeling. They also imply each other, causally, sequentially, symbolically, and so on. The relationship meanings are defined more differentially than, perhaps, items in a less deviant relationship. It is the privacy, or in other words the secrecy, that melds things together.

This internal language, though, is not only solitary and private; it is also much more self-styled than outer language. Ordinary language has a smoothed-over or idealized version, which Saussure refers to as language or "langue." And it also has a more stylized, idiosyncratic version. This is its spoken variety, which Saussure refers to as parole or speech. Parole is more heterogeneous than langue, given that the speaking process reflects the unique mentalities of individuals and subcultures.

But by the same logic, inner speech is even more individualized and heterogeneous than outer speech. *Your* spoken or outer speech is somewhat different from *mine*, and both are different from purified or formalized language. But your inner speech, given its elliptical, embedded, and egocentric qualities, is even more different from mine, and both are quite different from the outer langue. In other words, the gap between outer langue and inner speech is greater than that between outer langue and outer speech.

The peculiarities of inner speech are so stitched into the psyche, so personality dependent, that they differ considerably from person to person. This does not seem to be primarily a reference-driven variation, for everyone's inner speech has roughly the same, generic world of reference. The variation in the internal dialogue is largely due to the personal qualities of the speaker, to that person's particular ego needs and shortcuts.

We are little gods in the world of inner speech. We are the only ones, we run the show, we are the boss. This world is almost a little deviant, for it lacks the usual social controls, and we can be as bad or as goofy as we want. Inner speech does have a job to do, however; it has to steer us through the world. That function sets up outer limits, even though within those limits we have free rein to construct this language as we like.

There are similarities to the idealist worldview in inner speech. The philosophical idealists, especially George Berkeley, reduce the outer world to some version of an inner world. They internalize the external, as though it were all a dream, each doing it somewhat differently. For them all speech would be inner, since there is no outer. And since everything would be radiating from the self, everything would be connected via the self.

The Saussurean theory of linguistic differences, whether Saussure actually held it or not, is much like idealistic metaphysics. In both cases everything is dangling from a single string, and some kind of self is pulling the string. The late nineteenth-century British idealists thought all of reality was in relationship, and given that they had only an inner world, they referred to these as "internal relations" (Ewing [1934] 1961, 117–194).

Saussure uses this same phrase, internal relations, to refer to the differences among signifiers and signifieds. Whether he was aligning himself with the idealists or not, there is a similarity between his self-enclosed linguistic world and that of the idealists. It is the denial of reference, of an external world, that underlies this similarity. For Saussure this denial is merely a theoretical move, an "as if" assumption, and not an assertion about the real world. The idealists said there actually was no external world, and Saussure said he would pretend, for methodological reasons, that there was no external world. But regardless of how they get there, they end up in the same place.

If there is no reference, no external world, then the only way language can be defined is internally, by a system of differences. Saussure's purely differential theory of meaning follows from the loss of the referential. But if there is an external world, even for inner speech, then we are back to the dualistic semantic theory—that is, to some sort of balance between referential and differential streams.

Although inner speech is not idealism, in some ways it seems to be a more differentially defined universe than outer speech. Linguistic context is even more important than in outer speech. One reason is that meaning is so condensed on the two axes. But a second is that inner language is so pervaded with emotion. We censor our emotions in ordinary interpersonal speech, hiding our fear, our shame, our jealousy, our gloating. It takes a while for little children to learn this, but when they grow up they are all, men and women alike, pretty good at it. Inner speech is another matter, for it is brutally honest. And its emotional life is "anything goes." We can scream, whoop, and holler to ourselves. Or we can sob on a wailing wall. In fact, we probably emote more in inner speech to compensate for the restrictions on outer speech. Emotions pervade large stretches of inner speech, and they heighten the importance of internal relations.

The determinants of meaning in inner speech seem much more stark and unarguable than in outer speech. Inner speech is enclosed within us, and this seems to make it a more dense set of internal relations, both because of the intense privacy and the more spontaneous emotions. In these respects, inner speech gives a rich example of Saussure's differential meaning system.

Inner speech is also more obviously referential than outer speech. Ordinary speech is quite conventional or arbitrary, and when we say "dog" or "apple pie," the sign has no resemblance to its object. In inner speech, though, the signs are often images of their objects, bearing an iconic or mirroring relation to them. In other words, as mentioned before, there can be a heavy dependency on sensory imagery in forming an internal sentence.

For example, my wife, a social worker, tells me she chooses what clothing to wear in a way that is quite imagistic. "It's a court day, so I'll wear a skirt, a black one." At this point her mind's eye is scanning the hangers of her clothes closet, or rather the hangers are circling on a mental carousel. "Now what *with* the skirt? Here's my new blouse, which I like, but it's too bright. Maybe the beige or the white would be safest. The blue isn't washed. And easy on the accessories."

She reviews all these possibilities with imagery, not words, as she glances at her closet. She selects by slowing down the scanning process and resting on a single article of clothing. Again no words needed. There is just the feeling of attraction or rejection. She can initiate this inner speech process with the word "dress," do the bulk of it with the closet-scanning process, and then conclude it with "Okay." And she does all this not while looking at her closet in the morning but in bed the night before, waiting to fall asleep.

The imagery, primarily visual but also tactile in this case, is dominating in the inner language. These images function as various parts of speech, but they also function as signs of external objects. They refer to the contents of her closet. True, the images of clothing do have interrelations. They give meaning, such as color coordination, to each other. But they also refer to what is in the closet, and this referential meaning is powerful. Not only do the images resemble the closet items; they also lead practically to the actual grabbing and putting on of those items. The whole point is to figure out what to wear, put it all on, and then go downstairs for breakfast and the paper. If there were no reference (i.e., if the closet were empty), this daily routine would be meaningless, and she would not be living in the real world (of being a social worker, etc.).

In conclusion, Saussure's theory of semantics works well for some aspects of inner speech and quite poorly for others—that is, the more referential ones. Here, as in previous sections, we see that Saussure's questions or issues can cast a lot of light on inner speech. They are well worth considering. However, inner speech is quite different from outer speech, and the Saussurean issues must be handled in special ways. Inner speech is only partially fitting to Saussure's theories. New ideas are needed to resolve Saussure's questions.

Parole versus Langue

The last Saussurean idea to be considered is the distinction between parole or speech and langue or language. Parole is the way people actually talk, as it proceeds in the interaction order. Langue is an idealized or formalized version of the way people talk, with standardized semantics, idealized syntax, and a purified set of linguistic rules. "Language" is a simplified and academically more approachable version of speech. In this respect, it has some resemblances with Weber's ideal types, which try to get at the underlying meaning of historical tendencies.

On the face of it, inner speech seemingly exists only in the form of speech and cannot be rendered into the form of "language." Everyone speaks a different dialect of inner speech, and one could not reduce all this variation to something smoothed over and idealized. Inner speech is too wispy and vague to even be identified clearly as a parole much less as a langue.

But we do go back to the same linguistic forms, over and over, in our inner speech, so we must have a grasp of the parole apparatus in some manner. In fact, to be able to steer through the complex syntactical paths of this inner world, we also need some set of rules or practices (or langue). The structures of parole and langue will be different from those in outer language, but there must be some functional equivalents of these structures for the inner speech process to proceed at all.

If we want to make the analogy to the multiple speakers of external language, however, some sort of transformation will be necessary. There simply are not multiple speakers of our own inner speech but only ourselves. Saussure's category of speech comprises the actual speech of an indefinite number of speakers; his language is some sort of amalgamated version of all these individuals. So Saussure's categories cannot be used as they are presently conceptualized.

But if we remember that inner speech is imagistic as well as linguistic, a principle of differentiation is evident. This is in the elaborate assortment of imagist materials we can use for parts of speech. Since these are only loosely tied to the meanings they might represent, they can vary quite a bit. I suggest that the words of inner speech tend to be standardized and small in number, but the imagery is less standardized and larger in number.

Let us say, to use my favorite example, "I'd like a hamburger." There are only a few ways we can say this in ordinary, outer language but a large number of ways in inner language, without uttering a single linguistic word. And I can do so in a large number of individualized ways. This diversity, then, is the "parole," and the core meaning, the desire for a burger, is the "langue."

There is a second way we can use the parole-langue distinction for inner speech, which I explain at greater length. To do this I discuss the pronominal system of inner speech, especially the I-you-me triad, as the formal apparatus or langue. I ignore the vocabulary and syntactical rules. I treat this pronominal scheme as a niche or circuitry or set of channels within which inner speech goes on. The pronouns are the saddle, and if you want to ride through this linguistic land, you have to get on that saddle and inhabit the pronouns.

I think the best example of how this works is seen in watching a good movie. Other aesthetic experiences may have some similarities with this one, but I emphasize film. If the movie is effective enough, one will yield to it and allow it to enter the core of one's consciousness. If this is done, the viewer becomes totally absorbed by the movie, and the movie seems to be going on within oneself. In particular, I think a strongly internalized movie enters the niche of one's inner speech and seems to be oneself talking to oneself.

Of course, one knows it's "just a movie" as one usually does not know during a dream. The viewer could always kick the movie out of his or her consciousness completely or, not going that far, create some distance from the movie (e.g., by pinching oneself). The movie does not occupy one's inner speech channels as naturally and tenaciously as one's own self occupies them.

In addition, the self does not completely exit from the inner speech arena, even though some exiting is necessary for there to be room for the movie. I think the self partially withdraws from this place and partially remains there. This makes the experience one of "split consciousness," for the movie has been allowed into this chamber, but the self still remains there, on the periphery, so to speak.

If the movie flounders—for example, by slowing down, meandering, getting confusing, or losing plausibility—one might find it moving out of that inner consciousness and getting more distinctly external than before. We have now diminished our identification with the movie and placed it back in the category of the other.

But if the movie holds its grip on us, the whole thing is as though it were happening within us and, in a way, to us. The movie becomes our daydream, and it goes in the place of daydreams. Saying we are conscious of the movie is not enough. In a way, the consciousness of the movie *is* our consciousness. Normal consciousness gets suspended or peripheralized, and movie consciousness becomes us.

At the same time, the split consciousness, with the self still inhabiting inner speech, allows the self to carry on its own internal conversation parallel to the one in the movie. For a movie, as Eikhenbaum ([1927] 1974) points out, requires constant interpretation to fill in the gaps, explain the seeming discrepancies, and contextualize the experience, perhaps by comparing it to other movies. Even when we're totally absorbed by a movie, the processing and interrogating goes on. We still look at the movie from above and use inner speech to figure it out.

Notice the movie characters may inhabit one's pronouns (almost as actors inhabit roles). But they do not use one's inner vocabulary and syntax. In particular, their speech is not abbreviated or sped up. They say the same things they say in the movie, using speech patterns as anyone speaking in this language would do. It is an outer language, then, going on in the arena (or on the "screen") of inner language. Of course, it's not crammed into that ten-to-one ratio. A ninety-minute movie takes the full ninety minutes when we allow it in our inner consciousness even though the self, in interpreting this movie, is moving at full inner speech speed. In this way it resembles how the self gives a fast, running commentary on a conversation when we are talking leisurely with other people.

One can also notice the usefulness of Peirce's tuism. This is his idea that inner speech is the I talking with the you. In contrast, Mead says the main inner conversation is between the I and the me, the latter being the self as an object or in the accusative case. It is possible to combine Peirce and Mead into an I-you-me triadic conversation, as mentioned earlier. But in relation to movies, it is obvious that Peirce's model is superior to Mead's. Picture Clark Gable talking to Vivien Leigh in *Gone with the Wind*. The speaker, Gable, fits into Peirce's I niche fine, and the spoken to, Leigh, into his you. But if one tried to shoehorn these movie characters into Mead's model—that is, the I-me—there would be room for the speaker all right but not for the person being spoken too. The speaker (Mead's I) would be talking to him- or herself (Mead's me), and the movie would consist entirely of people talking to themselves. In other words, Mead's model wouldn't work for internalizing a movie or any other conversational script. Perhaps other art forms, especially the novel, might also inhabit the inner speech niche.

There are probably other imaginative experiences that enter the inner speech chambers and seem to be our natural consciousness. Many rituals (e.g., political, patriotic, or religious) can approach this status. People who watch athletic contests with intensity also seem to have internalized these dramas.

But all I need to show is that outer events can sometimes seem like inner speech, somewhat as parole can enter the arena of langue. When this happens, the boundary between inside and outside is traversed. An external event seems internal, which means a third person event has become first person. The identification has to be strong or the performance will remain at arm's length. But once intense identification begins, the outer consciousness permeates the inner. In particular, the personal network (i.e., the I, you, and me) that constitutes the core of the self will be inhabited, at least partially, by these visitors. And it will seem real. Not as real as the paranoid, who experiences completely unrealistic and inappropriate fear. Or the schizophrenic hearing voices, which seem to be those of an outsider. These are cases where the gradual integration of I with the preexisting me breaks down. These unfortunately disturbed souls are only "me's," like prehistoric humans may have been or the infant seems to be. And their "I's" are detached and outside their control, terrorizing them.

Still, the reality of these visiting consciousnesses, occupying the space of inner speech as a parole occupies a langue, is strong enough to give us an out-of-consciousness sort of experience. In this sense, we can say inner speech is hospitable to Saussure's parole-langue distinction, allowing for some redefinition of the key terms.

I have now shown how the Saussurean questions pertain to inner speech. In each case, the questions are only partly applicable, and I have to invent new concepts to answer them. Still, Saussure's categories are useful, acting as a light by which one can see some of the more hidden aspects of inner speech. While inner speech could be examined on the model of outer speech, the more noticeable conclusion is how different inner speech is from outer.

Chomsky's Inability to Explain Inner Speech

Chomsky believes his linguistics is fit especially for inner speech (see his statements quoted in the Introduction). He thinks his linguistic theory explains language, not as a way of communicating but as a way of expressing thought to oneself. This leads to several serious problems. Since I have already expressed these ideas in an article (Wiley 2014), I just list the main points here:

1. For one, using inner speech to communicate with oneself is using language for communication, even though Chomsky says it is not. The self is in two (or more) parts, and one part communicates with the other. This is different from interpersonal communication, but it is still communication.
2. Inner speech uses a much smaller vocabulary than interpersonal speech does. Therefore, if, as Chomsky says, ordinary language can generate an infinite number of sentences, inner speech can generate a much smaller number of sentences, certainly not an infinite number of them.

3. Inner speech uses a lot of nonlinguistic images; Chomsky has no place in his theory for these.
4. Inner speech usually lacks a subject. This is not allowed in Chomsky's theory of syntax and violates his universal grammar.
5. Inner speech has the same condensed quality in all languages. The primary language, from which inner speech is constructed, does not override the linguistics of inner speech. French, German, or English: they all funnel through Vygotsky's condensed syntax and semantics when rendered into inner speech. This suggests inner speech is a distinct language, separate from its underlying or originating languages.
6. Inner speech has no competence, only performance.

Conclusion

I have now worked my way through the Saussurean scheme. It seems that inner speech does not qualify well as a language, at least not with Saussure's concepts. The fact that inner speech is silent tends to disqualify it as a language from any linguistic point of view. A linguistic theory requires an external language, either in the sense of being audible or in writing. You could just ask a lot of people about their inner speech, the way people do research on dreams, but this would be cumbersome and would also only reach a portion of inner speech. A lot of inner speech is so private it is incommunicable.

I do not think inner speech would qualify as a language in Chomsky's terms, either. I am not referring to Chomsky's overtly political writings, which I think are wonderful and a great contribution to the American conscience. His approach to linguistics, however, seems to require written or spoken language. The striking thing about Chomsky's linguistics is how boundaried it is, not only from inner speech but also from the social sciences and everyday thinking. Chomsky has managed to more or less fight off endless critics for many decades, so he obviously has considerable strength in the field of linguistics, at least as it is practiced today. But, unlike earlier forms of linguistics, his ideas are not useful outside his field. This suggests that two kinds of linguistics are needed: something formal and highly specialized, such as Chomsky's version, and something more humanistic and interdisciplinary that can be useful to other disciplines. Saussure fills these latter requirements better than Chomsky does.

6

INNER SPEECH AND AGENCY

There is a well-known argument, discussed in Chapter 1, that thought is often exercised through inner speech. In this chapter I add the claim that action, too, is exercised through inner speech. We talk our thoughts, at least a lot of the time. But we also talk our goals, options, deliberations, plans, and moves. We talk our way through our actions.

In one sense, it is the whole self that decides and acts. But in a more localized or pinpointed sense, action is the work of the dialogical self conversing with itself in the arena of inner speech. Of course, action is often also exercised or carried out through the body, as when we use our fingers to dial a phone number or our legs to run. But inner speech is the controlling or directing factor in action. I apply the agentic model to George Herbert Mead's theory elsewhere (see Wiley, forthcoming).

In the first section I show why inner speech seems to be a necessary condition for agency. In the second section I discuss the structure or stages of action and how inner speech is the control for each. In the third section I discuss a specialized problem of agency: how the mental practice or performance of an act can perfect the motoric or "doing" part of an act.

The Link between Inner Speech and Agency

The term "agency" is not standardized, and the meanings that are used by social scientists vary quite a bit. I keep my definition simple, since I am primarily interested in the relation between agency and inner speech, not in all the intricacies of agency itself. I define agency as the process of conscious and purposive human action, as opposed to automatic reaction. The key word is "purposive." Habitual actions can be at the minimal pole of consciousness and purposefulness, but even in these cases we often make a conscious decision to engage or retain the habit. I do, however, emphasize the less habitual, more deliberate acts, for here is where inner speech has its strongest effects.

This process of agency involves (1) the mental construction or design of a possible action, (2) the actual choosing of this or perhaps some other action from the options at hand, and (3) the behavioral carrying out of the action. In agency we construct, choose, and enact. The following examples illustrate this process.

The kitchen sink is not draining properly, so I start mulling over possible solutions. I consider trying to fix it myself or asking my handy stepson to take a look at it or phoning a plumber. I take a close, mental look at each of the three options. I then decide which path to take. I will ask my stepson, Dan. Then I phone him and ask if he can come over and look at the sink. He fixes it in a snap. At every step I am telling myself what to do and how to do it.

I need a new project, so I consider writing a comprehensive book on inner speech, a book no one has ever gotten around to writing. I ask myself what it would look like, what issues I would consider, and how it would fit into social theory. I try summarizing some of the chapters. It seems to be a viable project, so I decide to start the actual research and writing. I begin churning out the chapters as conference papers and journal articles. The project is moving along, so I find a publisher, turn on the steam, and finish it. Again, I have talked myself through it, from start to finish.

Agency goes on during a series of processes. Action is not a single burst of energy but a buildup or construction that proceeds through a set of steps. It is parallel to speech itself in that it has meaning, proceeds chronologically as narrative, and obeys rules of practical syntax. Each completed action is a little drama, and you are the director of these performances. Agency seems to be located primarily in inner speech and not in some other part or process of the self. One argument for this is that you can observe the agentic process by paying attention to your inner speech. We can watch—or rather listen—to how the dialogical self creates action. It does so in stages, and this makes it easier to observe.

A classic task, at least for academics, is writing a Ph.D. thesis. The rumor is that graduate faculties like slow-moving theses because they keep grad students around a long time and allow universities to exploit their teaching as cheap labor. It is also easier to flunk poor students by wearing them out with delays rather than by summoning up the courage to tell them they are not good enough. Whether these rumors are true or not, a student's own inhibitions and fears probably contribute the most to the slowness of the task.

Another common story, though, is that once a lagging graduate student makes a decision to write the thesis, he or she can do it in a fairly short time. A decision of this nature must be more than just inner speech. Perhaps one's unconscious can contribute a "ripeness" effect. But in any case, it seems like an inner speech phenomenon. We decide, we get a flood of energy, we write furiously, and we hand it in.

If you watch yourself making a minor decision, such as picking a movie or ordering at a restaurant, you can usually hear yourself discussing it with yourself. You may also be discussing it with others, but this does not disallow or supersede the discussion within yourself. The two discussions work together, with the inner one providing interpretation and direction for the outer one. If it is an easy decision, you will just get the approval, so to speak, of the internal partner in your inner conversation. Usually, this inner partner is Peirce's "you." If the decision is a close one, say, between two good movies, you may stage a little debate with yourself. Is one of these movies leaving town soon? Which time of night is better? What am I in the mood for? And what does my spouse want? This dialogue might be lengthy and systematic, short and perfunctory, or so fast that it is more unconscious than conscious. Still, there is a conversation, and you can usually observe how the drift of the conversation leads to the choice.

In the case of more weighty decisions, such as buying a house or changing jobs, the inner conversation is longer and more complicated. And, as mentioned, it will be interspersed within, and even during, conversations with other people concerning this decision. It will proceed over as many weeks as it takes to make the decision. If the external act has stages, say it begins with shopping around for options, you may search for a while and then retreat to inner speech and look at the big picture again, to see if you still want to go through with it. Do we really need a new house? There can be an indefinite number of false starts, retreats to thinking it all over again, and making still more starts. Yet, despite complexity, the process is there, you can easily observe it, and it seems to be the boss or master of the action. We assess, pick, and even sometimes remake the act, and we do so by talking to ourselves about it.

At this point one cannot but remember the pragmatist idea that thought and inner speech are initially evoked by frustrations in one's flow of action. All four of the major pragmatists use this idea at times, but it is most explicit in Dewey's work (1910, 11–12). You want something, you try to get it, your advance toward this goal is blocked by some circumstance, you pause and ask yourself what to do next, and you respond by describing the nature of the impasse and by searching for a way around it. Thought and inner dialogue can be a substitute for overt trial and error. The pragmatists are not always clear about whether the relation between frustration and inner dialogue is first encountered by the species (phylogenetic), by each individual early in life (ontogenetic), or by people throughout their lives. Peirce's example of the burned finger, as he sees it, leads to the discovery of the self. Then, once discovered, you can talk to it in an I-me or I-you conversation. The pragmatists in general, though, merely assert a functional relation between frustrated goal-seeking and inner dialogue. Regardless of whether this actually explains the origin of internal dialogue, it clearly fits the idea that agency is directed by inner speech.

Of course, this does not mean that all inner speech is based on frustrated activity. Some is purposeless daydreaming or reverie. It can amuse one and thereby be an end in itself. Some inner speech is an end in other ways, such as exploring imagery or an idea. And some inner speech is so quiet, involuntary, and dimly conscious, such as the kind we engage in as we approach falling asleep, that the category of purpose does not apply at all. My point is rather that inner speech is often closely related to frustrations, even though many varieties of inner speech are not.

There are also many cases of frustration and agency that are emotional rather than instrumental. We are sad and depressed, but we are not sure why. It may be because of problems in our love life. We talk to ourselves about this sadness, trying to find the social cause, assuming there is one. A major component of this self-talk is the confusing emotions themselves. We try to produce the emotion in our consciousness and take a good look at it. Naming an emotion can sometimes help us find its cause.

It is also possible to "linguify" emotion—that is, to find a syntactical way to place it in our sentences. The emotion can function as a part of speech, especially as a substantive or modifier. This "sententializing" of emotion allows us to use the search function of inner speech to figure out the meaning of the emotion. I am a little angry. Why? Am I angry at someone? At myself? At my computer for not working well? For some unconscious or suppressed reason? I start saying, "I hate you" at all the suspects. I cuss out my computer, and I get a warm feeling in the pit of my stomach. Aha! It's the computer. Inner speech discovered the explanation for the anger and it did so via a verb (hate).

Emotional problems often lead us to other-talk as well as to self-talk. We can talk to friends, family, confidants, and various kinds of counselors. The power of the other can sometimes evoke emotions from us that we are not able to produce in self-talk. This interpersonal talk will be combined with self-talk.

My point in this aside about emotions, though, is to correct the perhaps overanalytical way I am looking at agency. The pragmatists emphasize the oversimplified problems of agency, such as fixing a car or curing an illness. But many problems of agency are emotional or semi-emotional, and they do not submit to analysis as easily as the more mechanical problems do. Still, to come back to my larger point, emotional problems respond, if anything, even more to inner speech than nonemotional problems do. So my argument for the connection between inner speech and agency seems well-founded.

A second argument for the agential role of inner speech is that people who have little or no ability to engage in inner speech also seem to have little foresight into the consequences of their actions. In other words, if inner speech is absent or impaired, people have a weakened power of agency. This applies to children with ADHD (Barkley 1997, 278–282) as well as to most children with autism (Whitehouse, Maybery, and Durkin 2006).

People with brain injuries that hinder inner speech also seem to lack foresight. Both physical and psychological tests reveal that these latter groupings have little use of inner speech (Morin 1993; Rohrer et al. 2008). It is also known that people with brain injuries frequently engage in actions that cause them frustration and difficulties. Since we already know, via self-awareness, that self-talk is a directing part of the deliberation process, and we can see that the absence of inner speech weakens agency, it seems reasonable to conclude that inner speech at least partially controls agency.

The former argument, then, from self-observation, indicates that where there is inner speech there can be planning and foresight. The latter argument indicates that where inner speech is absent, foresight is weakened. Together, they permit a fairly firm conclusion that inner speech is a necessary and more or less sufficient condition for intelligent agency.

The Stages of Agency and Inner Speech

I now look at the structural features of agency, the stages or parts, and how inner speech operates in these parts. The argument in the preceding section concerns the overall cause or relation between inner speech and agency, but the argument of this section, the examination of the stages of action, shows the more specific causal processes or pathways.

Defining

To define an action is to tell oneself what it is or, more specifically, what it means. This includes characterizing the nature of the action, placing it into more general categories, but more importantly, it entails examining the consequences of the act for oneself. In other words, we take a close look at an action and we run it through our system of beliefs, values, and desires. We inspect and we evaluate. We ask how the action articulates with ourselves. The whole time we are, so to speak, interrogating the option or "talking" the definition.

This talk may even construct the reality to some extent. In other words, the action we are talking about may become what we are saying it is. W. I. Thomas says, in a much quoted line, "If men define situations as real, they are real in their consequences" (Thomas and Thomas 1928, 572). Thomas's notion of definition may be an interpersonal process, based on what people say to each other, in which case it is social construction. But it can also be an individual process, based on what we alone say to ourselves, in which case it is psychological construction. Either way, Thomas's definition suggests that this process can entail two distinct relations to reality. We can both describe what it is and construct what we say it is. The line between these two processes is blurry, and we often cannot know which component is the stronger. I think, at least in the short run, describing is usually the stronger statement and constructing is usually a modest addition. But there are several contemporary positions that credit construction as the stronger component. In any case, the Thomas theorem suggests that inner speech not only helps us define an action; it can also to some extent create the action.

Another way of looking at defining is to say that we are often searching for an act with a particular goal in view. We want a means to an end. For example, we are bored and we want something to alleviate the boredom. We may consider having a drink, calling a friend, listening to music, taking a walk, or going to a movie. We list the possibilities to ourselves. And we may anticipate, mentally, the particular satisfaction each will give. This "tasting" of an act can sometimes tell us if it is the one we want—that is, the one that will most effectively relieve our boredom. We try out each act in our imagination and visualize its effect on our mood. This visualization, which can involve emotions and imagery as well as speech, may help us make the decision and find the act we want. But the searchlight itself is inner speech and related modes of dialogue.

Choosing

The process of choosing is much disputed in social theory, since it brings up the matter of free will. This is an issue that gets a divided response, since, as Samuel Johnson once said, "All theory is against the freedom of the will; all experience for it." Free will is an "essentially contested idea," by which I mean an idea that has one valid form of evidence arguing for it and another valid form of evidence arguing against it (modifying Gallie 1956 a bit).

In particular, as noted earlier, it seems to be a necessary condition for society that institutions presume nondetermination, or free will. In particular, rules pervade all societies and it is assumed that people have the capacity to obey or disobey the rules. If people were determined, or even thought to be determined, there would be no point in having rules. In democratic, industrial societies such specific rules as economic contract, civil and criminal law, and civil liberties also pervade the social fabric. So one can think or theorize in a determined world, but it appears one cannot live a normal life except in a world that assumes free choice. There is yet to appear a society that does not assume some freedom of choice.

It also seems unlikely that people would invest a lot of their inner resources thinking and planning to do things in a determined world if they then had to act in an indeterminate social world. Instead, they "think free will," even though this may be, in some technical ontological senses, a philosophical mistake. For thinking in a determined world and then being unprepared to act in a seemingly undetermined social world would be a bigger mistake.

The classical pragmatists themselves are of two minds about human freedom. On the one hand, they recognize the affinity between society and freedom. On the other, they see that the epistemology of natural science requires a cause for every effect, a system of determinism, and a complete absence of causal freedom. Peirce, James, Dewey, and Mead all have commitments to free will, but they also wobble at times and tend toward the determinism of empirical science.

It is possible that there is an objective ontological split here—that there is both a deterministic physical world and a nondeterministic social world. We live in both worlds, moving back and forth from moment to moment. We check the weather (determinism), and we decide to take a drive in the country (nondeterminism). We start the car (determinism), and we decide which music disc to pop into the player (nondeterminism). We feel hunger pangs in our stomach (determinism), and we start looking for a place to stop for lunch (nondeterminism).

I now set aside the choosing we do in the determined world, since we seem merely to rubber-stamp what nature requires of us anyway. As we say, we have no choice. Fighting against the determined world, for example jumping off a high cliff in hopes of defying the law of gravity, is something sane human beings rarely do. If we set aside the worlds of nature, then, this leaves the nondeterministic world, the part that has an intrinsically human component.

Speaking of mental illness, though, there seem to be two reasons people are committed to mental hospitals (i.e., declared to be mentally ill). If, on the one hand, you treat the deterministic world as though it were one where free will prevailed (i.e., if you start jumping off cliffs, etc.), you would be declared out of touch with reality and perhaps too dangerous to self and others to live in the ordinary world. On the other hand, if you treat the social world as deterministic, by ignoring rules, refusing cooperation, obeying impulse, and evading all issues of self-control, this might also get you locked up—for again, you are not living in the real world. You are out of touch with reality.

The world of social institutions, then, is the one the German social theorists had in mind when they distinguished the human sciences from the physical sciences (Windelband 1980). Weber calls the former sciences the sphere of culture. And in contrast to the sphere of nature, he claims that human beings "make" this world. By this he means that the social institutions are products or artifacts of human beings, somewhat in the same way that paintings, music, and literature are the product of human beings. Institutions are less obviously so, since their origins are often buried in the past, and their authorship is much less that of single individuals than is the case with the fine arts. Still, such social institutions as money, language, and law are obviously not given to us in the natural world. They are not like the planets, oceans, and continents. They are cultural forms and human products, however obscure their actual origins.

Decisions about the nonphysical world—that is, the human world—seem to have a voluntary or free component. But for any given act, the volition or freedom may be extremely small. As Marx has said, "Human beings make their own history, but not under circumstances of their own choosing" (1983, 287). He means, given that history has its own structure and tendencies, humans cannot change it as they will. The free play or optional space may be very slight indeed. This is true of individuals in their lives too. Still, in principle there seems to be a modest amount of freedom in human affairs, sometimes more and sometimes less. The result, for present purposes, is that in the choosing moment of cultural actions, inner speech has a more important role than it does in actions confined to the deterministic, physical world. This is because there is more to talk to oneself about.

In physical actions we merely tell or remind ourselves how to cooperate with the laws of nature: "Put that there, hit that first, glue those two parts together," and so on. But in voluntary actions we can both describe and persuade. The rules of society come into play, but one's own set of wants may also become engaged. Given the expanded options in a voluntary act, there are more "moving parts." There is also the whole cajoling or expressive vocabulary in play. "You can do it." "Try harder." "Make your (wife? father? kids? friends?) proud of you," and so on. In other words, the inner speech for physical agency and cultural agency differ a lot. Most inner speech is for the voluntary side of life.

I suggest that the dialogue in these cases is between our cognitive and volitional sides, our mind and our will. The mind says quite clearly that another drink at this cocktail party is a bad idea. It crosses the good health line, and it may hurt your night's sleep. The will, itself fanned by the emotions, says the drink will taste good, keep the buzz buzzing, and make you smarter. The will might convince the mind to alter the picture a bit, to make the drink look less menacing and more delicious. If this happens, the will is winning the argument. If, instead, the mind remembers something that toughens its stand—say, that you are near the legal limit for driving—the mind might start getting more insistent, and the will might get less pushy. The argument can go back and forth for a while, but at some point one of the voices wins.

This kind of dialogue seems to be behind all free choice issues. We are trying to decide which is the best course: engaging in the action under consideration or not. These two pictures will be present in our overall definition of the situation. One picture will look best at the point of decision as a greater good, a lesser evil, or possibly as an irresistible pleasure. The cognition—that is, what you picture and how you picture it—will usually determine the choice. We will choose what looks best, and looking best is the product of our own cognitive definition.

Of course, we did not make this definition out of nothing. We chose it, and the will or choice process had a lot to do with what the cognitive power elected to see. So the will determines the intellect and the intellect in turn determines the will. Both are boss, but in a circular fashion. This might seem like an unsatisfying evasion of the issue, but it has a certain familiarity to the way life goes on. Another way of saying almost the same thing is to adopt James's solution. He says he decided to believe in free will, and his first act of freedom was to believe in free will (Perry 1935, 323). His action, too, seems circular, but perhaps this is simply how things work.

Before leaving this section, let me point out how the self's argument over the next drink fits into the I-you-me scheme. The more cognitive, commonsense spokesperson, which I call the mind or intellect, seems to be the "I." But this "I" is drawing, reflexively, on the "me" by invoking the driving laws and the science of what alcohol does to the body. This bank of rules and information is stored in the generalized other and the memory, which are aspects of the "me." The eager beaver, pushing for another drink, seems to be the "you." For it is the "you"—that is, the self just coming into the present—that will be the "I" that actually makes the decision.

Enacting

Once a choice has been made, carrying out this choice is often simple. But in some cases, circumstances can add complexity. In the decision to commit suicide, to pick a somber example, there is usually a time lag between the decision and when one can carry out the decision. This delay would probably include plenty of internal dialogue concerning the action. For one thing, one might be thinking about the more specific planning details, such as how or where to perform the act. But one might also vacillate in the decision, particularly as the moment approaches (Firestone 1986).

Enacting can also entail several new choices. If you decide to sell your house, to mention another example, you still have to make new decisions about which one to buy. If you divorce your spouse, there are still decisions about what to do next. And, more trivially, if you decide to have a party, you still have to decide on the guest list, the refreshments, and so on. All this shows that enactment itself probably has stages of its own. Just as in the earlier stages of an act, this latter stage requires a lot of direction and the inner speech that guides that direction.

In law the enactment is more important than the decision. If you decide on, but do not act on, an illegal action, there is no crime. It runs the other way in some religious moralities. If you decide on a wrongful act, sinning in your heart, you may be as guilty as if you had carried out the act. I grew up on the South Side of Chicago in the Catholic church. In that setting all sex, including thoughts and fantasies, was a sin (unless you were married and the thoughts concerned your spouse). And all sexual sins were "mortal" rather than "venial" (i.e., they could put you in hell for all eternity). So a fleeting image that you were a bit slow to dismiss could be a serious sin. And if, as was always instilled in us, you were "hit by a car" and killed, you would go straight to hell. You hadn't actually done anything, but the imagery of your inner speech did you in.

Establishing Habits and Skills via Inner Speech

To discuss habits and skills it is necessary to stretch the notion of inner speech to include inner experiences that are slight variations from speech itself. In outer speech there are variations in such forms as body language, gestures, and mispronunciations. These spheres of signification are continuous with speech, and normally they can be interpreted as forms of speech, but they are still structurally a bit different from formal speech itself.

Inner speech also has a variety of peripheral forms. Imagery is an important area of inner experience. Yet images are not language as such, even though images can be incorporated into linguistic utterances. A special form of imagery is the mental practicing of some skill—say, artistic or athletic—as mentioned earlier. Daydreams, too, consist largely of imagery, although they can include dialogue and narrative. Night dreams are characterized largely by images, including emotional imagery, although these dreams can also have dialogue.

In near-sleep states, to continue the list of peripherals, humans can have inner speech, often with lots of uncontrolled imagery. The famous Molly Bloom soliloquy in Joyce's *Ulysses* was her half-asleep experience. These near-sleep events sometimes seem to be happening to someone else, even though they are present in our consciousness. The sensation of falling through space is common in the near-sleep state. A variant of near-sleep experiences are hypnagogic images, which are unusually sharp in their sensory features and often present in lucid dreams. Lucid dreams are dreams that we can control and that are known to be dreams, even as they are transpiring. Some people have lucid dreams and others do not.

Another kind of peripheral is the uncontrolled fantasy, which, again, seems to be happening to someone else. In particular, paranoid fantasies, in which the person seems to be in some kind of danger, can take over consciousness as unwelcome guests. It can require considerable effort to dispel these daydreams from consciousness. Finally, meditation, in which you concentrate, say, on your breathing and attain a state of deep relaxation, is related to inner speech. If you repeat a mantra or talk to your deity, this experience is explicitly linguistic. In the case of inner silence, however, the near suppression of inner speech is what organizes the experience, and it is, in a way, a variant of inner speech.

To take a comprehensive look at inner speech, you have to take into account all the peripheral forms, just as you have to for a comprehensive look at outer speech. Some of these nonlinguistic modalities can be incorporated into inner speech by inserting them into sentences. But much of the time these forms are simply on their own in our stream of consciousness. Inner speech not only has such formal functions as thinking and self-regulation; it also performs less controlled activities such as passive daydreaming, dialogues with visitors, entertainment, browsing, just hanging out in one's mind, and chatting with one's self. The peripheral forms of inner speech, perhaps better designated simply as inner experiences, tend to prevail in the less formal activities of inner speech.

Returning now to habit, James has an incisive discussion of this topic, including the way we might use determination and sentiments to make or break a habit (1950a, 122–123). But Peirce goes one better by suggesting that inner speech on its own can strengthen a habit; that is, we can practice a habit mentally and covertly, getting some of the same strength we would get by practicing a habit physically and overtly. His example, detailed in Chapter 8, is how his younger brother Herbert, probably in his mid-teens, acted when their mother's dress caught fire during a family dinner. Herbert extinguished the flames in a highly skillful manner. Peirce believed you could instill habits mentally, as his brother Herbert had done.

Peirce was a century ahead of his time with this insight. But he gives no other instances of how to do this—none from his own life, for example. Peirce seems to have thought inner speech was more important for self-regulation than it was even for thinking (Colapietro 1989, 99–118). And Peirce discusses self-regulation brilliantly in an abstract, semiotic manner. But he does not do the obvious thing and give us extended examples. My guess is that he attempted to break bad habits and instill good ones in his personal life, but he was not as successful as he had hoped. He may have been too embarrassed to recount his failures. Still, he is correct that working with habits is a major form of self-regulation.

The idea of mentally practicing a habit was not picked up by the other pragmatists, even though Dewey (1930) wrote a whole book on habits. Peirce's comments were in his personal notes, however, and his unpublished papers did not become available until 1956. Dewey uses the notion of habit as the unit of culture, thereby opposing the racist idea that the subcultures of ethnic groups are instinctive and biologically determined. Peirce does not use the notion of habit as the unit of culture, although he could have, since his notion of semiotics is almost the same as Boas's anthropological concept of culture (Wiley 2006b). Instead, he uses it as a way of explaining how self-control works.

Peirce's idea lay fallow for a long time, but eventually it was used to see whether artistic and sports skills could be practiced in the mind. Can you dance, play the violin, or paint better as a result of mental practicing? Or can you improve your swimming, diving, football punting, or basketball layups? In recent years a large number of surveys and experiments have been done in a variety of sports fields that show that imaginative practice can improve athletic skills (Holmes and Calmels 2008). Mental practice bumps into the issue of whether mental imagery is pictorial or, in a highly technical sense, verbal (Tye 1991; Kosslyn 1994). This issue is too complicated for this book, so I touch on mental practice only lightly.

Repeating an act—for example, swimming, overtly in the swimming pool—normally strengthens a habit. But repeating it covertly, in the mind, can also strengthen a habit. I call this inner activity "inner speech," since it can function as parts of sentences. But it is not just inner speech. It is also inner (or mental) swimming itself. And all forms of mental practice for any athletic or artistic skill are of the same nature. The mental use of injured muscles in the rehabilitation process is still another form of mental practice (Holmes and Calmels 2008). In all these cases, inner speech does not just direct activity; it *is* the activity. To put it another way, what is going on here is not so much inner speech as inner agency.

Another way in which inner speech can be useful for directing habits is in the area of mental health. For several decades now cognitive therapy has used inner speech processes to intervene in mental health. This started with mood, especially depression, but now this therapy is used for psychopathologies of all kinds. For my example I single out Donald Meichenbaum's (1977, 201–214) way of confronting phobias with inner speech. Meichenbaum is considered the leading expert on the topic of phobias. Unfortunately, he does not explain the inner speech aspect of his therapy in sufficient detail; he does not actually tell you what to do. So, given that this is an important but insufficiently explained issue, I discuss it at some length. After I show how inner speech can be used to crack open a hardened phobia, I suggest that this method can be used for a wide variety of psychopathologies.

I might first mention that it is currently unknown how much of an ordinary phobia is genetically determined and how much is learned. For the sake of argument, I'm going to assume it's fifty-fifty—that is, about half of a phobia is learned (and therefore treatable), and the other half is determined by your genes or the condition of your brain (and therefore less treatable).

In an ordinary phobic situation, then—for example, fear of heights—the person starts getting anxiety symptoms when he or she is in the frightening situation. These symptoms typically include shortness of breath, rapid heartbeat, sweating, muscular tension, and the feeling that one is no longer in control of one's body. There is also a typical inner speech pattern. The theme of this frightened speech is a frozen passivity, and it is characterized by terror, surrender, the feeling of being dominated, and the relinquishing of one's will. The inner speech might be something like "I can't," "This is too much," "Others will see," or "Get me out of here!" Both the physical symptoms and the mode of inner speech will be inflexible, ritualized, and paralytic. The inner speech, in particular, will be simple, in a narrow range of meanings, and repetitive.

It might not be stretching it too much to say the power of inner speech is, for all practical purposes, nonexistent in a terrifying situation. People can lose their outer speech during intense fear, finding themselves reduced to making a pathetic croaking sound. In nightmares, too, the power of speech can disappear, replaced by animal grunting. So the status of inner speech in fear can actually be paralyzed. When the voice freezes in terror, the job is to get talking started again. Any flowing of inner speech at all is a victory when in fear. But, of course, cognitive therapists want their clients to say particular things to themselves.

Meichenbaum thinks your inner dialogue is the crucial causal strand in these phobic situations. He encourages his clients to try to talk to themselves in some way that does not fit the terror. Instead of voicing despair, he asks them to say something that distances themselves from the physical symptoms. He does not give examples, but it is clear that he wants some kind of self-labeling that is incompatible with the fear reaction.

Staying with fear of heights, I give a hypothetical example of what Meichenbaum seems to be getting at. If you have this fear, and you are, for example, driving over a high bridge, you may find yourself experiencing some of the fear symptoms described above. If the symptoms are severe, you are an unsafe driver, but you still have to get across—or be driven across—one way or another. If the symptoms are not too severe, there are options for changing your inner speech.

Presumably, as you approach the bridge you are saying things to yourself about the frightening situation and also about your reaction to the bridge. In other words, you are saying that the bridge has overwhelming power over you and that you are unable to traverse it in a normal, calm way. You see and address the bridge as a unitary, undivided danger. What you need to do, Meichenbaum seems to be saying, is to start looking at features of the bridge other than its danger. This will not be easy, because fearful inner speech is tightly boundaried. It will be difficult to say anything that is not functionally related to the terror. But if the person, possibly with the help of a therapist, can use self-talk that breaks out of the terrified mode, the cure can begin.

The frightened driver might take a second look at that bridge. Bridges are high so that ships can cross under them. But they do not have to be, and usually are not, uniformly high over their whole span. They can be low and then high, or they can have a low middle with higher beginnings and endings. In other words, they can vary in how frightening they are. Since the driver is locked into a fear pattern, he or she may not notice that the fear stimulus is greater at some points than at others. The driver will be trapped into an unvarying fear pattern and inner speech response from beginning to end. But if the driver can say, "This middle part is not quite as scary as the beginning and end," this is a clue for varying the inner speech pattern. The middle part can be gradually transformed into a "time out."

What Meichenbaum wants is for the client to alter the inner speech pattern so that it begins to be incompatible with extreme, uniform fear. If the fear can go up, down, and then up again, along with the rise and fall of the bridge, the driver may be able to begin altering his or her internal dialogue. If one can say, "Now I'm extremely frightened," and then "Now I'm a bit less frightened," and then "Now I'm very frightened again," the client will have adopted an inner speech pattern that is beginning to be incompatible with a uniformly terrified response.

If the therapy process goes as it is supposed to, the terror should be getting a bit less intense. The fear response should be moving to a less extreme level. And the symptoms themselves should be starting to change from dangerous to neutral—and eventually even to a positive, energizing state. Dividing up the stimulus, the bridge, into parts of differing danger is the beginning of constructing an inner speech pattern that is less overcome with fright. If you can say to yourself, "This part is less frightening," you have begun to release the ritualized clutch of fear.

Another way one might find what Meichenbaum advocates is to divide the span itself into "going up," "at the top," and "going down" stages. If you can divide the stimulus into these three zones, you might be able to alter the nature of the fear reaction at each of the three moments. For example, you might say, "Going down is easier than going up. The height keeps decreasing, and my fear can decrease with it." Or maybe going up can be defined as less frightening than being at the top. The point is that dividing the span up in this way can again give you some cognitive flexibility along with some control over the stimulus.

What Meichenbaum seems to be getting at is having the client create some cognitive dissonance in the situation. This dissonance can serve as a lever for getting some purchase on one's inner speech and, as a result, on the symptoms themselves. Meichenbaum's method—learning to modify a frightened inner speech repertoire and thereby creating a cognitive structure incompatible with the phobic pattern—can be used for other psychopathologies. All phobias and compulsions might respond to this approach. An incessant hand washer can distinguish the wetting down, soaping up, rubbing around, and watering down, for example. And mood disorders such as depression have also been treated with inner speech modification. In all cases the therapist and the patient construct some kind of cognitive dissonance that raises the psychic costs of maintaining the symptom.

Conclusion

This chapter explores how inner speech intersects with agency. Inner speech is a fairly well-defined idea, but agency is much more open-ended. For this reason I had to choose which of the many aspects of agency I would consider. Agency is a sea of meaning because the self is also a sea of meaning. Self is one of our more or less limitless concepts, along with such notions as reality, meaning, truth, value, and so on. We sample elements of meaning from these big ideas, and everyone's sample is a bit different.

A theme I try to hit is that the self is an autonomous, *sui generis* entity. Whatever the self's ontology might be, its activity is largely controlled by its dialogical function. To quote Bakhtin, the self not only engages in dialogue; it is dialogue. Or with Mead, the self is reflexivity and reflexivity is inner dialogue. Or as Peirce likes to say, the self is a sign.

Inner speech is the key self process. Dialogue steers the self, acting as our compass through life. My diagram of the self (Chapter 4) is meant to show, in some detail, how dialogue controls the self. For John Maynard Keynes finance was the magneto of capitalism, and when the magneto failed, the whole system fell with it. Dialogue is the magneto of the self, the controlling process. The things being controlled are the structure and agency of the self, using these terms more or less as they were used in the debate between Anthony Giddens and Margaret Archer (Archer 1982).

In the self the social structure is located primarily in the generalized other. Mead's term suggests that we encounter the social structure as part of the internal dialogue. This is why he gives it the personal name of "other" rather than an impersonal name such as structure. For Mead the I-me dialogue is largely between the "I" and the generalized other—that is, the internalized social structure conceived as a conversational other.

When you add Peirce to Mead, the main strand of the internal conversation is between the "I" and the "you," although there is a simultaneous and indirect conversation between the "I" and the "me." Mead's conversation is now encompassed in a larger, more comprehensive conversation. And Peirce's conversation is similarly part of a larger conversation.

When we act, we draw on all our resources, including both agency (our ability to design and complete an act) and structure (our access to the social rules and resources). Along with the generalized other, we also draw on habits and memory. When, in Chapter 10, on theory, I describe the complex connections between the "me" and the "you," I talk about the connections between structure and agency.

The interaction of structure and agency seems wide open and undetermined from either direction. We choose how dependent we will be on the structure just as we choose how innovative we will be in action. How this balance works out depends on the circumstances, the internal conversation, and the free will of the agent.

The self is the crossroads of several ontological levels—culture, structure, person, physical body, and so on. A variety of influences come together and influence the life of the self. But it is the dialogical process itself that produces these outcomes.

7

PRAGMATISM AND THE DIALOGICAL SELF

The classical American pragmatists, Peirce, James, Mead, and Dewey, are known for their theory of meaning. The idea that the meaning of a statement is in its practical or activist consequences is considered their common denominator. But these thinkers also have innovative ideas concerning human nature and the self, the most central being that the self is an internal dialogue. In addition, the two ideas, meaning and dialogue, are connected. Humans pursue meaning by the dialogical method. This method is enacted both publicly via interpersonal and communal dialogue and privately by virtue of inner speech or the dialogical self. Inner speech is the key to the human semiotic or symbolic ability, itself the means of inventing culture.

Close examination of the dialogical self in the pragmatists is a fairly recent development, and I mention some of the important publications. Eugene Rochberg-Halton (1986, 24–40) took what I think was the first decisive step toward identifying the pragmatists' dialogical self, comparing the self theories of Dewey, Peirce, and Mead. Rochberg-Halton does not talk directly about inner speech, but he does show how the structure of the self, as seen by each theorist, allows and might conduct inner speech. Soon after Rochberg-Halton had unlocked this door, James Hoopes (1989, 190–233) opened it by systematically comparing the self theories of Peirce, James, and Dewey. And independently, Colapietro (1989) analyzed Peirce's theory of self at length, making the first sustained examination of the pragmatists' dialogical self. Then Perinbanayagam (1991a) wrote a book chapter on the dialogical self, discussing Buber and Bakhtin as well as Mead and Peirce. Later, I (Wiley

1994) compared Peirce and Mead, showing how each takes the theory of the internal conversation in a somewhat different but complementary direction. More recently, Archer (2003) made an innovative analysis and empirical study of pragmatism's theory of inner speech, covering James, Peirce, and Mead. Finally, Collins (2004b) showed the relevance of the inner speech discussion to a wide variety of theoretical issues.

Since this idea is now of considerable interest, it is important to understand how the notion of inner speech began to be discussed and developed among the pragmatists. This chapter is an overview of how the pragmatists treat this idea, touching on James, Peirce, Mead, and Dewey. I also discuss the views of two sociologists who followed the pragmatist tradition, Cooley and Herbert Blumer. Then I look at the pragmatist's theory of meaning, showing how it might include a sociocultural dimension and distinguishing it from the more private systems of meaning all humans seem to have. I conclude by listing the advantages of including the dialogical self as a central pragmatist issue.

James and Preliminary Concepts

As previously mentioned, there tend to be two approaches to self theory: that the self is a particular kind of feeling or emotion and that the self is a special cognition (Mead 1934, 173). The first is the self-feeling approach, and its prominent exponents are James and Cooley. The second is the reflexive approach, or the idea that the self is that which is aware of itself. Peirce, Dewey, and Mead follow the reflexive path. James has several ideas that are useful and foundational for the theory of inner speech, but he does not work with the idea as such. The theory of inner speech is a smooth outgrowth of reflexive theory, but it is only indirectly related to self-feeling theory.

Actually, Peirce wrote about inner speech well before James wrote his background concepts. But although James's ideas are not chronologically prior to those of Peirce, they are what might be called analytically prior. James's main two relevant ideas, then, are the naming of the "I and me" components of the self and the description of the stream of consciousness. He also gets close to the dialogical self, especially in the "divided self" section of the *Varieties of Religious Experience* (1970, 143–159). But he never specifically names and analyzes this idea.

As James puts it in originating the I-me distinction:

> We may sum up by saying that personality implies the incessant presence of two elements, an objective person, known by a passing subjective Thought and recognized as continuing in time. Hereafter let us use the words ME and I for the empirical person and the judging

Thought . . . if the passing thought be the directly verifiable existent which no school has hitherto doubted it to be, then that thought itself is the thinker, and psychology need not look beyond. (1950a, 371, 401)

For James, then, the "me" is the empirical person, and the "I" is the passing thought, which he equates with the thinker. These definitions are not the same as Mead's I and me, which are the elements of his internal conversation, but they are extremely close. James's "thinker" can easily be visualized as communicating with that thinker's empirical self. In fact, it seems highly likely that Mead's I-me dialogical self was formed by moving James's I-me a short step further.

James's identification and analysis of the stream of consciousness, as mentioned earlier, is a major contribution to the psychology of the self. This stream is the inner life, including all the feelings, sensations, and ideas that flow through the person. James does not emphasize language in this context, but the organizing principle of this stream seems to be language or inner speech. When Mead describes the I-me conversation, he is talking about James's stream of consciousness but with the emphasis on the directing or controlling linguistic feature of that stream.

Sometimes inner speech can just be a small aspect of the stream, but at other times it can embrace wide swatches of this stream. When James's stream of consciousness was used by James Joyce, Virginia Woolf, and other modernist novelists to get at the inner life of their characters, they drew on the linguistic aspect of this stream (Humphrey 1962). Like Mead, they pushed James a step further, centering on internal speech as the key ingredient of the stream. James constructs a powerful infrastructure for the dialogical self, even though he does not quite explicate the dialogical self as such (but see Hermans and Kempen 1993, 44–45, for the application of James's I-me distinction to contemporary dialogical self theory).

Peirce and the Rediscovery of the Dialogical Self

Plato made the point that thought is the self talking to itself. Subsequent to Plato there was little scholarly work on inner speech as such, as explained earlier. It was not until Peirce that inner speech was clearly identified, thematized, and analyzed. Peirce knew the medieval language of thought discussion, but he also knew the relatively slight writings on inner speech as ordinary language. For all practical purposes he took an idea from Plato and applied it to contemporary theory. He showed how inner speech fit into the theory of semiotics and also into the development of the person.

Although pragmatists have always been aware of Peirce's dialogism and its relation to his semiotics, Colapietro (1989) is the first to fully grasp the importance of inner speech for Peirce. Peirce has no treatise or extended discussion of inner speech, but he makes important brief comments here and there, including in his unpublished papers. Colapietro has pieced these fragments together and shows how Peirce uses them to explain the moral capacity of humans. In particular, Colapietro singles out the way Peirce views inner speech as the capability for self-determination and self-regulation.

A characteristic statement by Peirce is the following:

> A person is not absolutely an individual. His thoughts are what he is "saying to himself," that is, saying to that other self that is just coming into life in the flow of time. When one reasons, it is the critical self that one is trying to persuade, and all thought whatsoever is a sign, and is mostly of the nature of language. The second thing to remember is that the man's circle of society (however widely or narrowly this phrase may be understood), is sort of a loosely compacted person, in some respects of higher rank that the person of an individual organism. (1934, 421)

This text is full of ideas, and I have to ignore most of them to stay on theme. The most obvious moral point is that we check with our "critical self" in deciding what to do. This gives the individual a certain moral directionality or teleology.

But there are two other points in Peirce's writings that show more clearly how inner speech is involved in moral choice. One has to do with modeling our options, internally, so we can visualize the choices that lie before us. The critical self, which is more or less the conscience, may not give us detailed instructions on how to act. But if we attempt to foresee the various paths along which we might go, we can more clearly see what is right for us. Then we are faced with two distinct acts of choice. One is to choose the internal model, the inner speech scenario that looks best to us. This is already a pre-choice or a preparation for action. Then we choose which action to follow in the world of external behavior. This is choice in the usual sense of the word. But the pre-choice of the inner speech selection is a causal factor in how we eventually choose to act.

Peirce also discusses inner speech in relation to habit formation and choice, which is merely an extension of the point already made. Here Peirce proposes that one can break bad habits and institute good ones by internal modeling of the good. Now a single moral choice is turned into a series of such choices (i.e., a habit). Peirce believes that the internal conversation is a potent weapon for steering one's habits.

My impression is that he got these ideas from reading Friedrich Schiller's *On the Aesthetic Education of Man* ([1795] 1967) as a teenager (Wiley 2006b).

Schiller's intense book concerns the moral problem of striking a balance between one's physical and spiritual sides by using the aesthetic as a bridge. It was at this point in his life that Peirce conceived the internal conversation as going on among an "I," "Thou," and "It"—that is, the first, second, and third persons, grammatically speaking. His I-thou-it triad is close to my I-you-me triad, although Peirce does not say enough about his triad to permit comparisons. He may have also modeled these three pronouns against Schiller's triad—for example, the "I" as the mind or spirit, the "it" as the body, and the "thou" as the aesthetic bridge between the two. But this is a guess, and Peirce may have merely used the pronouns as pronouns.

In any case, Peirce seems to have stumbled onto inner speech in a moral context, specifically in the context of his own adolescent formation and quest for identity. Presumably, it did him some good in navigating through the teenage years, and it may have also served him in later years. But Peirce does not seem to have done very well controlling his bad habits, especially gambling, extravagant living, womanizing, and taking consciousness-altering drugs (though the latter may have been self-medication for a neurological condition).

My point, then, is that Peirce reintroduced inner speech into the history of thought (Archer 2003, 65). For him most thought is in inner speech, usually but not always in language. By and large, cognition is conducted within the medium of the internal conversation. But within this larger function, he emphasizes the power of agency and the moral leverage that inner speech can bring. The fact that Peirce himself did not seem very successful in using this agency is of interest, his bad habits controlling his life. But the tyranny of his habits does not lessen the importance of his rediscovery of inner speech.

Mead's Internal Conversation of I and Me

Here is Mead's version of the internal conversation:

> Thinking is a process of conversation with one's self when the individual takes the attitude of the other, especially when he takes the common attitude of the whole group, when the symbol that he uses is a common symbol, has a meaning common to the entire group, to everyone who is in it and to anyone who might be in it. . . . There is a field, a sort of inner forum, in which we are the only spectators and the only actors. In that field each one of us confers with himself. He asks and answers questions. He develops his ideas and arranges and organizes those ideas as he might do in conversation with somebody else. (1936, 380–381, 401)

As this quotation suggests, Mead contrasts with James in actually developing the I-me distinction into the basis of internal conversation and the dialogical self. But he contrasts with Peirce in the way he structures the internal conversation. For one thing, Peirce has the person or "I" talking to his "you," the "self that is just coming into life in the flow of time." But Mead has the self conversing with his "me," which is the self considered as an object. Temporally speaking, the me is in the past. Mead often said the me is the I of the previous moment, having passed into the past and having become an addition to the me. Peirce, then, has the conversation pointed toward the person of the immediate future, and Mead has it pointed toward the person of the immediate past.

There is also a noticeable ambiguity or vacillation in Mead over whether the I is talking to the me or to the generalized other. The me is yourself viewed pronominally as in the objective case, or temporally as in the past. The generalized other, in contrast, is the community viewed as a quasi-person. In particular, as Mead uses the term, it is the community's conscience or common morality. If the internal conversation is between the I and me, it works within the individual's own moral system. If it is between the I and the generalized other, it works within the community's moral system. These can be quite different things. For example, I am liberal in both my economic and cultural attitudes. I am often well to the left of the community's moral standards, taken as some kind of average or typicality. So my own internal conversation is almost always with my me. On rare occasions—for example, when I think an issue is so explosive it may end up in court before a judge or jury—I may want to check in with my community's standards (i.e., the generalized other). This version of my internal conversation is labeled by me as specialized or bracketed, because it is not dealing with my own morality.

This issue comes up in Archer's first book on inner speech (2003, 78–79), in which she says Mead has an over-socialized view of human beings. I disagreed with her in my review of her book (Wiley 2005), but I now realize she is right if she is emphasizing the fact that Mead often defined the internal conversation as going on between the I and the generalized other. That emphasis suggests that the person doing the thinking is committed to the generalized other (and is therefore over-socialized). So we are left with an awkward wobbler in Mead's position. When he has the internal conversation going on between the I and the me, he is open to whatever moral or political stance the person may have. But when he has this conversation going on between the I and the generalized other, he is leaning toward the politically conservative, over-socialized position. This means the reader had to make up his or her own mind which Mead to follow. I am personally a left liberal, so I almost always lean in that direction, including in my interpretation of Mead.

This pronominal difference between the "me" and the "you" is related to a functional difference in the way the two theorists treat the internal conversation. Both Peirce and Mead regard all thought as primarily conversational. But within this larger category, Peirce emphasizes the moral aspect, and Mead, while not neglecting the moral side, emphasizes the purely cognitive side. For Mead the internal conversation solves problems, typical ones being whether to use a shoe to pound a nail when a hammer is unavailable or how to jump across a ditch. There is also a persistent intellectuality in Mead's inner speech, somewhat as a professor might construct and rehearse a lecture. Emotion, especially emotional impasses and crises, is avoided. When I talk about Bahktin in Chapter 10, it becomes clear how the pragmatists intellectualize consciousness. James's self-feeling might be a useful bridge between Peirce's and Mead's cognitive tilt and Bahktin's greater concern with passion.

Mead also discusses how we talk with the generalized other to calibrate our actions with social morality. This is not the only cognitive function the generalized other has in his system (Dodds, Lawrence, and Valsiner 1997). When talking of his main ideas, "sensitizing" or loosely fabricated concepts that they are, Mead might use somewhat different language from time to time. Among his major concepts are the significant symbol, role-taking, the act, the me, the I, and the generalized other. This variation in language reflects Mead's metonymical tendency to use the part for the whole. A concept might have a half dozen key properties or features, and Mead might sometimes refer to it with one aspect and sometimes with another. This variability seems sloppy, but it merely reflects the fact that Mead was crafting his concepts as he went along. You have to watch closely to follow his mind.

You also have to interpret Mead as you go along; that is, you have to deal with his varying emphases and priorities. When you read people's discussions of Mead, it is common to find a fair amount of disagreement. Each portrait does not seem quite like the same Mead. Given the somewhat casual nature of many of his texts, it is impossible to find out exactly "what he said." And I do not think it important to strive for exactitude. Mead presents us with a rich array of theoretical resources, and it is up to scholars to, in a sense, pick and choose. Still, I think that with reasonable caution it is possible to come close to what Mead really thought. I also think it is possible for scholars to "take it and run," meaning to move Mead's ideas along and make something new.

There is also the issue Collins brings up (1989, 5): that Mead, who began as a religious person and had highly religious parents, may have felt uncomfortable about (seemingly) having become an atheist. As pointed out earlier, in the transition from medieval to modern philosophy, the soul was reconceptualized as the self. Mead reenacted this transition in his own intellectual transformations. Mead may have been a bit evasive about his atheism at times, to not offend his mother. This is similar to the idea that Vygotsky and

Bahktin had to pull their punches to not be in too much conflict with the Communist party line at times. There is not much a scholar can do about these ghosts standing behind a scholar's writings. One can just avoid or de-emphasize issues that might have been affected by some ideological force in the background. With Mead it is not too difficult to allow for his possibly softening his stand at times, but for Bakhtin it is a more severe problem.

Returning to Mead's concept of the generalized other, he seems to deal with several distinct facets of this idea. The best known is the moral one, and in this sense the term means roughly the same as the conscience or Freud's super ego. It is also pretty much the same as Peirce's "critical self." Moral rules tend to be institutionalized in religion and in public law, although more informally they are also enforced in primary groups and communities.

Mead also interprets the generalized other as a control over our common sense, logic, and scientific method. If you use the community's language, you have to follow the semantic and grammatical rules, as suggested by Mead above. More broadly, the community has rules concerning what is rational and cognitively acceptable. If one violates these rules, the result is cognitive error or perhaps the more fundamental problems of delusion and hallucination. These rules are institutionalized in the (constantly changing) theories of abnormal psychology and psychiatry, although they are also enforced in more informal social channels.

A third major way in which Mead uses the generalized other is to mean someone we might be talking to—a sort of imaginary companion, listener, or "everyman." Lonnie Athens refers to this version of the generalized other with his interesting concept of the "phantom other" (1994, 525). People who are quite religious might place God in their inner speech forum, either instead of or along with the generalized other. Mead seemed to be fleeing from God, and he did not mention this possibility.

If we interpret Mead's generalized other as always and only the conscience, it might appear that his internal conversation was overwhelmingly moral, even more so than Peirce's. But, as said, his generalized other has at least three major aspects: a conscience, a logic machine, and an "anyone" with whom we might be conversing. So it is simultaneously moral, cognitive, and a sort of placeholder. I think the generalized other also has additional complications, but these three seem major and they help us understand the subtlety of Mead's theory of inner speech.

An additional confusion, as discussed a little earlier, comes from the fact that Mead tends to place the generalized other in or near the "me." Sometimes we have an I-me conversation and sometimes an I–generalized other. Mead does not explain this seeming ambiguity, but perhaps it is not hugely important. Given that the me also has several aspects of its own, the combination of the me and the generalized other would have to be treated carefully.

This is the way it is with geniuses, especially those who are constructing systems of basic ideas that did not previously exist. They are confusing. But if we do the job of carefully unraveling their lines of thought, the work is well worth it.

Dewey and the Mental Experiment

Like the other pragmatists, Dewey thinks inner speech is a way of solving problems without overtly carrying out a trial-and-error process. This ability developed in evolution, and it was the distinctive human process—that is, the key to human intelligence. As Dewey explains it:

> Deliberation is a dramatic rehearsal (in imagination) of various competing possible lines of action. It starts from the blocking of efficient overt action. . . . Then each habit, each impulse, involved in the temporary suspension of overt action takes its turn in being tried out. Deliberation is an experiment in finding out what the various lines of possible action are really like. But the trial is in imagination, not in overt fact. (1930, 190)

Dewey's inner speech is a search process, seeking the best way of reaching some goal. It fits with the thought of James, Peirce, and Mead, but it adds an emphasis on genesis, on how blocked action triggers inner speech. This happened both phylogenetically in the primates and ontogenetically in the human infant. Dewey was impressed at what an advance inner speech is in the process of evolution and how it lifts the moral importance of human beings.

> The modern discovery of inner experience, of a realm of purely personal events that are always at the individual's command, and that are his exclusively as well as inexpensively for refuge, consolation and thrill is also a great and liberating discovery. It implies a new worth and sense of dignity in human individuality. ([1929] 1958, 172)

Here Dewey adds "refuge, consolation and thrill," suggesting that inner speech has a wide variety of uses other than just basic cognitive search. Dewey does not talk about daydreaming, but this process is evoked by his language in the preceding quotation.

Cooley and the Imaginary Companion

Cooley got most of his insights concerning child development from observing his own three children (Jacobs 2006). He adopted the view that thought is a process of talking to oneself. And he noted that his children initially thought out loud and later submerged this conversation into silent inner speech. This resembles Vygotsky's line of thinking, the one I disagree with in Chapter 2. But Cooley had the unique view that early thought occurs when talking to one's imaginary companion. Evidently because his own children had imaginary companions, he assumed that all children do. As he says:

> When left to themselves children continue the joys of sociability by means of an imaginary playmate. Although all must have noticed this who have observed children at all, only close and constant observation will enable one to realize the extent to which it is carried on. It is not an occasional practice, but, rather, *a necessary form of thought*. . . . Thus the imaginary companionship which a child of three or four years so naively creates and expresses is something elementary and almost omnipresent in the thought of a normal person. ([1902] 1983, 88, 96; emphasis added)

Cooley evidently thought the imaginary companion, whom he regarded as present in the lives of all children, was the precursor of the "generalized other" whom, according to Mead, adults tend to address when they talk to themselves. However, Marjorie Taylor (1999) finds that only about 65 percent of children have imaginary companions, and other scholars have reported similar findings. I think this conclusion of Cooley's is what is called "being right for the wrong reason." He is talking about Mead's generalized other as placeholder, or Athens's phantom other, but I think he has the genesis wrong, at least for the other 35 percent of the population.

For people who lacked an imaginary companion in childhood, the "anybody" of the internal conversation must be an ordinary abstraction or generalization, formed much like any other abstraction. For the 65 percent or so who began with an imaginary companion, this generalized other may have a much more intimate and emotionally tinged quality than it has for other people, but there seems to be no research on this question. Despite what seems to be a partial error on Cooley's part, he does cast light on the "generalized other" issue. There is a convergence among Mead, Cooley, and Athens on this question.

Cooley himself was personally troubled by several minor flaws and disabilities. He had a high-pitched voice, spoke with a stutter, was slightly deaf, and was extremely shy. As a result, he lived in his own mind to a great extent (i.e., valuing inner speech more than outer speech). Did he also have an imaginary companion, and if so, how long did he have it? He does not explicitly tell us, but his comment about an imaginary companion being a necessary form of thought suggests that he did. Overall, his interpersonal problems sound like strengths for his scholarly interests. He was researching the self or mind, and since his phobias constantly drove him into the inner reaches of his mind, he seems to have put his disabilities to good use.

Another distinction of Cooley's is that he preceded Mead in his theories of child development. In particular, although Cooley did not develop the inner speech model as extensively or as well as Mead did, he had the idea of inner speech ([1902] 1983, 88–97) well before Mead first wrote on the topic (1909 briefly and 1913 extensively). Mead did not give credit to Cooley for his intellectual priority. Also, after Cooley died, Mead wrote a highly critical and, in my opinion, inaccurate appraisal of Cooley's work (Mead 1930; Wiley 2011b). My impression is that Cooley and Mead had some kind of falling out when they were both on the faculty at the University of Michigan, Cooley as a teaching assistant and Mead as a junior professor. They were perhaps the only two people at this university working on the social self, and this may have placed them in competition from the start. They were both disciples of Dewey, who was also on the Michigan faculty at that time, and my guess is that they fought over Dewey's approval of their ideas. There is some documentary evidence for my interpretation, but it is not completely conclusive (see Cook 1993, 199n19).

Blumer and Agency

Blumer was a graduate student at the University of Chicago, and he was given Mead's classes when Mead died in 1931. Blumer was the major interpreter of Mead for a long time. He was also the founder of a substantial school of thought called symbolic interactionism, which was based on Mead's theories. Blumer was not only an important scholar; he was also a somewhat larger-than-life, almost mythical personality. He had played football at the University of Missouri, and later he played for the Chicago Cardinals, a professional team. He was famous for coming to his Monday seminars with a bandaged face from the Sunday game. He was also friendly with criminals and social revolutionaries.

Among Blumer's concepts is inner speech, which he refers to as "self interaction." He sees all action as directed and guided by inner speech. As he says:

> By virtue of self-interaction the human being becomes an acting organism coping with situations in place of being an organism merely responding to the play of factors. And his action becomes something he constructs and directs to meet the situations in place of an unrolling of reactions evoked from him. (1969, 73)

Blumer is here arguing against both behaviorism and over-socialized views, which visualize action as a kind of unrolling of built-in and normatively regulated responses. Blumer is emphasizing the deliberation and thinking-it-over, which, as he sees it, precedes action and takes the form of inner speech. Here Blumer is reminiscent of W. I. Thomas's definition of the situation, although Blumer's definition is usually a redefinition for any given situation. Blumer liked to slug it out with his intellectual competitors, especially Talcott Parsons and functionalism, which he thought presented an over-socialized view of action and needed inner speech as a corrective.

In relation to the determinism of human action, Blumer says:

> Yet, one must consider the contention that the process of self interaction has an intrinsic character or logic that prevents the resulting action from fitting into a determinist framework. (Quoted in Athens 1993, 171)

Blumer, then, brings up two issues that broaden the inner speech discussion. One is that all human action, not just the more deliberate variety, is guided by inner speech. The other is that inner speech might be interpreted as weakening the deterministic framework that some apply to human behavior. In other words, it might be our means of voluntary choice, a position I also take in Chapter 6, on agency.

This review of pragmatism and the dialogical self shows a distinct coherence and thematic unity. The pragmatists have an extremely complex and usable theory of the dialogical self, even though it takes some selection and interpretation to piece it together.

The review shows that James prepared the conceptual foundations for inner speech, and Peirce, Mead, and Dewey each had distinct insights concerning this theory. The terminology differs from theorist to theorist, and this hides the thematic unity to some extent. Peirce tends to talk about "thought" or "dialogue," Mead refers to the "internal conversation," and Dewey uses the terms "deliberation" and "dramatic rehearsal." Cooley speaks of "imaginary conversations," and Blumer uses the term "self interaction." Yet they are all talking about inner speech. Another noticeable feature of the pragmatists is that they use very few examples, either from their own self-observation or from that of others. They also ignore soliloquies and stream of consciousness dialogues from literature. These omissions held them back, and made it more difficult to theorize inner speech. Yet this is by no means an irredeemable deficiency. Instead, it invites further research (for example, that of Archer [2003]).

Regarding the uses or functions of inner speech, we again see diversity among these thinkers. Each of them emphasizes cognition in the broad sense, but they also hit on special uses. James introduces the context (the stream of consciousness) and the I-me distinction. Peirce is especially interested in

TABLE 7.1 PRAGMATISTS' POSITIONS ON THE DIALOGICAL SELF

Theorist	Terms	Emphasis
James	Stream of consciousness	Monitoring experience
Peirce	Dialogue	Self-determination
Mead	Internal conversation	Problem solving
Dewey	Deliberation	Mental experiments
Cooley	Imaginary conversations	Imaginary companion
Blumer	Self interaction	Agency

inner speech as it allows self-determination, both for individual actions and for the formation of habits. Mead is interested in how inner speech allows the discovery of solutions, especially for everyday problems. Dewey emphasizes the systematic way we might run through a series of hypotheses or paths of behavior. Cooley points to the way the otherness of the dialogical partner bears a resemblance to the child's imaginary companion. And Blumer, in the spirit of Peirce, focuses on the question of agency and how inner speech helps us form choices. This discussion of terminology and emphases is summarized in Table 7.1.

Despite the variation in how the pragmatists treat inner speech, there is a substantial unity in their discussions. This issue runs like a bright thread through the pragmatists' writings, making it an important candidate for identifying the main theses of their philosophy.

Pragmatism's Theory of Meaning

Having shown how pragmatism might include the dialogical self as one of its central interests, I now show how this interest relates to the theory of meaning. It should be pointed out right away that I suggest two distinct theories of meaning. One is the public sense of meaning, as, for example, it is used in language. This meaning is intersubjective and social, and it is sometimes thought to be the only theory of meaning. But there is also a private or personal sense of meaning, which is the meaning peculiar to one individual. Everyone has personal, possibly quite idiosyncratic, meanings, peculiar to them. These meanings are especially present in their internal conversation or inner speech.

Public Meanings

I first consider public meaning, for personal meaning can be more easily defined once public meaning has been delineated. The pragmatists define meaning as consequential in a behavioral or action-related sense, but this is only loosely defined in their writings. Peirce, James, Mead, and Dewey each define meaning, but their definitions do not fit perfectly well together. One can simply take these as they are and claim the unity of a family relationship, or one can try to make the formulation more precise. Mead and Dewey are pretty close to each other on this issue, and I do not think they are the problem. Instead, the difficulty is in reconciling the near-positivist statements of Peirce with the near-idealist statements of James. These two are the outliers in the discussion, and if they can be fit together, Mead and Dewey will fall into place in the middle.

There are three major meanings of "consequences" in pragmatism: physical, social, and individual. In his Metaphysical Club statement (1878), Peirce emphasizes the physical properties of an object—for example, that a "hard" object such as a diamond is difficult to scratch. As he puts it, "Consider what effects, which might conceivably have practical bearings, we conceive the object of our conception to have. Then, our conception of these effects is the whole conception of the object" (Peirce 1986, 266). In his critique of Descartes, however, Peirce's arguments against intuition and for a semiotic view of cognition imply a cultural view of meaning. He allows social as well as physical consequences. And finally, at the nonphysical extreme, James introduces consequences for the individual, which might be present and meaningful only for that individual. Sometimes James connects these consequences to religion as in his "will to believe."

James had willed himself into believing in the existence of God, the immortality of the soul, and even in free will. These three entities had meaning for him because they had consequences for him as an individual. They felt true and had soothing effects, and this satisfied James's widened notion of meaning.

These soothing effects differ from social consequences in several ways. They are restricted to the individual. They can be constructed in the short-term. And they are sometimes deliberately or intentionally created. In contrast, the consequences implied by Peirce's semiotic theory are widely social, constructed over long periods of time, and unconsciously or indeliberately formed. Peirce was quite uncomfortable with James's pragmatic theory of meaning, and he distanced himself from it by calling himself a "pragmaticist."

As I interpret Peirce, physical consequences were eventually regarded as too restrictive. The physical version did not have room for his semiotics; nor did it allow for such nonphysical entities as money, language, law, and other social institutions. However, individual consequences, as found in James's version, were too unrestrictive. They were not anchored in society and culture. Sociocultural consequences, then, became the core idea of the pragmatic test; that is, pragmatic meaning was cultural meaning, or how people act in relation to an object. The physical consequences were still there; for example, a mirror reflects objects, but it also allows the social process of grooming. This notion of meaning fit Peirce's theory of signs. His semiotics implied both intersubjective and intra-subjective dialogue—this dialogue being inherently social.

This formulation excludes Peirce's more positivist definitions of meaning and James's more idealist or wishful thinking versions. Peirce's physical consequences are still allowed, but they coexist with sociocultural consequences. And James's cultural consequences are included but not his idiosyncratic personal ones. In other words, until now I have traded inclusiveness for clarity. Instead of a widely scattered spread of definitions, the formulation I suggest disallows the more extreme definitions but has more unity and clarity.

This formulation also clarifies pragmatism's relation to the social sciences. Peirce's highly empiricist, 1878 formulation was fit for the physical but not for the social sciences. It excluded those from having meaning. The sociocultural version, however, not only allows room for the social sciences; it can also act as a paradigmatic starting point or meta theory for these sciences (Wiley 2006b).

Personal Meanings

Now that public meaning has been defined, let me return to its opposite—that is, personal or private meaning. People sometimes make up their own meanings. These may be variations on public meanings: a word or phrase reflecting some experience we attach to it; a strong emotion, love or hate, getting linked to it; or a simple drift in what we allow something to mean. But people can also construct meanings more or less confined to themselves. Ordinary language can be given new meanings, as when people think in a condensed or egocentric manner (Vygotsky 1987b, 274; Wertsch 1985, 124). Any sound or signifier can be given a novel meaning in this way, a process limited only by the human imagination. One's psychopathological symptoms, however mild, can also condition one's semantics. I think the linguistics of everyone's inner speech—that is, its semantics and syntax—is substantially different from everyone else's. This seems to have been Joyce's belief when he structured the inner voices of his main characters in *Ulysses*.

And, as stated before, I would also add the view that nonlinguistic elements, such as sensations, emotions, and kinesthetic routines, can function in one's internal linguistic system. I formed this hypothesis from self-observation, talking with colleagues, and, again, from Joyce's *Ulysses*. Not only can these elements affect meanings as context; they can also act syntactically as parts of speech. I will not say much about the language of thought, the medieval version of pure abstractions, the contemporary one of computer messaging, or any other version. But if any of these semantic streams existed, they could intermingle with the elaborate structure already described. In other words, instead of, or in addition to, words or sensations or kinesthetic routines or emotions, one could also have "thought," in whatever sense one might give to that term. This new stream of meaning, depending on how one used it, would make an already quite private conversation even more private.

The reason I look at private meanings is that they seem to function quite centrally in our flow of consciousness and therefore in the way we regulate our lives. Private meanings, even our own, are not easy to fix on. Reflecting on them may distort them, so we can catch our own meanings only by a kind of peripheral vision. Still, it seems useful to describe the private meaning system here, particularly as a contrast to public meaning but also as the road into a person's consciousness. Much as Freud thought dreams were a window on the unconscious, inner speech seems to be a window into consciousness. In fact at times, such as the uncontrolled inner speech before sleep, it may also be a glimpse into the unconscious.

To return to the larger theme, public and private meanings can both be defined as consequences. But the consequences of public meanings are physical and social, never purely individual. While those of private meanings are also physical and social, their defining quality is individual consequences. As already pointed out, these personal meanings can draw uniquely and idiosyncratically on several varieties of semantics. This can make them not only nonpublic but intensely personalized and private.

Yet both streams are dialogical. Public meanings are communicated in the public community, with the dialogue varying from cooperation to competition and conflict. Private meanings are communicated in people's inner speech. The two streams, public and private, interlock in complicated relations of cause, effect, competition, coexistence, domination, and so on. I do not try to analyze these relations except to point out that they connect two different semantic regions. Public meanings draw on public consequences, and private meanings are built on private consequences. The first is the home ground of Peirce and the second is that of James. Together in relation, they reflect the tension that united, and sometimes disunited, the classical pragmatists. They also reflect the two interests I see as central to pragmatism, the theory of meaning and that of the dialogical self.

Conclusion

I conclude by pointing out some advantages of centering pragmatism around the dialogical self.

First, the theory of meaning, which has usually been thought of as the central theme of pragmatism, is somewhat confusing. It differs substantially from pragmatist to pragmatist, and even its author, Peirce, changed his formulation from time to time. The dialogical self is a much more coherent theme, integrating the relative contributions of the major pragmatists. In addition, it explains the process of interpreting meaning. In other words, the dialogical process explains the theory of meaning, and meaning motivates the dialogical process.

Second, the pragmatist theory of meaning was often thought to be a variant or precursor of logical positivism's theory of meaning. Thus, when logical positivism declined, pragmatism also suffered a loss. But if the theory of meaning is both reformulated and linked to the dialogical process, this distances pragmatism from logical positivism and gives it a clear and original focus of its own.

Third, the theory of the self shows how pragmatism influenced modern social sciences. In particular, the anthropological concept of culture, which is the meta-paradigm or umbrella concept for the social sciences, is virtually identical with Peirce's concept of semiotics (Wiley 2006b) and is also implied by the pragmatists' theory of the self. The dialogical self is also a central concept for social psychology and sociology, including the theory of social construction.

Fourth, the dialogical self is a distinct version of the "decentered self," a central idea of postmodernism. Derrida was influenced by Peirce's idea of semiotics as an endless process of interpretation, but the dialogical self shows how pragmatism had many of the ideas of postmodernism.

Fifth, the dialogical self is now a popular concept, used in areas ranging from psychotherapy to film theory. In other words, the dialogical focus places pragmatism at the heart of much contemporary thought.

Finally, to shift directions, pragmatism's dialogical or semiotic self shows how people's minds and not their physical or racial traits create cultures and subcultures. This idea of the self explains the fundamental equality of human nature and the foundation for egalitarianism, giving it an affinity with democracy (Wiley 2006b).

To put this another way, pragmatism created the intellectual premises for both egalitarianism and democracy. In this way it supplied the cognitive resources for smashing racism. These premises make this philosophy a deeply American contribution to social justice.

This chapter argues that American pragmatism, usually viewed as an action-based or practical theory of meaning, might also be regarded as a theory of inner speech or the dialogical self. James invented background concepts in the I-me duality of the self and the stream of consciousness. Peirce introduced inner speech itself, showing how this process is central to the human moral and deliberative capacities. Mead showed how we solve everyday problems with inner speech. And Dewey pointed out how we run mental experiments with the inner conversation. Taken jointly, these thinkers constructed a complex and far-reaching theory of the dialogical self. A second issue I consider is pragmatism's theory of meaning and how it relates to the dialogical self. I argue that the theory of meaning is best understood as including a sociocultural component. And further, this public theory of meaning should be distinguished from a second kind, the personal or private variety. I conclude by showing the advantages of orienting pragmatism toward both meaning and inner speech.

8

THE PRAGMATIST THEORY OF THE SELF

The nature of the self has already been discussed, drawing largely on Perinbanayagam's ideas. This chapter concentrates on the same topic, but it shows how the American pragmatists have a highly developed theory of the self. Their theory stands behind the one I sketch in Chapter 3. One purpose of reviewing pragmatism's theory of the self is to show the larger psychological context within which inner speech goes on.

This review is limited to four major pragmatists: Charles Sanders Peirce, William James, John Dewey, and George Herbert Mead. Although other pragmatists could have also been included, I prefer to use workable boundaries and concentrate on these four. Despite the general lack of work on the pragmatist theory of the self, some important analyses can be found in the writings of Archer (2003), Shalin (1984), Rochberg-Halton (1986), Rosenthal (1986), Colapietro (1989, 1999), Hoopes (1989), Joas (1993), and Perinbanayagam (2000), among others.

The pragmatists did not create fully developed theories of the self. Instead, they worked with rough-cut approximations, which were often lying in their writings as bits and pieces. Many of Peirce's best ideas on this topic are in his unpublished papers (Colapietro 1989). Mead's materials are largely student notes from his unpublished lectures. Dewey, who wrote a great deal, wrote little on the express topic of the self, although his paper on the reflex arc was quite innovative (Dewey 1972). James, despite his systematic and lengthy chapter on the self (1950a, 291–401) left us with a distinctly "divided" self, in both the theoretical and moral senses (Gale 1999).

These materials are a bit like clay; to form them into a coherent statement takes some selecting and combining. To do this I take ideas from each of these pragmatists and try to fit them together. From Dewey I take the self as actor or agent, from Mead the social self, from Peirce the semiotic or significative self, and from James the emotion of self-feeling. I proceed by going from Dewey to Mead to Peirce to James, adding concepts as I go along. This is not a chronological order but one that was chosen for the fluent presentation of ideas. There should be an increasing cognitive momentum as the portrait fills in. After going through the four pragmatists, I list the overall characteristics of the theory. Then I present a concluding section. Altogether, this chapter has six sections: one on Dewey, one on Mead, one on Peirce, one on James, one on properties of the overall theory, and the conclusion.

Finally, a point about method needs to be mentioned. When scholars are dealing with the history of ideas, especially the ideas of a great thinker, a choice has to be made between two objectives: what he or she said and how to develop or advance these ideas in the best way. This is the distinction between the close caretaking attitude of exact analysis and the more relaxed attitude of intellectual synthesis. There are also intermediary positions between these two extremes.

Problems exist with both objectives. There is no exactness to what anyone said because, assuming that the master wrote quite a bit, there are always gaps, variations, omissions, and contradictions in the master's writings. Derrida made a career out of finding these contradictions, a process he calls deconstruction, first finding them in Husserl and then in everyone else. Anyone who writes much contradicts him- or herself at times. Consequently, the disciple who wants to explain exactly what the master said is bound to fail, because inexactness is built into the intellectual process. If you think big at all, there will be cracks in your thinking. These cracks are, or can lead to, the self-refutation process, and all systematic intellectual products, as Kurt Gödel shows for mathematics, tend to be self-refuting.

The other objective, to take the ideas and run, can also quickly get out of hand. You can run too fast and lose all connection with your starting points. If you are choosing between two or three differing tendencies in your master, there will always be arguments about the wisdom of your choice. In addition, the people doing these two styles of scholarship—the "what did he or she say" people and the "what might he or she have said" people—can waste lots of time bickering with each other.

So I try to do both. I attempt to be as faithful as possible to the four key intellectuals, and I also try to move these people along a bit. To attempt a pragmatist theory of the self, building on these four thinkers, requires some connecting of the dots. Laying down four somewhat discrete theories side-by-side would be pointless. I have to try to integrate them to some extent.

These thinkers each use somewhat different concepts and at times they seem to have somewhat different views of the self. They are looking at the self through different windows. I think James, in particular, goes in a different direction than the other three. James's key concept is self-feeling, and this is, in a specialized way, an emotion. Dewey, Peirce, and Mead have a more cognitive approach, with a concept like reflexivity as their key idea. There are also differences among Peirce, Dewey, and Mead that require some attention.

I nevertheless attempt to move toward a pragmatist theory of the self, being reasonably fair to the four thinkers while also trying to put them together into something a bit new. Scholarship is a cooperative enterprise, and my hope is to stimulate more thought. I am also aware that other pragmatist scholars might have combined these thinkers in a completely different way. This is the nature of the scholarly process.

John Dewey

Dewey is distinct from the other pragmatists in having a populist style, emphasizing ordinary life, practicality, everyday problems, common sense, and the improvement of life for the average person. He is suspicious of theory and analysis, preferring practice and synthesis. In relation to the self, Dewey emphasizes the process of solving problems. This means the aspect of the self that he pays most attention to is practical action or agency. In fact, in his "reflex arc" article (1972), one might say Dewey created the contemporary concept of agency. All the pragmatists emphasize practice, and the term "pragmatism" tips the discourse in that direction. So it makes sense to use Dewey's agency as the overall framework for the theory of self. Dewey's idea of agency, however, also has room for pure cognitions or theory, for he recognizes that thought can sometimes be relatively distant from goal-seeking or practice, even though he himself was disinclined from this type of thinking. Within the overall agentic loop there can be one or more purely cognitive sub-loops. Still, he sees agency as the overall framework within which all thought, no matter how abstract, operates.

Dewey is also of the opinion that all thought originates in agency and in the frustrated goal-seeking that stimulates inquiry. Consequently, all the pragmatists' theorizing of the self fits within Dewey's concept of agency. In other words, agency is an umbrella concept for this entire chapter.

For Dewey action or agency has two stages: rehearsal and enactment. He distinguishes them as follows: "An act overtly tried out is irrevocable, its consequences cannot be blotted out. An act tried out in imagination is not final or fatal. It is retrievable" (1930, 190). This distinction again opens up the agentic process to a number of early, preparatory stages. People have been known to think for indefinite periods of time before engaging in such actions as getting married or divorced, picking or changing an occupation, going into or out of psychotherapy, actually writing their Ph.D. dissertation, killing themselves, curing themselves, and so on. So thought can be a preparatory as well as an intermediary stage of agency.

In rehearsal we are defining and modeling the act, not executing it. We are also trying out the choice to see how it feels. As Dewey says, rehearsing is less committing than action itself, for you can back out of it. You are usually not morally and legally attached as you are to overt action. In contrast, action is unchangeable. Once we do it, not in our minds but in the external world, it cannot be undone. Dewey is especially insightful in mental experimentation, where we can try out, imaginatively, the various options and see which one seems to work best. As he puts it, "Deliberation is an experiment in finding out what the various lines of possible action are really like. It is an experiment in making various combinations of selected elements of habits and impulses to see what the resultant action would be like if it were entered upon. But the trial is in imagination, not in overt fact" (1930, 190).

A good example of Dewey's distinction between rehearsal and execution can be seen in the boyhood of Herbert Peirce, the younger brother of Charles Sanders Peirce. Charles Peirce tells of the incident:

> I well remember when I was a boy, and my brother Herbert, now our minister at Christiania, was scarce more than a child, one day, as the whole family were at table, some spirit from a "blazer" or "chafing-dish" dropped on the muslin dress of one of the ladies [their mother] and was kindled; and how instantaneously he jumped up, and did the right thing, and how skillfully each motion was adapted to the purpose. I asked him afterward about it; and he told me that since Mrs. Longfellow's death, it was that he had often run over in imagination all the details of what ought to be done in such an emergency. It was a striking example of a real habit produced by exercises in the imagination. (1934, para. 487n1; see also para. 538)

Fanny Longfellow had died in a dress fire in 1861, when Herbert Peirce was about twelve. Fanny was pouring candle wax to seal an envelope, and her gauze dress caught on fire. When she screamed, her husband, napping in the next room, immediately got up, grabbed a rug, and began to put out the fire. But the rug was too small, and in her panic, Fanny pulled away and ran across the room. Then, after losing precious seconds, she ran back to her husband, and he extinguished the fire. But by then Fanny's body had been blackened, and she lived only a few more hours (Wagenknecht 1956, 242; McFarland 2004, 243–244).

This story was repeated throughout Cambridge, and, I think we can assume, everyone was concerned with having the right size rug at hand. Herbert, who evidently never wrote about his action, must have been mentally practicing how to seize the right rug, encircle some woman's enflamed body, and put out the fire. Of course, young boys are always engaging in self-heroic fantasies, but in this case the fantasy came true. It also gives a crisp and dramatic example of Dewey's distinction between rehearsal and execution.

This deliberation process is also, in large part, a matter of inner speech or internal conversation. All the pragmatists recognized this process at the core of the self. Thought and planning are central to this activity. It seems as though freedom of choice itself, to the extent that we have it, is also partly a matter of inner speech. We first exercise choice in inner speech—we say to ourselves that we are going to do it. Only later do we externalize it in action, and at that we sometimes back out. Making a pre-choice in our inner speech is, in a way, a stage between deliberation and overt action.

Another one of Dewey's major concepts is habit. In his revised edition of *Human Nature and Conduct* (1930, viii), Dewey explained that between the 1922 and 1930 versions of the book the discipline of psychology had changed from an emphasis on instincts, which were thought to be biologically innate forces that determined people's personalities, to habit, which was a largely symbolic or semiotic concept. This was a shift from racism to a cultural approach. For Dewey habit was the unit of culture. Anthropologists nowadays say the symbol is the unit of culture, but Dewey meant approximately the same thing by using the word "habit."

Peirce and Mead also use the term "habit," and for them it is a semiotic response that is repeated and patterned. For Peirce the meaning of a sign is the habit it produces. James uses the term both for a physical response and a significative one. So, all four pragmatists use this term in about the same way. And for each it is associated with the emergent (i.e., nonbiological) self and with the system of culture. Dewey uses habit in multiple, highly nuanced ways. It is his tool for exploring the complexities of the self.

Dewey was always both personally and intellectually close to Mead. In 1931, after Mead's death, he said he had great respect for and agreed with Mead's theory of the self (Dewey 2008). This was quite an admission. Since Mead's self-theory is extremely complex and pretty much his own invention, Dewey seems to be subordinating himself to Mead with this statement. Dewey had been Mead's academic sponsor, getting him jobs for many years, but this admission gives another slant on their relationship. It was an exchange. Dewey helped Mead institutionally, but Mead helped Dewey theoretically. Dewey's use of habit also shows his closeness to Mead's significant symbol. We can assume, then, that if Dewey were to flesh out his agentic scheme, he would fill it largely with Mead's ideas. When I turn now to Mead to present his own ideas, it should be understood that I am talking, indirectly, about Dewey as well.

George Herbert Mead

According to Mead, the key feature of the self is in its being an object to itself (1964, 243). The self is a recursive, reflexive, or looping entity that turns back on itself. This is what allows it to be aware of itself. The relation of self to itself, which is self-awareness, entails a sort of split in the self between a reflecting and a reflected aspect. For Mead the reflecting aspect is the "I" and the reflected aspect is the "me."

What I have just described is ordinary or first-order reflexivity. But sometimes the self jumps to a higher level and reflects on its entirety—that is, on both the I and the me. In this case it is aware of itself, not in a partial manner, such as a thermostat or other feedback device. These self-regulating machines, as touched on in Chapter 3, have two parts, the part being reflected on and the part doing the reflecting. And the latter part can never reflect on itself. This makes mechanical reflexivity only partial. In contrast, the self can reflect on the totality of itself. This is because the reflecting device is, so to speak, another self; one that is meta to the one being reflected on. In this case the self does not really split into two parts like self-regulating machines. It doubles up into a first order and a second order or meta self. Thus the entire self is in the "reflected on" position, and another version of the entire self is in the "reflecting" position.

Sometimes people say that mechanical reflexivity devices are "selves," because they share the property of reflexivity with selves. This belief is behind the idea that computers are people or that people are computers. Machines can be engineered to be quasi-reflexive. But they are reflexive in a more limited sense than selves, and the attribution of selfhood to these devices, such as thermostats and computers, is fallacious. In other words, the self can engage in total reflection because it can go meta to itself. Reflecting physical objects, such as thermostats, can only engage in partial reflection because *they cannot go meta to themselves.*

Mead also argues that this reflexivity is a transformation of the infant's first social relationship, the one formed between the baby and his or her caretaker. This argument is a complex but breathtaking insight, and it takes several pages to explain. The reflected, as opposed to the reflecting, self is a generalized form of the caretaker, now incorporated into the self as an internalized other. Mead sometimes refers to the me as a "generalized other" (1964, 246).

In other words, the self, being an internalized and condensed social relation, is modeled after an interpersonal relation. This relation is usually that of infant and mother. In what appears to be a small minority of cases, the close caretaker is a male, normally the father. Sometimes there is more than one close caretaker. But the most common case is one in which the close caretaker is the biological mother. Baby begins with a strong identification with the mother but gradually separates into a semi- and then more or less completely autonomous self. Just how close the original identification is, how long the separation process takes, what stages it goes through, and so on are matters of discussion in child development literature.

The relation between child and caretaker becomes internalized so that it exists inside the infant, even in the absence of the mother. When Freud's grandson tossed the spool and then happily pulled it back by its string, he was, as Freud saw it, testing the internalized relationship with his mother. The inner mother gradually becomes more plasticized and generalized so that anyone can occupy the space that was initially occupied by the mother or close caretaker. Finally, the internal dyad, though based on the child-mother bond, is transformed into two aspects of the baby's self. This is what Mead refers to as the dialogical self and what he calls the "I" and the "me." The mother has become the me.

The internal society, baby and caretaker, becomes the form of the self. The self is a two-sided or social relationship that can house not only the caretaker but also anyone else. Baby's first relationship to the caretaker becomes the template for relationships with other people. First these others are family members and close intimates. But gradually this dyadic form can accommodate anyone else as the partner to the infant. This partner or other gradually becomes an aspect of the self. For Mead the self-caretaker relationship broadens into a self-other relationship and this becomes a self-self or "I-me" relationship. So as the relationship internalizes, it passes from "I-mother" to "I-other" to "I-me." Mead's self is the internalization of the social relationship.

The pragmatist version of the self, including both male and female selves, is usually modeled after the mother. In other words, even though the self has sometimes been given what could be interpreted as a highly separated, masculine tilt (e.g., by Descartes), for the pragmatists it is usually the product of a mother's love and therefore might be said to have a feminine ontogeny or tilt. This tilt shows how profoundly feminist pragmatist philosophy is, and it fits the antiracist, civil libertarian premises of this philosophy.

This bit of pragmatist child development theory fits the psychoanalytic view of Nancy Chodorow (1978), although her critical period comes somewhat later in the infant's life. She compared the outcomes of the Oedipus and Electra complexes as they occur in males and females. She concludes that in the female case the child remains somewhat under-separated from the mother. This explains, according to Chodorow, why women are usually more skilled with emotions than men and also why they tend to be better mothers (i.e., close caretakers). Men, she concludes, experience the opposite effect of being over-separated from their mothers and thereby from all women. This makes them usually less skilled with emotions and child-rearing.

From a pragmatist point of view, the reason why women tend to be under-separated and men over-separated from their mothers is because both genders are outgrowths of their mothers in the first place. Women's Electra complexes are continuous with this feminine origin, and it is understandable that women would remain close to (or under-separated from) their mothers. In contrast, men, who are told to identify with a gender other than that of their mother, would initially have the same tendency as women—that is, to stay close to their mother. But since males are not allowed to indulge this natural tendency, they have to try extra hard to find their gender. In fact, they have to be over-separated, not only from their mothers but from their selves. The solution to this problem would seem to be to allow men to be less "masculine" and more like women. This may, in fact, have been the case before male work became separated from the farm and home with the Industrial Revolution (Laqueur 1990, 149–192). The Meadean theory of the self, then, explains the fundamental similarity between men and women and the reason why men in industrial society are often uncomfortable in their gender.

The reflexivity of the self, which is the key to thought and language for Mead, is a product of the internalized social relation. The condensed relation to the mother permits the self to relate to itself, which is what is meant by reflexivity. This reflexivity permits the self to role-take, which is Mead's term for being able to understand and communicate with another person. The major functions of the self are closely interconnected for Mead. The social origins of the self, in the condensed relation to the caretaker, lead to the thinking, linguistic, communicative self. These capacities, in turn, lead back to the mother. There is a loop in the infant, then, from (a) mother-as-caretaker to (b) the internalized social relation to (c) the linguistic-communicative capacity and then (d) back to mother (and anyone else) as an autonomous, thinking, and talking human being.

There is one point Mead does not fully clarify, and that is how the internalized other goes from particular to general. The mothering one invokes the generalized other as society's regulatory standards or, one might say, conscience. This moral reference point is general, to be sure, but I am asking how this general other enters the internal conversation in the first place. Baby has learned to engage in dialogue with the mother, even when she is absent. But this dialogue is with a particular mother. How does this "particular person to particular person" conversation transform into a conversation between a particular person and a general person? Put another way, how does "she" become "they"?

Mead does not explicitly say how the mother becomes a general "person" in baby's inner speech, but I think this point is implicit and partially developed in his writings. It is true that the mother tells baby there is a "they" behind the rules, that people or society require certain behaviors. In this sense mother introduces the general other and introduces it into baby's inner conversation. But I think the mother goes a step further, and it is here that we can see how internal dialogue is transformed into a "self-other" dialogue that partakes of generality.

When the mother urges the general rules onto baby, *she transforms herself from a particular person into a general person.* She speaks as a corporate person, one who represents the culture. She takes on the voice of society. She talks to baby as the general person to the particular person—that is, the general other to the particular other. When this happens, baby can talk back to her as a particular baby to a general mother (or "other"). The mother may even start looking like an abstraction or corporate entity, so to speak. Normally, she looks affectionately and even smiles at baby. But when events heat up and baby needs to be told the social rule—concerning eating and drinking, hitting people, breaking objects, early toilet training, and so on—the mother gets a serious look on her face and just looks at baby. This conscience mom is an impersonal mom, a woman who could step right into one of Weber's bureaucratic roles. And when baby sees this serious, rule-enforcing mom in his or her mind, baby can talk to a general force. She presents herself as general, and baby can respond to her as a general force.

So baby's internal dialogue can learn to cope with general forces because the mother teaches baby to do that. The mother pretends she is the general force—perhaps in a gradualist, little-by-little manner—and baby adapts to the mother's transformation. No doubt baby will also learn the process of logical induction in which we reason from the particular to the general. But the mother's dialogical maneuvers—going from the particular to the general—may be the template for this logical process. In other words, baby may learn the generalized other from the mother's playing the role of the generalized other. And then other generalizations—those that we make throughout life—may draw on this initial moral generalization with the mother. In other words, she may be the metaphor for how we learn to find and logically manipulate other generalities.

One can understand why Dewey was impressed by Mead's theory of self, for it is both original and ingenious. I have the impression that, given Mead's loss of early religious faith, he decided, rather obsessively, to replace religion with reason. In particular, he wanted to explain everything traditionally attributed to the soul in naturalistic terms. He wanted to explain all the mysteries with a purely secular theory of the self. I do not think he completely succeeded, for he never could explain the phylogenetic origins of the self in primates, which in religious terms would be the creation of the soul. But he may have come closer than anyone else. In any case, he has the most developed theory of the self of all the pragmatists.

Mead's reflexivity has another quality that should be mentioned. The nature of a reflexive relation will depend on which aspect of the self is being known and looped through. Mead's reflexivity is between the I, the subject and center of the self, so to speak, and the me, which is an object and is in the past. Peirce's notion of reflexivity, to anticipate this point, is between the self and the "you," which Peirce defines as "that other self that is just coming into life in the flow of time" (1934, para. 421). Peirce's you is the self of the immediate future. The temporal passage of the self is from you to I to me, or in other words, from future to present to past. These temporal positions can be conceived and experienced as either physical or psychological or both at the same time. The combination of the two modes of experiencing the flow of time can be quite complex.

Given these two modes, Mead's reflexivity is a looping between subject and object or present and past. In contrast, Peirce's reflexivity is a looping between two subjects, that of the present and that of the imminent future. If we accept both Mead and Peirce, it seems that the self has (at least) two modes of reflexivity, Mead's to a past object and Peirce's to a future subject. Another way of saying this is that inner speech has two major voices—to the past and to the future. These two voices have different moral qualities. As Dewey says, "Authorship and liability look in two different ways, one to the past, and the other to the future" ([1929] 1958, 233). In other words, the past is, to a great extent, morally settled; the future is morally open.

The two voices also have different communicative and signifying qualities. The voice to the past deals in rather stable states and certainties. The voice to the future deals in unstable configurations and uncertainties. These two reflexivities seem to be able to talk to each other, and they constitute a distinct layer of the dialogical self. For example, you can say (to the future), "Shall I let myself fall in love with this person I am already leaning toward?" and you can also say (to the past), "What have I learned from my previous fallings in love?"

The distinction between Mead's me and Peirce's you also suggests a way that pragmatism can explain self-deceit, or what Jean-Paul Sartre (1957a, 47–70) calls bad faith. Your past is more or less settled and done with, allowing that it is always subject to reinterpretation. Your future is open and indeterminate. Your choices are primarily for the future, not the past. But people sometimes falter when they face a tough decision, pretending that one particular option, usually the safer one, is the only one they have. For example, you keep quiet when an evil act is being committed, afraid to risk speaking out. You could try to stop the evil, but you pretend that there is no avenue but to close your eyes. You kid yourself to avoid the pain of facing your cowardice. When you do this, you are pretending that the open future is like the fixed past, determined and closed. You are facing your you, which is the self that is soon to come to be, and you are seeing it as a me, the self that has already been and is sedimented into your past. Sartre refers to this as mistaking "being for itself" as "being in itself"—that is, taking the conscious and free, to be without consciousness and inert. But I think the pragmatist formulation of mistaking the you for the me is a simpler and more compelling explanation.

At this point I must make a short digression. I am aware that when using the terms "me," "I," and "you," it may sound like I think there are little people or homunculi inside people's heads. I may seem to be hypostasizing or reifying these ideas. But this usage is merely a literary device for facilitating communication. It must be decoded. These phases of the self, the you, I, and me, are actually part of a continuous process. Our personal time is breezing along inside James's stream of consciousness. It is rolling and fluid. It does not have stops, let alone little islands that have names. But we can still distinguish the future from the past. And we can identify the present, both the theoretical or knife-edge present and the felt or saddle-back present. This latter point in time can be referred to as I or even as "the" I. The future can be called you and the past can be called me. These words are a convenience for conveying a particular idea about the flow of time. They are also built into ordinary language. Time itself actually flows continuously, but we can divide it, analytically, into past, present, and future (or the self-in-time as me, I, and you). So when I refer to what may sound like little people inside our heads, I am actually talking about the process of temporal passage and how we, somewhat artificially, slice it up.

It is also important to remember that these self-pronouns have reflexive meanings. "I" does not refer to some fixed person. It refers to whomever is saying "I." The same is true of you and me. And "you" has the additional ambiguity of referring, à la Peirce, either to the future of whichever "I" is at center stage or to whomever we might be talking to. It can be the other me, approaching the present from the future, or it can be our interpersonal or conversational partner.

Beyond this, these three pronouns, at least as I use them, are relative to the flow of time. "I" refers to time at the precise moment when we utter the word "I." You and me are also relative to the temporal flow. So the pronouns are twice relative: to the person doing the talking and to the stream of time. I use the terms "I," "me," and "you" somewhat flexibly, for analysis calls for this usage. But when we unfold these terms and apprehend their precise meanings, we find the complex pair of relativities just described. Nevertheless, if we spoke with all the precision and nuance that these ideas carry, the discourse would be opaque with congestion. Therefore I say "I," "you," and "me" with the understanding that I am referring, for ease of utterance, to something far more wordy and conceptually complicated.

Having concluded the digression, let me return to two earlier points. Bad faith or self-deceit, in pragmatist terms, to conclude my original comment, is the mistaking of the future for the past, the you for the me, or freedom for determinism. It is a particular form of sin or moral flaw—namely, the violation of our best possibilities or dignity.

And returning to my larger point, both Mead's and Peirce's reflexivity fit into Dewey's agentic self. In the kind of action that the agentic self is engaging in, we are facing the future and dialoging it to find the right path to take. We are also dialoging the past to find out which actions have proved to be unsuitable. When Herbert Peirce was thinking about Fanny Longfellow's death, he was dialoging the past. When he was thinking about how he would act if he were ever faced with such a challenge, he was dialoging the future.

Charles Sanders Peirce

Turning to Peirce, his definition of the self is in terms of meaning or significance. As he says, humans are "signs" (1934, para. 314). As such they are composed of iconic, indexical, and symbolic signs—that is, the whole range of signification. This definition is perhaps a bit cryptic, and I devote much of this section to expanding it.

Peirce's theory of signs was derived from his argument against Descartes and intuition. An intuition, in the specialized sense in which Peirce uses the term, is an idea or proposition that is self-validating or self-evident. It needs no previous proposition from which it is derived or any future evidence to give it confirmation. It is clearly true as it stands.

Peirce's position was that there are no intuitions. Ideas, he held, were signs, and as such they had to be interpreted. They were never clear and distinct in themselves. They had to unfold gradually, and they had to do so by way of an interpretive process engaged in by individuals and communities.

Peirce's favorite example of an invalid intuition is Descartes's "cogito, ergo sum" ("I think, therefore I am"). Descartes thought this statement was self-evident, that to think this proposition was to be convinced of it. Peirce argues that there is no direct cogito. We encounter the self indirectly and never intuitively. As I mention in Chapter 2, he used the child's burned finger as an example of how we might have first encountered our self.

One striking feature of Peirce's semiotic definition of the self is that it makes no reference to the body. It is merely implicit in his definition that humans are bodies. The self actually is a property of the body and it gradually evolved in the body. But the self, with its lofty semiotic properties, has outshone the body. Human selfhood is more distinctive than its body-hood. So it is tempting to define humans primarily in terms of their selves. The traditional Scholastic definition of humans as "rational animals" does include the body, but all the emphasis is on the term "rational." Rationality denotes the self, not the body.

Peirce ignores the body in his definition because his key idea is the "sign," an idea more suggestive of the self than of the body. The result is that Peirce is the first major philosopher to define human beings without including the body. His intentions here were solely intellectual, for he was reacting against Descartes and substituting the fallible sign for Descartes's allegedly infallible intuition of the self. Peirce seems to have had no political intentions whatsoever. In fact, his politics seem to have been aggressively conservative and *antiegalitarian*, as the following quotation suggests:

> If they were to come to know me better they might learn to think me ultra-conservative. I am, for example, an old-fashioned christian [*sic*], a believer in the efficacy of prayer, an opponent of female suffrage and of universal male suffrage, in favor of letting business methods develop without the interference of law, a disbeliever in democracy, etc. etc. (Peirce 1910; see also Hardwick 1977, 78–79)

It is possible that Peirce was exaggerating in this note, for his second wife was quite feminist, and he was supportive of his brother James Mills Peirce, who was a homosexual (Pencak 2007). He also wrote something that had a Christian socialist flavor (Peirce 1982, 285–307). So his precise politics or political mix remains something of a mystery. My only point is that his politics seem to have been, for the most part, conservative, and he did not intend his definition of humans to lead to a left-wing interpretation.

Still, once an idea is placed in the public domain and becomes what Durkheim calls a social fact, it can develop in a way different from what its author may have intended. Ideas are public goods, and there are always constituencies and pressure groups seeking to move them in the direction of their interests. The idea that humans are signs and that this definition transcends the body had, as it turns out, a lot of potential for a politically liberal interpretation. The most obvious implication is that it can be interpreted in such a way as to refute racism. "Whites" and "blacks" have the same definition, for their definition is nonbiological. Peirce may have been conservative, but the other key pragmatists, James, Dewey, and Mead, were distinctly and increasingly liberal as time went on. These three all used Peirce's momentum, including his theory of the self, in an egalitarian manner.

Peirce's semiotics also contributed to anthropologists' notion of culture. Culture is composed of signs and symbols. When Boas created and developed this concept, he was not drawing directly on Peirce's ideas, but he was drawing on the general pragmatist and social science atmosphere Peirce had helped to establish (Wiley 2006b). So it is reasonable to say Peirce had a strong, if indirect, effect on the idea of culture.

It was the theory of culture that smashed the various forms of racism—in the scholarly and also (gradually) in the legal world. Cultural anthropologists showed that there is equality among all cultures and that humans in preliterate societies think with the same logic as those in literature societies. Anthropology promoted a nonhierarchical view of cultures, societies, and human beings.

Peirce's semiotic self and the related anthropological notion of culture led to the idea that all selves, being plastic and of highly malleable possibilities, are therefore fundamentally the same. Peirce's self seems to be an empty template for a sign—that is, for any sign and any number of signs. All empty templates are alike. Peirce's self-sign resembles Locke's "tabula rasa," in being undetermined and open to any meaning. But Locke's mind *has* a tabula rasa, whereas Peirce's self-sign *is* a tabula rasa (or generic sign).

Peirce's semiotic self also resembles Sartre's idea that the self is, in some respects a "nothingness," remembering that Sartre's nothingness has the technical meaning of an absence or privation (Sartre 1957b). Accordingly, Sartre's nothingness, like Peirce's semiotic self, can become an indefinite variety of "somethingnesses." In other words, Peirce's self has unlimited potential; as a sign it can become a sign of anything.

As mentioned previously, Peirce formed this notion of the self for logical, not political, reasons. He was evidently quite racist, patriarchal, and the like, making him a man of his times. But sometimes ideas have their own ideas—that is, they have implications that were unforeseen by their originator. This is a property that Robert Merton calls "unanticipated consequences" and Max Weber calls "elective affinity." In this case the ontological or structural similarities of all semiotic selves strongly suggests that biologically determinist and racist theories of the self are erroneous and that selves are formed by purely symbolic processes.

Peirce's notion of the self did not come a moment too soon for American politics. It took several decades for Peirce's idea to take on its political role, but gradually, and with the help of other pragmatists and social scientists, the pragmatist notion of the self became a cultural weapon. It became a means of checkmating racism, at least in its intellectual form. This conflict came to a head around the time of World War I in the controversy between the racist Americanization movement and the more liberal ideas of the pragmatists and the social sciences, in particular anthropology and sociology (Higham 1988; Wiley 2011a).

This controversy extended over several years, and in the process, the egalitarian theory of the self was gradually worked out and honed. In other words, the biologism and racism of the Americanization movement pushed pragmatism's theory of the self even more in the opposite—that is, the cultural—direction. All four of the major pragmatists as well as the many secondary pragmatists contributed to this controversy. Dewey describes, in restrained language, the victory of the liberal side:

> When this volume was first produced, there was a tendency, especially among psychologists, to insist upon native human nature untouched by social influences and to explain social phenomenon by reference to traits of original nature called "instincts." Since that date (1922) the pendulum has undoubtedly swung in the opposite direction. The importance of culture as a formative medium is more generally recognized. (1930, viii)

The moral and legal equality of all humans was slowly recognized, if not always acted on, in the 1920s and later. In practice this idea implied the equality of all subcultural groups, including race, gender, age, ethnicity, sexual orientation, and so on, although it took decades for these democratic implications to work themselves out.

Glassy Essence and the Double Mirror

Peirce also likes to refer to the self as a "glassy essence," taking this metaphor from Shakespeare (Harrison 1948, 756). A common interpretation of Shakespeare is that he is referring here to the fragility of glass, suggesting the delicacy of the human spirit. I interpret this phrase in the plain, ordinary sense of a mirror, although I give it a new twist. Drawing on Peirce's definition of humans as signs, particularly using my interpretation of a potential sign, takes us close to a mirror analogy. A mirror in itself is merely emptiness and possibility, but once something is reflected in it, the mirror becomes a positive representation of that thing.

The mirror suggests how the self can reflect anything, and this goes a long way. But it would be better if this analogy could also capture the most distinctive feature of human nature, which is self-awareness or reflexivity. The self is an object to itself in that it can loop around and be aware of itself, as though looking from the standpoint of another. Kant thinks self-awareness is always present when we are conscious at all. This looping or reflexivity is not a simple mirroring relation. The mirror represents only linear cognition but self-awareness is curvilinear. It is us looking at ourselves from an outside vantage point. Mead refers to this process as "role-taking," which is his term for reflexivity (although he also uses this term in other ways). Mead's reflexivity is usually represented by a curving line of 360 degrees, which goes out from the self, takes a twist and comes back to its starting point, our self. It is not like us holding a mirror out to reality. Rather, it is like us looking into a mirror at ourselves. In other words, it is a second mirror analogy.

What is needed here is a way of representing both mirroring functions, the one that pictures the outside world and the one that pictures our self, in the same metaphor. I suggest the following idea, which I think is merely an extension of the thought of Peirce and the pragmatists. Picture two mirrors in the self: one reflects the outer world, and the second reflects the first mirror. In other words, we watch ourselves as we watch the world. As we listen to the world, so to speak, we eavesdrop on our listening process. The first mirror has an implicit form of self-awareness, for we know it is us doing the watching. But the second mirror gives us a more express, explicit, and pronounced form of self-awareness.

The double mirror analogy also evades the awkwardness of the bent sightline. To look out and somehow loop back, 360 degrees, and see ourselves, is not how the eyes or sightlines work. But the two mirror analogy respects the linearity of the sightline. To sum up, the first mirror gives us phenomenological consciousness and the second gives us self-consciousness.

Other animals have only the first mirror, phenomenological awareness, and even their first mirror is not as strong as ours. They do not have self-consciousness or the second mirror. Babies start with only the first mirror, and gradually, in ways that are not yet fully understood, they attain the second mirror (i.e., self-consciousness). It also appears that certain kinds of brain damage, as well as intrusive medications or chemicals, can weaken or remove the second mirror, leaving you unaware of who you are.

The Dialogical Self

Peirce is also responsible for the revival of the dialogical self, an idea found in Plato and in the Middle Ages but ignored since the time of Descartes. This idea, too, has egalitarian implications, for if humans are self-steered by a dialogical process, this is clearly a nonbiological, cultural force. I have already pointed out that Peirce's definition of the self *without the body* probably made it easier to combat racism. His notion of the semiotic self and the dialogical process also both are radically egalitarian. Peirce, then, is a striking example of unintended consequences, for his purely analytical ideas gradually flowed through an interpretive, elective affinity process and became foundational for American political liberalism.

William James

James invented the term "stream of consciousness," an idea almost bursting with meaning. For one thing, it points to consciousness as the life of the mind, a category completely inaccessible to contemporary materialism. We live in the sea of consciousness, and it is our window into reality. We wake up to this reality, and as we awaken, the world of consciousness envelops us as an extension of our self.

Another characteristic of consciousness is that we experience it in the "first person." It is not another's consciousness (second person); nor is it the community's (third person). It is ours, and we experience it in a sightline that leads right back to our selves. Just as our eyes lead directly, in linear fashion, to what the eyes see, our consciousness leads back in quasi-linear fashion to ourselves as the subject of consciousness.

Consciousness also has a unique set of meanings, which are called "qualia," a term that means about the same as "quality." When we are conscious, we perceive the sensual imagery of the world around us. We also perceive the non-sensory imagery of emotions and kinesthetic feelings. In addition, we experience meanings and understanding of the world surrounding us. We perceive and understand the world in the field of consciousness.

This experience is also located in the medium of time, and the passage of time makes it appear as a river or "stream." This passage gives a temporal dimension to consciousness, and we regularly organize our experience along this dimension. For the individual this flow becomes a biography and for the community it becomes a history.

James's stream of consciousness describes the experiential parameters or "world" of the self. Within this stream the human being is on a kind of boat, navigating the stream and moving toward wherever the stream (i.e., history), is going. An active, self-possessed person can sail through the stream in a reasonably controlling, self-directing fashion. But a person without internal direction or controls will simply reel down the stream wherever the current and wind takes him or her.

When modern novelists, such as Joyce and Woolf, explored the flow of consciousness, they focused on inner speech as the main content of consciousness. The subjective turn of the novel is called "stream of consciousness" literature. This literature suggests that the main thing we notice in our consciousness is not the scenery or the imagery or even the emotionality but the dialogical flow of inner speech. Consciousness, then, is not only self-consciousness; it is consciousness of our internal conversation and related experiences. This conversation can be imagistic as well as verbal, but in either case it is dialogical. To the extent, then, following Bakhtin and Peirce, that the self is dialogical, consciousness itself is largely our communicative confrontation with ourselves.

When James's stream of consciousness is interpreted as a flow of verbal meaning, as the modern novelists understood it, the "flow" and the temporal traits become less important. Instead, we are now talking about the owner, the organizer, and to some extent, the creator of this consciousness. Instead of gravity pulling the stream toward its goal—for example, toward a lake or one of the oceans—the controlling force is now human attention.

In this situation where we more or less rule over the stream of consciousness, the self has two major powers: cognition or knowing and volition or choosing. Agency is an extension of choosing, but I ignore agency for now. Knowing tells you what is there, in the stream around you, and choosing allows you to get, or at least attempt to get, the things around you. The self obviously uses both powers to live a life. But theorists tend to emphasize one side, usually the cognitive side, in their description of the human process.

The reflexivity or cognitive mode is what most philosophers, including the pragmatists, tend to emphasize. James made the opposite choice by selecting the emotion of self-feeling as his key to explaining the self. The other three pragmatists, especially Mead, chose to emphasize reflexivity, which is the cognitive side. Actually, you do not have to make this choice; you can work with both capabilities together, but this is not what happened.

James was aware of the cognitive side; in fact, his I-me distinction became the basis for Mead's reflexive theory. Still, James did not develop this reflexivity insight. Instead, he was more impressed with self-feeling as the key to the self. Two quotations give an idea of what he had in mind:

> *In its widest possible sense*, however, *a man's Self is the sum total of all that he* CAN *call his*, not only his body and his psychic powers, but his clothes and his house, his wife and children, his ancestors and friends, his reputation and words, his lands and horses, and yacht and bank-account. All these things give him the same emotions. (James 1950a, 291; emphasis in original)

> *The words* ME, *then, and* SELF, *so far as they arouse feeling and connote emotional worth, are* OBJECTIVE *designations, meaning* ALL THE THINGS *which have the power to produce in a stream of consciousness excitement of a certain peculiar sort.* (James 1950a, 319; emphasis in original)

This way of coming at the self is quite different from the I-me distinction, for it is not cognitive but emotional. The I-me reflexivity approach divides the self into parts that differ in self-communicative function. The self-feeling approach divides the self into parts that differ in our feelings about ourselves.

It might have been better if James had stayed with the I-me distinction and simply added the self-feeling perspective, for they are both valid and powerful views of the self and both seem true to experience, but he did not. James begins his analysis of self-feeling with a property metaphor, as though the things to which we give self-feeling or ownership become extensions of the self. Self-feeling is somewhat undefined in James, and it has perhaps several slightly differing meanings. I would like to take hold of the expression "excitement of a certain peculiar sort" and give this an interpretation.

The word "excitement" suggests that James has something extraordinary and unusual in mind. But since James does not give any precise definition to self-feeling, the concept seems quite open to the reader's interpretation. Perhaps it is not stretching things too far to suggest that James is here getting at the particular charisma that is characteristic of the human self, particularly in modern times. This seems to be what underlies the excitement of the self.

The self is sacred, according to Durkheim, and this mana or sacredness can extend to the things that one loves or is closest to. Mana is contagious; it jumps from person to person and from center to periphery. Durkheim's sacred is similar to Weber's charisma, particularly as it is exercised by a charismatic leader. The charismatic person, too, has a somewhat contagious charisma, as people who are close to the leader feel energized by contact with the charisma.

In contemporary times, as mentioned earlier, the self is the most sacred of entities. For many people and certainly for most legal systems, it is more sacred than a religious entity. The sacred self, then, resembles the charismatic leader in having a glow of value or holiness. James himself did not give much theoretical development to the notion of self-feeling, but I am engaging in what I think is a reasonable interpretation. Cooley also used self-feeling but in a slightly different way than James. He looked at feelings the self has about itself, and he drew the important insight of the "looking-glass self" (Cooley [1902] 1983, 183–184; Scheff 2005), later richly developed in Goffman's works and discussed at length in Chapter 9 of this book. Nevertheless, I want to take James's concept in a different direction than Cooley did.

More generally, I decided to make this chapter tilt in a cognitive (i.e., not an emotional) direction. The pragmatists all comment on emotions, but putting these comments together and integrating them with the cognitive side is a task for another time. It is pretty clear that most emotions will fit into Dewey's agency scheme largely as sources of energy, pro and con, for action (Collins 2004b). Also, I think the cognitive aspect of the self is what makes humans most obviously distinct from other animals. Human emotionality is also probably distinct, but the distinctness seems less striking. An additional reason for leaning in a cognitive direction is that this issue is what the American "politics of the self" was fought over. As mentioned earlier, my view is that in the early twentieth century, the United States was drifting in a nondemocratic, authoritarian political direction, the Americanization movement being central to this drift. The influence of the pragmatists and the

University of Chicago sociology department (Wiley 2011a), largely based on the cognitive and cultural nature of the self, helped swerve the United States back toward the democratic center.

Another way of saying this is that the pragmatists finished off the still inconclusive Civil War, especially in its underlying ideological fight. This war was in large part over the morality of slavery. It took a while, but when the pragmatist theory of the self gradually developed its fully egalitarian implications, the United States could finally see what the fight was about. It could see that it is a violation of human nature to have slaves, and it could also see in what deeper sense African Americans are equal to and the same as all other people. It took a clarified theory of the self to explain this issue.

Returning to James's notion of self-feeling, this idea appears to be ripe for development. One obvious way to do this is to connect it to the sacred self of Durkheim and Weber, as I have hinted. I do not pursue this connection extensively at this time, but it suggests how the value of the self fits into the pragmatists' theory. Although James had a reflexivity theory of the self, he also had a quasi-religious one, in which the self is permeated with a sacred feeling or emotion. This emotion is similar to Durkheim's religious awe. This quality of the self is not explicated by Peirce, Dewey, or Mead, but it is compatible with their views of the self.

The pragmatists also attribute other features to the self, but these four—agency (Dewey), sociality (Mead), symbolicity (Peirce), and self-feeling (James)—go a long way to constructing a theory of the self. The self has goals and it can exercise meaningful self-awareness in pursuit of these goals. This self-awareness also creates value, for the self evokes an awe and reverence in other people—that is, in the community. This profile of the self can be seen in the example of Herbert Peirce saving his mother's life. I have already pointed out how agency, in both its deliberative and active stages, is strikingly visible in this example. Herbert was rehearsing with the signs and symbols of Fanny Longfellow's death and also of the undetermined person whose life he was preparing to save. His thoughts would also be characterized by Mead's reflexivity and sociality, for this is arguably the nature of all thought. And Herbert's self-feeling would be intensely engaged as he anticipated the dress fire and the life saving of someone he loved. These concepts work together rather well to describe the actual practices of selves, and it seems clear that they constitute a coherent and powerful theory.

I do not suggest here that the pragmatist's conception of the self is by any means finished. But no school of philosophers—Greeks, Medievalists, British Empiricists, German idealists, or contemporary poststructuralists or postmodernists—has a finished theory of the self. Their theories would probably all have as many weaknesses as the one I am working with. But as Peirce says, the point is for the community of thinkers to keep on thinking.

The General Properties of the Pragmatist's Self

This theory can also be described in a brief list of its characteristics. Up to now I have been talking about four discrete theorists. Now I talk about the four of them collectively, treating each characteristic as a shared idea. This is a loose list, and I mean it to be an umbrella over the theory.

Irreducible Self

The self cannot be reduced to some other kind of thing, either upward or downward. Upwardly, the self could be erroneously reduced or dissolved into language or culture, which would render it a form of nothingness. Downwardly, the self could be absorbed into physical, chemical, or biological processes, ceasing to be a supra-biological entity and therefore becoming another form of nothingness. But the pragmatist self is a *sui generis* entity, incapable of reduction in either direction. This irreducibility has implications for the dignity of the self. If there is no self; that is, if it is subject to reduction, then the whole human drama is a sham. Rights, consciousness, self-worth, conscience, and love, to mention some features of the self, would all be a delusion. All the human values, in my opinion, assume an irreducible self, and the pragmatist's self is of that nature.

Dialogical Self

The core process of the self is dialogical. The self functions by exercising a dialogue with itself as well as with others. This is how we think, how we plan, and how we steer ourselves through the world. When people are emotionally disturbed, inner speech becomes damaged and loses some of its function.

Internal dialogue is at the core of the healthy self. There are also unconscious processes, both emotional and cognitive, and these are distinct from the conscious dialogue. But the conscious process is probably the most important part of the self. And in any case, the unconscious processes may themselves be dialogical.

Decentered Self

The self of the pragmatists lacks a dominating center, for it is divided into discrete and semi-autonomous parts. Mead's I and me are certainly a decentered self. If you add Peirce's you, there is more decentering. And James's network of possessions that share in self-feeling also add to the decentering. Descartes's "I" is the powerful center of the self. Nothing else in his self has this centrality or rootedness. The "I" of the pragmatists is more like an equal partner with several other important players. This I is a kind of administrative center but not necessarily at the center of meaning or feeling.

Relational Self

If the self is not a Cartesian substance and is not reduced to physicalist or postmodern nothingness, the only serious category left is that of relation. Relations are pairs that are connected in some way. In the case of the self, they are pairs connected by reflexivity—that is, by a looping back onto itself. All aspects of the self are aspects of the reflexive relation. This relativity is basic to the self's decenteredness. It also underlies the internal dialogue, for one part of the relation addresses the other part. I see the self as a triad, embracing the I, Mead's me, and Peirce's you. This triad is the combination of two relationships: Mead's I-me and Peirce's I-you. The self, then, is composed of many relationships, which means its basic kind of reality is the relation.

Egalitarian Self

There are several important egalitarian strains within the pragmatist theory of self. Peirce's self is the most strongly egalitarian of the four. His self-as-sign is a kind of rubber band or putty that can be stretched or formed in an indefinite number of ways. Equality is rooted in this flexibility. Dewey's self is a distinctly ordinary man, contradictory to all versions of inequality. Mead's self is anti-patriarchal, initially a female and then branching out into the two genders. His self also has Peirce's plasticity. And the charisma of James's self is one of equal and inviolable value. The sacred self, in contemporary times, is the source of Weber's substantive rationality. This is his category of the good-in-itself. All selves are sacred in the same way, and this makes them all of equal value.

Voluntarism

The pragmatist self is goal seeking and self-determined. The agency framework implies voluntarism, and the term "pragmatism" suggests the self-steering of practice. Similarly, inner speech seems to be the place where choices are initially made and tried out. Social institutions in all societies, including the regulatory or legal system and the family, assume that people make choices and are responsible for these choices. It is difficult to see how these institutions would have evolved and remained in place if the actions of human beings were completely determined. Therefore, the pragmatist position on self-determination seems to fit the practical realities of life.

Cultural Self

Pragmatism's self is culturally driven, although bodies obviously have a huge influence on the self. Nevertheless, the distinctive features of the self are cultural or symbolic. The particular way culture animates and steers the self explains how human lives develop. Symbols steer them, not genes or other biological traits. Culture is composed of signs and symbols. So semiotics—which is the study of signs—underlies culture. The pragmatists had a semiotic view of the self, meaning the self, like culture, is primarily composed of signs and symbols. To say that the self is semiotic and to say that it is cultural is to say the same thing. These concepts also lead to the egalitarian self, for all selves are made of the same plastic, highly malleable "stuff."

Social Sciences

The pragmatist theory of the self is closely related to the social sciences, especially as they developed in the United States. I have already mentioned that the pragmatist notion of the self runs parallel to the anthropological concept of culture. The social sciences have also used some form of Mead's social self for a long time. In addition, the pragmatist theme of the dialogical self has a counterpart in social psychology. And the pragmatist theory of meaning, given a semiotic or cultural interpretation, underlies all of the social sciences.

Field Theory

All the pragmatists can be interpreted in field theory terms (Martin 2003; Fligstein and McAdam 2012). This idea has been applied most extensively to James (Fontinell 2000) and Mead (Wiley, forthcoming), but it also fits Dewey and Peirce. A field theory, drawn by analogy from the field theories of physics, is based not on causality but on context. This context is a setting or atmosphere or subculture, most evident in the ethnographies of cultural anthropology and the neighborhood studies of the 1920s Chicago school of sociology. These contexts or fields influence anything in their space, somewhat the way a cocktail party's ethos influences anyone at the party. This idea is still something of a sensitizing concept, and there are several versions of it, but it is gradually becoming a major resource in social theory.

Conclusion

This discussion of the pragmatists' conception of the self has profound implications for several broader issues, which I now briefly touch on.

Form versus Content

A formal property of the self can be defined as a feature that is claimed to be part of all selves at all times and places: for example, Peirce's idea that selves are symbolic or Mead's idea that they are reflexive (i.e., self-aware). In Chapter 4 I distinguish generic traits of the self from those concerning identity. I am now equating formal properties with generic traits. The discussion in this chapter is primarily at the generic or formal level.

A substantive feature of the self would be a matter of content as opposed to form. A particular identity, for example, or a self-concept of some kind would be at the level of content. The boundary between form and content is not always clear, and sometimes only time can tell which is which. For example, saying the self "maximizes" hedonistically or economically seems formal, but it may come and go with modern capitalism. Even if traits were around for centuries, such as male hegemony, Christianity, or what Weber calls modern capitalism, they would still be matters of content—having the quality of (long-term) transiency. Content can come and go, but the formal qualities remain. In Chapter 2, where I look at a dozen or so anti-self arguments, the issue often turns on a form/content distinction. The pragmatist theory of the self concerns only the form. This mode of existence should be distinguished from content, which constantly varies throughout time and across cultures.

Family Resemblance

The unity of the pragmatists seems to be one not of essence but of a Wittgensteinian family resemblance. Wittgenstein uses this term in two senses: structural and stylistic (suggested to me by Perinbanayagam 2006, 63–67). Wittgenstein's list of family resemblances includes "build, features, color of eyes, gait, temperament, etc." (Wittgenstein 1958, para. 66, 67).

The first four items are structural features of the body. But the last one, temperament, is more a matter of emotional style. Certain ways of smiling, laughing, frowning, and so on sometimes run in families. These are the emotional expression or style of the bodily structure. If we follow the now common practice of applying Wittgenstein's family resemblance analogically to other kinds of groupings, such as clusters of scholars, we might look for two kinds of similarities: structural and stylistic. Among thinkers, structural similarities would be ideas that they, more or less, hold in common. Similarities of style would seem to be matters of presentation and logic, including informal logic and logic-in-use. The pragmatist theory of the self, for example, entails these structural features: agency, symbolicity, goal directedness, internal plurality, dialogicality, and interpenetration with society. The pragmatists place different nuances and emphases on these ideas, but they have enough in common to say they have a family resemblance in the structural sense. The pragmatists also share such stylistic features as an emphasis on consequences rather than antecedents, a concern for the tangibility or observability of concepts, a suspicion of dualisms, an acceptance of the first person perspective, and a relational view of the self. The unity, then, of the pragmatist theory is the resemblance, in both the structural and stylistic senses of the word.

Theory of Mind

Cognitive science has been working on the theory of mind—that is, of the mental properties of oneself and others—for two or three decades, and it looks as though pragmatism has neglected this problem. But the pragmatists have been theorizing the theory of mind for a long time, although they have used a different terminology (Wiley 2013).

Humanism

This philosophy insists that humans actually exist and that their existence cannot be explained away by dissolving them into some other reality, such as language or computers. The pragmatist position is that humans are pretty much as we experience them. We think that we see and hear, and we actually do see and hear. We seem to choose, and we do choose. We seem to have some kind of agency or center of action, and we do have this center. We seem to think our way through life, and we do think our way through life.

In addition, pragmatism sees humans as having intrinsic value and inviolability. We have rights, and these rights come from the nature of our selves, not from governments. And the rights are equal, not only in the United States but throughout the world, at all times and in all places. Men and women also have the same rights, all racial, ethnic, and subcultural groups have the same rights, and the Declaration of Independence, with its radical egalitarianism, pretty much describes pragmatism's ethics.

Finally, pragmatism is humanistic in being comfortably suitable for democracy. This philosophy and American democracy have had a back-and-forth, causal dialogue for many decades. Democracy, with its system of voting, civil liberties, and equal rights, assumes a particular kind of human nature or "self." And this "self" seems quite close to the one I describe in this chapter.

9

BAKHTIN'S VOICES AND COOLEY'S LOOKING-GLASS SELF

A theme of this book is that the self is largely the product of inner speech. One way in which this process works is Cooley's looking-glass self. We talk to ourselves about other people and their attitude toward us. I look at this process and add a new ingredient to the discussion—Bakhtin's theory of voices. First I review Cooley's idea and see how it has held up in the literature. Then I describe Bakhtin's notion of voice along with related concepts. Then I look at Cooley's limitations. And finally I integrate Bakhtin's ideas into Cooley's theory.

Cooley's Looking-Glass Self

The looking-glass self idea was stated by Cooley in 1902, rather early in the history of American sociology (Cooley [1902] 1983, 183–185). The core of this idea is that people tend to internalize what they imagine or think other people think of them. If they think others think they are ugly, they tend to think of themselves as ugly. If they think others think they are kind, they tend to think of themselves as kind. Sometimes one person, one opinion, is enough to activate and imprint a trait into the looking-glass self.

This process works most strongly if one is emotionally close to the other—for example, as a family member or a friend. It also seems more powerful if the other is of higher status. The process probably gets less important the older one gets. People commit to traits as life goes on, narrowing the options for change and making a person less subject to suggestion from others.

Still, adults in love seem to have enormous power over each other's self-concept. Love opens your boundaries, your fences.

When the self is first formed in infancy, in the ontogenesis process, the significant other or others become part of you and prop you up. These supportive loved ones, especially the mother, act as a kind of lynchpin in the self. They are the foundation that holds it together. Over time, their presence may seem less important, for you start getting an autonomous self, which can, more or less, stand on its own. But if they withdraw from you for some reason, you might start getting quite uncomfortable. You still need them to keep your self-process going, and their withdrawal can still destabilize you.

Sometimes one might go through what could be called a second ontogenesis process, a "born-again" feeling. It might happen because of some kind of conversion, religious or political, that gives you a new psychological structure and a new lynchpin. The Stalin purges of the 1930s in the Soviet Union seem to have had a psychologically devastating effect on their victims. The targets of these purges had identified too strongly with the Communist Party, and they were vulnerable to a major looking-glass self disruption.

This same born-again process can come about in a love affair. Let us say you are so much in love that the new person starts replacing your mother as your lynchpin. Your welfare and ontological security are now dependent on this loved one as an essential constituent, and that person's basic security may also, in turn, be dependent on you. Now you have a new looking-glass self. This self thrives on the love and recognition you get from this loved one. Those resources are what make you strong, happy, and whole. They are your positive looking-glass self.

But if for some reason that loved one withdraws his or her love and recognition and instead starts attacking your "self," he or she has the power to disintegrate you (by removing the lynchpin). Then you have to wiggle out of this mess by repairing this relationship, finding another lynchpin, becoming your own lynchpin, or degenerating into a highly disturbed person, probably with a severe depression. This is an extreme case of the looking-glass self, where the self as such starts to disintegrate and disappear. This disruption is not yet well understood, although Thomas Scheff's (2005) analysis of shame comes pretty close. Cooley, however, was too innocent to envision this psychological disaster.

And, going back a step, Cooley is not explicit about how we learn others' opinions of us—for example, whether we learn this directly, indirectly, or by guesswork. This knowledge might be based on something a third party said. Or it might be based on the look in someone's eye or on his or her tone of voice. Or someone may have spoken openly, confronting us with an insult or seeking us out with a compliment. We can work around Cooley's imprecision here, although when I introduce Bakhtin, indirect or implicit communications become more important.

The looking-glass self idea has now spread into social psychology as a taken-for-granted truth, with the patina of a classic. There are also a variety of other ways in which social influences—for example, one's parents' political or economic attitudes—affect the self, but this is not quite the looking-glass self. These social attitudes are not about us; they are about the social order and what is right or wrong. The looking-glass self, in contrast, is about your traits and your identity.

We are affected, then, by the ordinary opinions that others seem to have of us. This influence is not necessarily based on logic or evidence but simply on the raw power of the other person's views, particularly if we have identified with them to some extent. Social influence is as much emotional as logical. If the other has a certain opinion of you, you can take his or her role and picture yourself with that trait. You might say no, but that picture can linger. This might be especially true if you are denying some trait you are ashamed of and someone nudges you about it. The other person may weaken your defense and remove the veil you have been using to hide that trait.

In Cooley's writing the looking-glass self idea was hedged considerably, and others have added to these cautions (Gecas and Schwalbe 1983; Reitzes 1980; Yeung and Martin 2003). Cooley does not by any means portray a passive or over-socialized self (Jacobs 2006, 91–92). On the contrary, he says we constantly filter others' opinions of us. At times others do influence us. But sometimes—for example, if the opinion is just too unwelcome—we resist being influenced. We can also manipulate the opinions of others, so that we can, in effect, create a flattering looking glass.

What we say to ourselves is also a kind of looking-glass phenomena, given that the inner dialogue is a bit like a conversation with another person. This means daydreams, positive or negative toward the self, can be a kind of self-work. Since we engage in this self-talk more or less all day long, we are constantly primping the self-concept. Depressives, to mention a more difficult case, get stuck on worry and self-criticism, operating as a negative looking-glass on their moods. People who worry too much have something of the same problem.

Mead also has the concepts for a looking-glass self, especially with the notion of role-taking, but he does not use them in this way (Wiley 2003). In particular, Mead does not use the idea of self-feeling, which for Cooley is the core of the self and the energy behind the looking-glass self. Self-feeling is our sense of "mineness," and it refers to anything we might be attached to or cling to, such as our bodies, our family, our friends, or our property. Its central idea is the way we evaluate and cling to ourselves.

Mead (1934, 173) thinks reflexivity or self-awareness, which is the cognitive view of the self, is more important than self-feeling. This may be true for the genesis of the self, which is what Mead has in mind, but the development of the self seems to draw heavily on self-feeling. In fact, self-feeling *is* a form of self-awareness or reflexivity. My own preference is to use reflexivity and self-feeling together, thereby combining Cooley and Mead (Wiley 1994, 110–117). In the case of the looking-glass self, then, Cooley has a powerful insight that Mead does not quite have.

Cooley's idea has now been around for over a hundred years, and to some extent it has settled in as a received truth. There are two scholars, however, who have used Cooley's idea in novel ways in recent years. For one, Goffman (1959) wrote extensively about the "presentation of self." This theme concerns our attempt to cope with and sometimes even control the social looking glass. Goffman's books have been quite influential, but, not unlike Weber, he lacks a clearly communicable method, and he has not inspired a lot of research.

A related line of scholarship is that of Scheff (2005) on shame. Cooley thinks that shame is a major motivator in accepting or resisting the opinions of others, and Scheff explains how this works. If a perceived opinion seems to shame us, we might do almost anything, including changing the self, to avoid the shame. Alternatively, we might brood, perhaps somewhat unconsciously, about the shame for an indefinite period of time. Shame seems to hurt the self more than any other emotion, possibly because it dismantles our self-feeling. Scheff has gone deeply into the structure and byways of this emotion, probably more so than anyone else, and in doing so he has created new understanding of the looking-glass self.

I should also mention Garfinkel's (1956) "degradation ceremony" as an insight into the looking-glass self, even though Garfinkel does not explicitly make the connection. The degradation ceremony is a formal and ritualized action in which someone's self is degraded or stigmatized. Examples are a criminal conviction, a mental health commitment, or a dishonorable discharge from the military. Garfinkel thinks this process is one of diminishing an identity by way of public shaming. This emotion links Garfinkel's idea both to the looking-glass self and to Scheff's work on shame.

Opposite processes are ceremonies that elevate the self, such as awards and educational credentials. These seem to work with the emotion of pride, which is the opposite of shame. These ceremonies are not the opinions of individuals but those of society. Yet they probably affect the looking-glass self at least as much as the opinions of individuals.

Cooley never intended the looking-glass self to be a major theory or a systematic explanation of social influence. His main source of information was observations of his three children in Ann Arbor, Michigan. His book *Human Nature and the Social Order* ([1902] 1983), which is where the looking-glass self idea appears, is largely about growing up in the United States. He is concerned about the relation between the development of human nature and the social order, particularly in how the latter influences the former. The looking-glass self is one such influence, though by no means the only one. Still, the looking-glass self idea has entered what might be called the heroic past of social theory, and it makes sense to evaluate this idea today. I hope that by adding Bakhtin's concept of voices, the looking-glass self can be applied in novel ways.

Bakhtin and Voice

If Bakhtin were forced into an intellectual niche it might be that of literary critic and literary theorist, but it would not be a completely comfortable fit. Russian history is noticeably different from that of Western Europe. They had no Reformation, no Renaissance, no Enlightenment, and no capitalism, let alone democratic capitalism. Russia's categories or major concepts are more Eastern than the West and more Western than the East. For this reason it is not easy for Europeans (or Americans) to classify their thinkers or even to fully understand their thought.

Bakhtin's writings overflow with ideas, but it is difficult to fit them into European grooves. Still, his ideas are far-reaching and they have distinct implications for the social sciences. Since I am mainly interested here in Bakhtin's notion of voice, I do not try to give a comprehensive description of his contribution but concentrate on voice and closely related ideas. After laying out these ideas, presenting them as conceptual tools, I show how they can be applied to Cooley's looking-glass self.

Bakhtin develops the notion of voice mainly in his analyses of Dostoyevsky's novels (Bakhtin 1981, 1984, 1986). Here Bakhtin is seemingly talking about literature rather than life. But his insights are so profound they constitute a broader social theory, not just about literature but about reality itself. One reason these novels glide into life is that Dostoyevsky gives an unusual amount of freedom to his fictional characters. He gets them started with his own voice but then releases them. This allows them to speak as they will, each with a distinct voice and each with a certain amount of social distance from the author. This process is similar to a daydream that starts with our active imagination, but then, releasing itself from us, it gradually moves along on its own.

Basing his ideas on Dostoyevsky, Bakhtin uses the concept of voice with a rich set of attributes. For one thing, there are no simple or single voices. All voices are multi-vocal, polyphonic, and replete with sub-voices. This plurality can be understood phonetically to indicate the different sounds a voice might have, authoritatively to indicate forcefulness or power, emotionally to refer to feeling tones, and linguistically to draw on semantics and syntax. There might be a central or core voice, but there are also an indefinite number of variations. The central voice might be loud and insistent, but there might also be voices that are peripheral and barely audible. This makes Bakhtin's voice complex and alive. Its effect on the looking-glass self is also complex and alive, for interpreting a voice saying something about you may be no easy matter.

Along with voice, Bakhtin uses the notion of dialogue, so that voice always means voices in dialogue. The dialogue may be explicit, as when two voices actually do communicate with each other. Or it may be implicit, as when a voice is speaking to an imagined or anticipated voice. This implicit voice might be that of a single person, a group, a category of people, or any other social entity. For Bakhtin we are always in dialogue in some sense, even if the dialogue is not fully articulated. When a voice says something about us, we can respond in dialogical form. This response might be confined to our inner speech, but it is still part of a dialogue.

In the case of dialogue, the speaker's voice has what Bakhtin refers to as addressivity and answerability (Perinbanayagam 2000, 61–62). By the former, he refers to the hailing and naming of the dialogical other, the person or person-like entity being spoken to. We might use the person's name, we might say "hey," or we might merely make eye contact. But in any case we are locking into intersubjectivity with that person. We are creating a flow of interaction, and this flow is open to a give-and-take process. Moreover, this addressivity is open to being answered, it has answerability.

Entering into interaction with another is a change in our being. We go from the psychological world into interaction *sui generis* (Rawls 1987). This causes a change in the tone of our consciousness, in our personal boundaries, and in the nature of our privacy. We also move into a new dialogical stance. When alone, most people are more or less constantly engaged in an intrapersonal dialogue within themselves. But when they interact with another, they add an interpersonal dialogue. These three dialogues, the two intrapersonal ones and the interpersonal one, constitute a mixing of three worlds. For Bakhtin a major dialogical process is conflict (rather than cooperation), and the two internal conversations vie in attempting to steer the interpersonal dialogue.

The nature of the address already says something about how the speaker is structuring the relationship. If one uses the other's last name, the address is formal, if one uses the other's first name, the address is informal, and if one uses a commanding phrase, such as "you" or "boy," the address is one of domination. The nature of the addressivity may have a strong effect on the looking-glass self process—that is, the interactants are not only saying something to each other; they are also saying something about each other.

Although all communication is, for Bakhtin, dialogical, this relation can be suppressed, and the communication will seem to be a monologue. A typical professor's lecture or scholarly article is formally a monologue. It is rounded off, objections are met as the argument proceeds, and when it is complete, it stands as a polished, finished work. The statement may suggest questions, but the monologue itself does not ask for them. In contrast, a dialogue is expressly addressed to other voices. It is open to questions, disagreement, development, and interaction. It is porous, with permeable boundaries. It is a conversation. Bakhtin prefers dialogue to monologue, and he regards it as the more creative way to engage in voice. In fact, he defines the self as dialogue—that is, it is not an entity that engages in dialogue; it *is* dialogue (Bakhtin 1984, 293). This is similar but more forceful than the dialogical self of the American pragmatists.

Both dialogue and monologue enter into the looking-glass self. But a dialogue does so directly and observably. A monologue is more indirect and implicit. You have to peel back, let us say, the professor's ceremonial language to find his dialogical attitude. He or she may, for example, be projecting an attitude of superiority, which implies inferiority in the listeners.

Bakhtin also speaks of voice as sometimes a silent and implicit kind of utterance. He finds voices in social forces, the surrounding community, and historical currents. Any social element that has a meaning also has a message, and this message can be decoded into a voice. These structural voices, so to speak, are usually inaudible, but they have a powerful influence over the humans in their range. And with enough attention they can be decoded (Bakhtin 1981, 341–350; John Shotter, pers. comm., 2008).

Institutional voices position you into a particular set of dos and don'ts, even though this positioning might be implicit. Everyone experiences this, but it is most powerful for minority groups. The elderly might be in a setting that glamorizes youth. Blacks might be in a place that has exclusively white symbols. The disabled might be in a situation that neglects their needs, suggesting that they are nonentities. Women might be in a place that has a choking masculine atmosphere. Little people might be in a setting where everything is too high. And gays and lesbians might be in an environment that emphasizes male-female romance. These settings are all silent voices that denigrate a minority group, lowering what might be called the group looking-glass self. Later I give concrete examples of this from my years at the University of Illinois.

Bakhtin's insight into the environmental voice is just a variation on Marx's idea that the superstructure tends to protect the capitalist class system. For Marx the implicit voice of this structure is "obey the bourgeoisie." Weber had generalized Marx by finding status and power conflicts as well as class conflict. And in a similar way, Bakhtin took Marx's talking social structure and gave it a broader range of messages.

In sociological terms, Bakhtin transforms structure into agency, structure being calcified or inaudible voice and agency being audible voice. He dissolves congealed and hardened discourses into vocalized and discernible ones. As he puts it:

> The process—experimenting by turning persuasive discourse into speaking persons—becomes especially important in those cases where a struggle against such images has already begun, when someone is striving to liberate himself from the influence of such an image and its discourse by means of objectification, or is striving to expose the limitation of both image and discourse. (1981, 348)

Another social concept that Bakhtin uses in his theory of the novel is that of inner speech or self-talk. This process is used a good deal in Dostoyevsky's novels. These, of course, predated Joyce's famous use of this device in *Ulysses*.

Bakhtin's deepest treatment of inner speech is in his analysis of Raskolnikov, the tormented killer of *Crime and Punishment*. Dostoyevsky's description of Raskolnikov's inner speech and Bakhtin's analysis of this inner speech is one of the most perceptive pictures of the human self and the inner torment of guilt in all of literature (Bakhtin 1984, 251–266).

Another concept in Bakhtin is that life is narrative (Rankin 2003; Perinbanayagam 2006, 18–21). Life is a set of facts and events, but it can also be characterized as a story, stretched across time. This means it has a plot, much like a literary work, and that this plot has a meaning. A narrative is an explanation that both individualizes and generalizes. It tells the story of an individual, but it also shows how this story partakes of the larger human story. A given life is an individual passage through a journey that everyone takes.

The voices, then—those of oneself, of others, and of the social environment—make one's narrative. This concept should be added to Bakhtin's notions of inner speech, voice, dialogue, structure-agency, and the addressivity-answerability relation. These conceptual tools are all relevant to social theory, and I try to show this by applying them to Cooley's looking-glass self.

Cooley's Limitations

Returning to Cooley, some weak spots in his own looking-glass self are the following:

1. He does not mention inner speech in his analysis of how we use the looking-glass self. He is aware that people are selective, filtering and sometimes even manipulating the looking-glass self. He is also aware of how inner speech functions in psychological life. But he does not put the two together. He does not show how we use inner speech in the processing and orchestrating of the looking-glass self.

Here are some of the ways in which this might work. We might hear (or hear of) someone saying something about us such as, "You are stupid" or "You are intelligent." And this person might have a certain intonation and facial expression. Our evaluation might be more vivid if we place this comment in our inner speech. We might, for example, repeat what this person said in our own voice and with our own force of statement. We might intensify the comment if it is flattering, to see how gratifying we can make it sound. Or we might exaggerate a negative comment, the way depressed persons dwell on their sadness.

Minorities are especially vulnerable to what people in the majority are silently thinking about them. If someone gives you a "look" that suggests some kind of emotion, it might also suggest what they are saying about you to themselves. Minorities imagine or guess at others' inner speech—that is, what others are thinking about them. This image is probably an important influence on their looking-glass selves.

In a related point, Cooley does not mention how we can, in our own minds, flatter or denigrate ourselves. Depressives get stuck in a stream of self-disparaging thoughts. These are insults that we deliver to ourselves and that undoubtedly hurt our self-esteem. The cognitive therapy approach to depression is to get control of negative inner speech and substitute positive self-attributions. This is not always easy to do, but when it is done, it seems to be as good a treatment for depression as any antidepressant chemicals. In ordinary (i.e., nondepressive) thought processes, self-compliments seem to be a useful way of controlling mood and sometimes even for handling such psychopathologies as phobias.

2. Cooley does not have a sense of how dialogue figures into the looking-glass self. We not only hear, or think we hear, people talking to and about us. We also, at least in our minds, interrogate them, ask for examples, sass back, and yell. In the case of compliments, we may feign modesty, smile appreciatively, and compliment in return.

Another way we might neutralize a negative comment is by saying it in such a way that it does not hurt as much, or even at all. If we repeat the comment in a mocking or silly way or in a way that makes the other sound foolish, we might find it easier to absorb or even resist the comment. All this may go on primarily in the head, as inner speech, but these processes constitute conversation or dialogue with the voices that stimulate the self.

3. Cooley also has a somewhat narrow notion of voice. But there may be other messages that do not come in the form of conversational voices, real or imagined. As noted earlier, social practices and institutions may have messages that apply to us. Laws and rules tell us who is right or wrong, good or

evil. These messages may sometimes detour through and get internalized by our selves, particularly our moral standards and conscience. But often they are completely external, much as the flattering or insulting neighbors are external.

These might simply be called "institutional facts," much as Durkheim had in mind with his term "social facts." These facts tell us what to do or what not to do. And they also tell us, depending on our conformity, what kind of person we are. These facts, then, are talking to us, and they are saying that we are or are not a good person. To hear their voices we have to transform social structure into social interaction, or institutions into conversations.

This decoding practice also helps explain how we can cope with the looking-glass self. To cope effectively we have to detect and monitor all the messages that enter into this self process. If there are some that have an effect on us but one that we are unaware of, we cannot cope with these kinds of messages. Cooley does not concern himself with the technology of protecting the self, but a closer acquaintance with Bakhtin shows how he might have done this.

4. Cooley does not take into account how the actions of others toward us can also enter the looking glass. He confines himself to language, but sometimes actions speak louder than words. When people who expect to attend some social function do not get an invitation, this can be quite hurtful. In fact, people often remember these slights indefinitely. The message of the non-invitation is that you are not important enough to invite, or even that they do not really like you.

More serious is actual abuse, both physical and sexual. Children who are abused may suffer because of it their entire lives. These traumas can be forgotten—that is, enter Freud's unconscious—but there is probably some kind of inner speech in the unconscious. This is also probably true of the new unconscious, referred to as the cognitive unconscious. My wife, a social worker, once did group therapy with teenage girls who had been sexually abused. The treatment was largely one of verbalization. The girls wrote letters to and gave speeches to the abuser. The looking-glass selves of these girls had been seriously damaged, and the group therapy and confrontation of the abuser was meant to cleanse the abuse.

5. Cooley based his research primarily on his observations of his three children, growing up in Ann Arbor, Michigan, in the nineteenth and early twentieth centuries. This was a distinctly white, middle class, privileged sample. He did not ask if minority groups or imperiled communities might have a different looking-glass self more dynamic than his three children did. Cooley's ideas are not inapplicable to low power groups, however. He simply does not

say much about people in these situations. Minority group members are subject to many more negative judgments than others. This kind of steady assault must harden the self and create a vigilance at its boundaries. In this chapter I try to restore the balance and pay special attention to minority groups.

6. Finally, Cooley's unit of analysis is the individual—that is, the person with the looking-glass self. He does not apply this concept to social groups or categories. But minorities are subject to a great deal of group social attribution as well as individual evaluations. They have a group or collective looking-glass self as well as the usual individual one.

Even though Cooley does not pay attention to this issue and his concepts are built solely for individuals, Bakhtin's concepts can address this problem. In particular, the institutional and structural voices are especially powerful in the way that they denigrate minority groups. This is the difference between institutional and individual racism, sexism, ageism, gay-ism, disability-ism, and so on.

The discussion so far can be summarized in Table 9.1, which describes two versions of the looking-glass self, that of Cooley and that of Bakhtin. Bakhtin's profile leans toward institutional voices, minorities, social types, inner speech, dialogue, narrative, and fighting back when necessary. Cooley's leans toward interactional voices, the average person, the individual, outer speech, monologue, the factual, and adjusting by way of coping. I say "leaning" because these distinctions are too sharp and extreme to be accurate as they stand—and Bakhtin is definitely not a categories or tables kind of thinker. I make the comparisons this way to be as clear as possible about the conceptual space between the two theorists. Still, the two thinkers and their versions of the looking-glass self are actually tendencies rather than stark, binary opposites.

Some of these distinctions are not explicit in Cooley, although he can be approached with them. If I am to add Bakhtin to Cooley, though, the contrast

TABLE 9.1 BAKHTIN'S LOOKING-GLASS SELF VERSUS COOLEY'S

Bakhtin	*Cooley*
Institutional voices	Interactional voices
Minorities	Average person
Social types	Individuals
Inner speech	Outer speech
Dialogue	Monologue
Narrative	Facts
Fighting back	Coping

has to be made on what might be called Bakhtin's terms. Cooley has to be placed on Bakhtin's turf, which is what I try to do.

Integrating Bakhtin and Cooley

I have laid out a set of new tools, and it is only in the use of these tools that their value can be discovered. Still, it is possible right away to mention some of the gains that Bakhtin gives to Cooley.

In the section on Cooley's limitations, I have already made some connection between Bakhtin's ideas and the looking-glass self. The question of institutions is a major point in the table. By paying attention to institutional voices, the looking-glass self can be made considerably more powerful. People are shaped not only by voices that they hear (or hear of) but also by those they do not hear. Everyone lives in a sea of unheard voices. According to Peirce, everything and anything can have a semiotic or signifying function (Ponzio 1984). Commercial products have voices, the built environment has voices, and the entire sociocultural system consists of meanings that can be vocalized. In other words, the social structure is a complex of signs and voices.

How does one decode these messages, and where does one begin? The answer depends on the individual case and on the aggressiveness of the person in question. The obvious place to look is where your interests are most at stake. Your income and economic class, your prestige or status, and your social and political power have interfaces with the social environment. These interfaces may seem to be saying that you are being treated fairly and that you should be satisfied with what you have. But if you look, or listen, more closely, you may find contradictions. Gunnar Myrdal (1944) found that the American Creed, as embodied in the Declaration of Independence and in the Gettysburg Address, preached equality, but the racial realities produced inequality. This set of contradictions was embedded in the voices of the social structure.

Obviously, the decoding of one's social environment is a matter of interpretation and may be subject to considerable controversy. But even Cooley's looking-glass self has plenty of controversy. If someone says something to you in a nasty tone of voice and you confront her, she might simply deny the nasty tone of voice. Cooley's looking-glass self would be rife with disagreement and struggle, particularly if one resisted unwelcome attributions. Decoding institutional voices is more of the same. The recent history of minority group protest—concerning language, laws, the mass media, sexual mores, employment and market practices, and so on—provides plenty of examples of confronting the institutional looking glass, even though it has not been conceptualized in that manner.

One way of giving flesh to these ideas is to look at an extended example. Consider the University of Illinois at Champaign-Urbana, where I taught from 1968 to 1995. During my tenure there were several confrontations between student minority groups and the official institutional structure. These conflicts can be translated into how institutional voices affect the group's looking-glass self. I do not single out this university because I think it is a bad example. It was probably typical of all major universities at the time. I choose it only because I have a participant observation window on what happened there. My examples emphasize women, African Americans, and gays and lesbians.

During the 1970s the law school started increasing its proportion of female students, largely because more women were applying for admission. One problem was that as female enrollment increased, there were not enough women's bathrooms. The law school was slow to keep bathrooms on an even keel with the sex ratio. As a result, women students were seriously inconvenienced—by long lines and lateness for class—and they loudly complained. The voice that some heard was that they should be embarrassed about their bodies, particularly their need to use bathrooms, and that the issue was of little importance. The problem simmered for several months.

A second example concerns race. In 1968, as a result of the assassination of Martin Luther King Jr., the university instituted the Project 500 program for black students. Previously, the university had a low proportion of black students, but on this solemn occasion the administration went out of its way to recruit five hundred black freshmen. Recruiters went into black neighborhoods and institutions to find black enrollees. Since this was, it would seem, a good-hearted and liberal move on the part of the university, it was expected that the black students would be appreciative of what was being done for them. The program included various forms of financial aid so that poor students would be able to afford attending this university. University housing was also included as a form of financial aid (Williamson 2003).

Unfortunately, some of the details, including both room assignments and financial aid, were not handled well, and some students found themselves in difficult circumstances. Female blacks were especially disgruntled, and it appears they were in the leadership. The blacks responded by holding a sit-in in the student union. The student union building was the hub of student activities. One went there for food and drink as well as for other conveniences. It had meeting rooms for student clubs, and it also had seventy-two overnight rooms for campus visitors. In addition, it housed the bookstore. The student union was also full of mementos, signifying the past glories of the university. Among these were about a dozen large oil portraits of the current and former presidents of the university. These were the people who ruled this university, and they were, unsurprisingly, all white males.

As one walked through the corridors, these well-clad, confident, white men looked down at you. They seemed to be saying, "We run this place, and, of course, you will do what we say." In any event, that is the voice the blacks participating in the sit-in seem to have heard. The response was to take ballpoint pens and deface several of these portraits. The protesting blacks also took over the union building and did not let anyone in, although there is uncertainty as to exactly what happened. But their loudest, and one might say most screeching, message was made with the ballpoint pens.

In all fairness to the Project 500 students, it should be pointed out that there were townie blacks as well as university blacks participating in the sit-in. There is no way of knowing who actually defaced the portraits. But it is reasonably clear that the portraits of the white male authorities, were, under these circumstances, offensive to blacks, and the marking of these portraits was the political response.

The university did what it could to remedy the snags in the program, and the sit-in was eventually terminated. But the program was pushed off course—and race relations on campus were given a reality jolt. In particular, the institutional complacency of the university, confident that blacks would be happy to just be there, was rebuked. And the university, never too successfully, attempted to restructure its voice for blacks.

A third example concerns the uniforms of the girls' basketball team in the early 1990s. A local sportswriter said in a column that these uniforms were baggy, ugly, and insufficiently feminine. He also suggested that these uniforms were related to the allegedly large lesbian presence on the team. He compared the team unfavorably to the girls' volleyball team. As the sportswriter put it:

> Herbert [the volleyball coach] has turned out attractive teams in every meaning of the word—rangy, athletic and remarkably handsome women who are well-spoken and talented. From Chancellor Mort Weir on down, local people are proud to support them. These women have contributed to a family atmosphere that . . . was not present in women's basketball.
>
> To build a strong following in an overwhelmingly heterosexual community with typically conservative Midwestern values, you must offer a conservative, heterosexual image on the court. Illinois women's basketball teams projected a different image. (Tate 1992)

The symbolic point here is the allegedly lesbian-looking baggy uniforms. The sportswriter was defining or voicing this institutional fact in a way that was offensive to lesbians. Of course, this was also an attack on the entire homosexual community at the University of Illinois and in the surrounding community. Given the anti-gay/lesbian backlash in the country at this time, it looked like Tate's aggressive column might be a trial balloon for a statewide antihomosexual action of some kind, whether he intended this or not.

On the day this column appeared, one of the sociology professors, who had a lesbian daughter, asked the university president to answer this column. The president asked the chancellor, Morton Weir, who had been named in the column, to write the letter. And Weir told the sociology professor he would do so. His letter read:

> In his Dec 14 column, Loren Tate appears to attribute views to me that I cannot let stand. . . . Tate's implication that it is important for women athletes to be attractive and heterosexual is outrageous. . . . At this campus, we are committed to providing an environment that enables individuals to study, work and participate in extracurricular activities in an atmosphere free of discrimination, including discrimination based on sexual orientation. Tate is free to write as he wishes, but he would do better to leave me out of it. (Weir 1992)

What happened here was that a local spokesman tried to push the university in an antihomosexual direction. But his attempt backfired, for the response was that the university made the strongest pro-homosexual statement it had ever made.

As I said, these three examples are not meant to slam the University of Illinois. The university performed reasonably well on all these issues. My purpose is solely to give examples of how the social environment can be offensive to minority groups. The missing bathrooms, the white male pictorial dominance, and the comment about the uniforms were all institutional voices. They have obvious implications for the selves of the minorities in question, most of whom were female. And notice that the three voices all have a shaming edge to them. Bathrooms, alleged black ingratitude, and baggy, ugly lesbianism all attack the selves of the groupings, especially the female ones, in question. Institutional attacks on the looking-glass selves of minority groups not only tend to be tacit and indirect; they can also be sniggering and highly disrespectful. In these ways they illustrate how Bakhtin's concepts can add to Cooley's looking-glass self.

Conclusion

Bakhtin's ideas are not completely new to sociology, but they complement and strengthen several existing ideas. Labeling theory in the social problems literature (Best 2004) is somewhat akin to Bakhtin's approach. People are labeled by voices, and the peeling off or modification of labels is facilitated by a close attunement to voices. Bakhtin suggests new ways of finding and dealing with labels.

Another relevant idea is social construction, which has to do with the free play or cultural relativism of what we see "out there." The modes of social construction and their means of defining reality are largely a matter of voices. Bakhtin's approach is useful for understanding how social construction works.

Also the notion of positioning, which is presented as a more robust notion than that of role (Davies and Harré 1990), is done largely through institutional voices. To understand how one has been positioned, and to attempt a repositioning, will depend largely on how one handles Bakhtin's version of the looking-glass self.

Finally, Bakhtin's analysis is quite useful for understanding social movements. Oppression is largely enacted via voices, and it can be fought by attacking the sources of voices. Social movements often rise directly from a Bakhtinian view of oppression. Of course, as with labeling theory, minorities can effect resistance only if they organize and take political action. The mere identification of labels and voices is just a preliminary stage. Still, it can be a powerful and indispensable preliminary stage.

In summary, Cooley theorized the looking-glass self in his 1902 book, *Human Nature and the Social Order*. His idea was that people tend to internalize the opinions that they think others, particularly intimate others, have of them. There are now lots of qualifications and hedges to this idea, but it is still a powerful insight. I add to this discussion by applying Bakhtin's notion of "voices" to Cooley's looking-glass self. You can find Bakhtin's voices in anything that has language, a message, or even a meaning. One important if silent voice is what others are saying to themselves about us. We can guess at their inner speech, particularly if there are clues in their body language. Your social environment—that is, social organization, social structure, and the built environment—can also be transformed into voices that are saying something to and about you. If you dissolve social elements into voices, you can more easily attend to them, correct them, resist them, and perhaps "orchestrate" them. This task is especially incumbent on people who are being pushed around by their social environment. Two glaring examples are people in minority groups and people who are classified as disabled.

10

INNER SPEECH THEORY

This chapter creates a framework for combining two important theories of inner speech: that of the American pragmatists Charles Sanders Peirce (1839–1914) and George Herbert Mead (1863–1931) and that of the Russians Lev Vygotsky (1896–1934) and Mikhail Bakhtin (1895–1975). The two approaches are somewhat different but still similar enough to be compatible. If they were combined, the overall theory of inner speech would be stronger.

The two Russians did not know about the two Americans, who preceded them by several decades, or their ideas. Nor did the Americans know about the Russians. The Americans had backgrounds in science—Peirce in chemistry and Mead in biology. The Russians had backgrounds in the Russian literary tradition and in ethics. These differences in backgrounds contributed to differences in modes of theorization. It is unfortunate that the two pairs of thinkers did not know each other's ideas. If they had, the theory of inner speech would probably have been pushed along much farther by now.

In addition, the two Americans had little influence on each other, and the two Russians also had little or no influence on each other. There are almost no citations of each other's work, and their bodies of ideas seem to have been independent creations. A factor here is that Peirce was somewhat unconventional in his moral lifestyle, particularly living with his second wife before they were married. Mead, who seems to have been morally quite conformist, may have been hesitant to recognize Peirce's scholarship for fear of guilt by association, although this is a guess. Also, several of Mead's ideas, especially meaning as triadic, resemble earlier ideas of Peirce, but Mead does not cite him.

In 1892, two years before Dewey went from Michigan to Chicago, taking Mead with him, Peirce was turned down for the Chicago post on grounds of unconventionality. This would probably have been gossiped about in the Chicago philosophy department by the time Mead got there, and he must have known about it. If Peirce, instead of Dewey, had gotten this job, Mead would probably not have gone to Chicago, and he might have had to stay at the University of Michigan. As it was, Peirce was full of novel and important ideas, but he did not develop them adequately in his published writings. A position at Chicago would probably have enriched his career considerably.

Another difference between Peirce and Mead was personal wealth. Peirce had a government surveyor's job for much of his life, and his salary gave him and his wife an adequate living. But his one academic job at Johns Hopkins lasted only five years, at which time he was fired for living with a woman he had not yet married. In his late years Peirce was penniless and at times lived on the street. In contrast, Mead always had a professor job, and he was married to a wealthy pineapple heiress from Hawaii. When Mead died in 1931, he had in excess of $500,000 (according to a probate court document), which would be worth over $7 million in 2015.

Given the differences between the two Russians as well as between the two Americans, the result is that these four theorists produced four independent lines of development. In a sense, I not only have to make a frame for combining the two dyads; each pair of thinkers, too, has to be placed into a sub-framework of some kind. Still, both dyads (i.e., all four thinkers) have broadly similar ideas of the self, including an emphasis on the social origins of the self. And both pairs think that inner speech is a central and vital function of human life.

Peirce and Mead

The notion that thought is inner speech, as mentioned earlier, was stated by Socrates and was often repeated by philosophers over the centuries. But no one paid much attention to it until Peirce explored semiotics in the mid-nineteenth century. Instead, Catholic philosophers from Augustine onward regarded thought as a sequence of pure abstractions, not words, and developed a theory of what they called "mental language." This theory finally declined with the onset of modern philosophy.

Today, the idea that thought is embodied by inner speech is robustly defended and developed by a small corps of thinkers (Carruthers 1996). But this approach is outnumbered by those who regard thought as an unconscious neurological flow, much like the flow of computer information. Some theorists may regard thought as largely linguistic, but this, so goes the computer analogy, is supposedly an illusion. We actually think in nonlinguistic media, according to this analogy, at the same time we seem to be thinking in linguistic media.

Peirce and Mead developed the notion that thought is linguistic before the computer was invented. Both Peirce and Mead also developed theories of the self, the self being the larger entity within which inner speech flows. One needs at least a minimal theory of the self to theorize inner speech because one has to specify which aspect of the self is talking to which other aspect. You have to show that the self has parts, that two (or more) of these parts talk to each other, and that these parts fit into a functioning totality.

Both Peirce and Mead regard inner speech as the internalization of outer speech. First we learn to talk to others, especially our close caretaker or caretakers. Gradually, we use language within an internalized replica of the outer conversation. We import the conversation with close family members into our internal psychological structure. I hold an opposed position, as mentioned in Chapter 2. I think inner speech begins with infantile imagery and pre-speech symbols, eventually combining around age seven with internalized language. But since that point is new and sketchy, it is held pretty much in abeyance in the present chapter.

Mead claims, as stated earlier, that the present self, which he calls "I," talks to the past self, which he calls "me." He is fascinated by the I-me distinction, and he bases several important ideas on this difference. He places the conscience, which he calls the "generalized other," in the me or closely attached to the me. And he places freedom, meaning the capacity of acting with novelty and indeterminacy, in the I.

Usually, Mead refers to the I as the knife-edge or instantaneous present. But he also sometimes uses another temporary criterion by placing the I into what is called the saddle-back or felt or specious present. The former I is in the physical present, but the latter I is in the psychological present. If the I can occupy two different temporal niches in its relations to the me, including the relation of the internal conversation, then these possibilities complicate the inner conversation enormously. The felt I is clearly poaching or trespassing on the territory of the me. Mead does not develop this idea, but it shows how complex his model of inner speech can become.

In contrast, Peirce's two communicating aspects of the self are what he calls the "I" and the "you." He does not say much about the I, but he defines the you as "that other self that is just coming into life in the flow of time" (1934, para. 421). Peirce's internal dyad, in contrast to Mead's I-me, is the I-you. Peirce's you is in the future-cum-present—that is, in the future as it travels down the time line toward the present. Peirce also uses the notion of "you" to allow for visitors to the internal conversation. If you are rehearsing an important business conversation, such as making a purchase or a sale, the person you are talking to is occupying the place of "you" in your mental conversation.

In general, Mead's me and Peirce's you offer distinctly different takes on how the inner conversation works. Each of their approaches has certain strengths as well as certain weaknesses. My position is that these two approaches can be integrated and that the inner conversation is the I, or present self, talking to the you, or future self, about the me, or past self. As mentioned earlier, I am not really hypostasizing or reifying the I, you, and me. I refer to these three positions as though they are substances, but I just do this for ease of utterance. It is easier to speak of these three as though they are entities than to constantly use precise linguistic formulations. So I am aware that these are merely aspects or facets of the self, even though I use the convenience of referring to them as though each were an entity unto itself.

When Peirce and Mead talk about inner speech, it is usually to show how it functions or performs in the life of the individual. They do not pay much attention to the more pedestrian uses of inner speech, such as daydreaming or sexual fantasizing. For both of them this process is the way thinking works. Since thinking is our steering device for traveling through the world, inner speech is the indispensible flashlight, so to speak, for getting from one dark place to another. Thought lights the way.

Since Mead uses me and Peirce uses you, they seem to be getting at different aspects of the thinking process. To oversimplify, one might say Peirce's model has us using the future to understand the past, and Mead's model has us using the past to understand the future. My I-you-me combination of the two thinkers is an attempt to place both of their insights into one theory of how thought works.

Peirce also emphasizes agency and habit-changing in his analysis of inner speech. He thinks that if we talk to our future self and thereby plan a new action of some kind, we will be better prepared to execute this action in the future. This hypothesis has recently been tested and proved, particularly with athletic performances (Hardy 2006, 206), but also with other kinds, such as artistic and musical performances. Peirce also thinks we can substitute good habits for bad ones via mental practice, and this looks like it may be at least a partial truth.

What is noticeably absent in Mead and Peirce are examples of inner speech. Peirce uses slang such as "I says to myself," but he does not say what one "says" to oneself. He does not fill in the blanks. Mead goes a touch further by saying that he "chides" or "plumes" himself in his inner speech, or that we "pat ourselves upon the back and in blind fury attack ourselves" (1964, 288), but again, no concrete examples are given. This omission seems strange since both thinkers had their own inner speech going all day long. They may have been intimidated from this information because of the criticism of introspection in psychology. Also the possible examples, especially if taken from their own thought processes, may have been too personal for them to use. Mead often rode his bicycle the mile or so from his residence to his university office, and he also sometimes took his dog. He must have had regular thoughts about the bike and the dog. But it would have been quite un-Mead-like to give examples of such ordinary practices.

The Russians, as I point out, use examples but not from their own thoughts. The first theorist to use his own inner speech for concrete examples, as far as I have noticed, has been Collins (2004b, 201). After his breakthrough, the use of personal examples became routine and acceptable.

For a long time in sociology Mead's I-me dialogue was the only recognized form of inner speech (Mead [1913] 1964, 1934). But this formulation was considered imprecise, opaque, and not readily available for empirical research. It did not help that Mead stayed quite abstract, giving no illustrations of the internal conversation. But when Colapietro wrote his pathbreaking book, *Peirce's Approach to the Self* (1989), piecing together important ideas that were buried in Peirce's unpublished papers, Peirce's version of inner speech theory became, for the first time, easily available. Colapietro's book also had the indirect but important effect of bringing Mead's dialogical self to life. With this new window into Peirce, it is possible to see that his version of inner speech theory differs from but can still be combined with that of Mead. The combination yields a synthesis that is far superior to the work of either thinker taken alone.

When Mead and Peirce are combined, the dialogical self is the I talking directly to the you and indirectly or reflexively to the me. Of course, this proposition entails two versions of reflexivity: the well-known backward one to the me and the novel forward one to the you. Still, the internal conversation is an I-you-me loop, a triadic reflexivity, encompassing a more comprehensive version of reflexivity than either of the two dyads can do by themselves.

Implications of the Peirce-Mead Approach

I now make several comments on the I-you-me triad to show its implications and to consolidate its relations to neighboring concepts. A central concept in this analysis is time. A leading theorist of human temporality is Michael Flaherty (2000, 2010), and I draw on his ideas. These comments may become rather abstract, but abstractness is the only medium that will allow one to take a close look at these reflexive qualities of the self.

Network Theory

People in traditional settings with dense networks and strong "me's" tend to solve problems by consulting the me and the generalized other. Using their stock of habits, they look to the past. People in looser, more creative networks tend to solve problems by talking to their you about novel options. They look to the future. In other words, the I-you-me triad is in good fit with network theory. Of course, the optimal stance is to look in both directions, past (me) and future (you) to seek solutions. But some people are sealed into traditional networks, and they neglect the future, the "you" and novel solutions.

Ecstasies

Mead talks of an I-me fusion as an elevated experience (1934, 273–277). How about the I-me-you fusion? Wouldn't that be even more ecstatic? The ecstasies themselves have been called "peak experiences" (Abraham Maslow), "oceanic" (Sigmund Freud), and mystical (St. John of the Cross). If ecstasies are experiences that allow us to transcend time, then they should include past (me), present (I), and future (you).

Structure and Agency

The I-me loop is into the past. It is a 180-degree, semicircular view, to use a visual metaphor. The I-you loop is into the future. It is also a 180-degree view. But when you combine the two, as people often do, both in their inner speech and in their thoughts, you have a 360-degree view—that is, you can see your entire range of temporality. You can envision both the past and the future, along with the present, simultaneously.

This omniscopic vision allows one to go back and forth from past to future, in a search of some kind, and also to see the two together. If you can simultaneously see your settled habit system (me) and your options for some new—that is, non-habitual action (you)—you can more easily integrate the two practical resources, structure and agency. The structure-agency issue can be viewed from several ontological levels, such as the person, the group, and the larger social organization. I agree with Archer (2003, 64) that inner speech is often the meeting ground of structure and agency (also referred to as the macro and the micro).

A diagram of the Peirce-Mead dialogical self is presented in Figure 10.1. The me, I, and you are on the same line, the time line. I list five attributes of the me, approximately as Mead does. Peirce places the critical self in the you, but Mead places this faculty in the generalized other or the me, so, for present purposes, I follow Mead. The generalized other is Mead's catch-all category, for it includes all sociocultural standards—that is, moral, cognitive-logical, and aesthetic (Athens 1994; Dodds, Lawrence, and Valsiner 1997). The generalized other also implies a personalized sense of society and culture, for an "other" is a person.

```
         _____
      /         |            \
     /  Generalized other     \
    |   Habits        |        |
    | Me  Memory      I    You |
    |   Interface with boy    |
     \  Self-concept          /
      _____|_____/
```

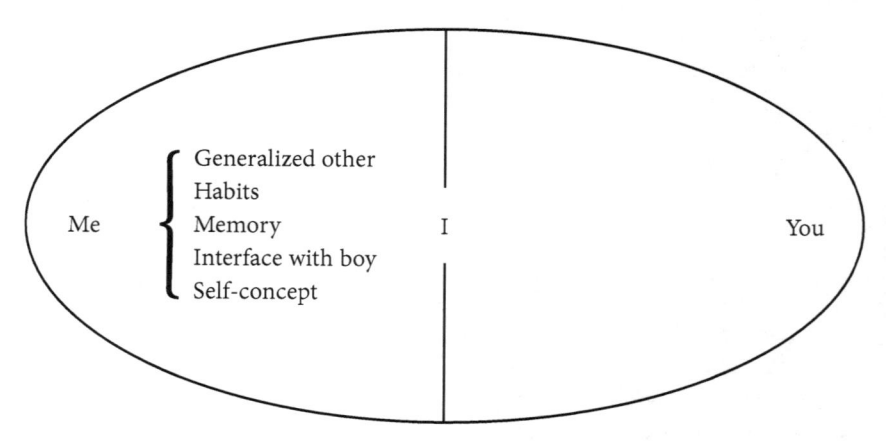

Figure 10.1 *The Peirce-Mead dialogical self*

The generalized other suggests an affinity with Durkheim's collective consciousness. The habits are habits in the ordinary sense. Pierre Bourdieu's "habitus" is a more inclusive term, encompassing both ordinary habits and elements of the generalized other. Mead does not mention memory as part of the me, but it is implied. Memory is simply all of our experiences, and it trails off into the unconscious, of both the Freudian and the cognitive studies varieties. The self does not include the body as such, but it does include a sense of, or interface with, the body. The traits of the body, including emotion, interpenetrate the self. Mead does not have a self-concept under that name, but, again, it is implied, and it seems to belong in the me. The self-concept includes everything we think about ourselves—that is, our self-esteem and our acknowledged traits. It is closely related, causally, to Cooley's looking-glass self. The notion of self-feeling, which James and Cooley think is the defining feature of the self, can also be understood as part of the self-concept. Mead prefers the concept of reflexivity to self-feeling, and he is cool toward this latter term, perhaps because he seems to have been threatened by and was in competition with Cooley (Mead 1930). So I leave it out, although it could be a process leading into the self-concept.

This illustration of the self is not meant to be a definitive portrait. Others might view the Mead or the Mead-Peirce self differently. Still, this picture seems reasonably usable to me at present, and I hope it provokes others to think further on this issue.

Human Temporality

Another advantage of combining Peirce and Mead in this triadic way is that it gives a sharper picture of how humans engage with temporality. We are three-legged stools, standing simultaneously in the past, present, and future. From the point of view of natural science, we are in the present empirically and in the past and future only imaginatively. But physical science has a limited view of how humans inhabit time.

For the human, time is primarily felt rather than measured by the clock. In this sense—that of psychology rather than physics—we can be in the past and present existentially as well as imaginatively. The exact way in which we experience the three tenses depends on how we are, at any given moment, oriented toward the three temporal facets.

At one extreme we can include all of the future and all of the past into an all-encompassing present (Mead [1932] 1964, 23–24). But more often we have a present consisting of some meaningful or workable chunk of time—that is, James's saddle-back present (broader than his knife-edge present)—with futures and pasts that have the sizes we want them to have. The precise way in which we package the three facets of time depends on our purposes and in particular our projected and anticipated actions. The size of the felt present is in constant fluctuation.

In addition, we are always in motion through time. The future of one instant is the present of the next—and the past of the one after that. The self, moving down the time line, is in a constant process of emergence. Our bodies grow old but our selves are ever new. We are always moving through James's stream of consciousness, although we are sometimes in a much larger swatch of that stream than he seems to have thought.

Comprehensive Dialogicality

Another advantage of connecting Peirce with Mead is that we can now see both speaking poles of the conversation and how the dialogical self works. For Mead it is difficult to see the I-me dialogue. He gives no examples, particularly of the me talking to the I. His me is in the past and he confines the possibility of action to the present, so in terms of his own theory, only the I can talk. But the possibility of the me responding is always implicit in Mead's notion of the specious present. If the felt present were enlarged enough to include the me, the me could speak. In physical time the me is in the past, but in psychological time the me could be in the (now enlarged) present. The me could say, "No, we've tried that." "We need something new." Or even, "That's sleazy, don't even think about it." Indeed, the me, in its capacity as the generalized other, is constantly disagreeing with the I.

It is Peirce's inclusion of the you in the conversation that makes it obvious that the I is not the only speaker, for the you talks, and it does so in two senses. As just mentioned concerning the me, the you can be in the felt present in such a way as it can stand on the speaker's platform and engage in speech. In addition, even in physical time, it is approaching the present, the status of I, and will soon be able to talk in that capacity. It is Peirce's addition of tuism that discloses the truly two-sided, dialogical character of inner speech. In fact, if all three facets of the self are together in the specious present, there is no reason why all three cannot take turns speaking, and for the dialogue to be between the me and you, as well as between the me and I (or the you and I).

This triadicity also makes the pragmatists more open to the Russians, Vygotsky and Bakhtin, who are much closer to the actual data of inner speech. The combining of Mead and Peirce facilitates the merger of them both with the somewhat different dyads of Vygotsky and Bakhtin. Mead and Peirce tend to be formal and proper, emphasizing the thinking and self-regulating functions of inner speech. Vygotsky is much more detailed in treating the semantics and syntax of inner speech. And Bakhtin, particularly in his discussions of Dostoyevsky's tortured characterization of Raskolnikov, shows the closeness of inner speech to the life-defining existential emotions.

If thought is largely in the form of talk, the I-you-me triad shows how the thought medium works. The triadic reflexivity can find and disclose more subtle connections within the self than a dyadic reflexivity can. The you gives you access to the future, to problems that are coming down the road, and to opportunities for actions. The me gives you your memory, the insights and practices of the culture, the habits and trajectories of the past, and the results of previous actions. The you-me arc is the pincer, which allows the I to grasp anything in one's world. This linguistic device is your mind, surveilling the world, to cope with your problems and desires. Thoughts are abstractions designated by words, inner as well as outer. The key words are—in my opinion—I, me, and you, for they designate the structure of the self, which is a linguistic thinking machine. The combination of Mead and Peirce seems to shed new light on how thought and the mind works.

Enlarged Structural Picture of the Self

Another result of the Peirce-Mead combination is that it gives a richer view of the structure of the self. Mead, as well as many others, define the self as self-awareness or reflexivity. This is an intuitively attractive definition, for it is self-awareness that seems to differentiate the self from all other entities. Everything that the self does goes on in the arena of self-awareness. But Mead's self-awareness is attributed to the I-me relationship, which ties it to the limitations of that dyad. If Peirce's I-you is added to the definition of the self, we have a much bigger and more complex structure of which we are aware. The definition of the self is enlarged to include more features of the self. Just as reflexivity goes from a 180- to a 360-degree scope, self-awareness goes from 180 to 360 degrees. Awareness of the me is one thing, but awareness of the me and the you, including the relation between those two spheres, is considerably more. The Mead-Peirce combination gives us a more comprehensive definition of the self.

Peirce's Tuism and Subjectivity

The relation between Mead's I and me is between subject and object. But the relation between Peirce's I and you is between two subjects. The I is the subject now, and the you will be the subject when it travels down the time line and reaches the present. Still, even when the you is in the future, it is a subject in the grammatical sense (i.e., "you" is in the nominative case). When we think of the you as in the specious or felt present, the you is also a subject in a nongrammatical—that is, ontological—sense.

Being two subjects, the I and you, we can enjoy the intimacy only available to two subjects. Peirce's tuism has two aspects: one's relationship to one's you and one's relationship to any other person—what Goethe (1974, 205) calls a "guest" to his inner speech but I call a "visitor"—construed as a you. Both tuisms have the immediacy of two subjects. According to Alfred Schütz (1962, 172–175), the self, being a subject, can have a closer relationship to another person than it can have to itself. He valorizes the relationship between two "I's." But this is only true if you define the self as an I-me relationship, which Schütz does, following Mead. If instead you think in terms of Peirce's I-you relationship, you have the same interpersonal intimacy within the I-you dyad of the self. When Husserl gives an example of inner speech and says, "You must stop this" ([1913] 1982, 279–280) or when Jerry Fodor says to himself, "You can do it, Jerry" (Gopnik 2009, 157), they are talking as I to you or subject to subject, with all the intimacy that that relationship can carry.

Emotionally Enhanced Self-Awareness

The I-me-you triad, as a definition of self-awareness, has two features that make it more powerful than the usual I-me definition of the self. For one, the self is self-aware of more features of itself, thereby making it a richer reflexive bundle. But in addition, the self is also closer and more enmeshed, so to speak, with itself. I-me is formal and somewhat distant, but I-you is emotionally close and allows more intimate emotions in the intra-psychological sphere. Peirce's formula allows more easily of self-acceptance and even self-love, which is always an aspect of the self. In other words, Peirce's you is the self in a more intimate way than Mead's me is the self. Therefore, the I-me-you circle allows of more internal closeness than is allowed in the I-me formula.

Grammatical Personhood

Another nuance of the I-you relationship is that, unlike the me, the you is in the second person. The you has considerably more otherness than the me, which, like the I, is in the first person. So one internal dyad, Mead's I-me, is confined to the grammatical first person. But the other internal dyad, Peirce's I-you, has a less confined grammatical niche. This grammatical location reflects the greater ontological sweep of the I-you relationship. The temporal zone between the I and me is inside the self, but the temporal zone between the I and you is, so to speak, outside the self. The past is in the self but the future is not. This is another sense in which the I-me-you self has more reality or being than Mead's I-me self has.

Decision Making in Felt Time

Another advantage of the Peirce-Mead fusion is that it helps explain how we can make decisions well before the chronological moment of choice. Take New Year's resolutions. You decide to lose some flab. You can wait for the battle at the moment of choosing—that is, when you are having dinner or possibly drinks afterward. But this is dangerous because your opposition, the chubby or wine-loving you, will have the advantage. He or she will tempt you with the anticipated tastes. And all the precedents, habits, and sensory memories will be lined up against you.

What you need is a head start. If you draw on the I-you-me scheme and define yourself as existing in a band or "swatch" of time, you can start the fight ahead of time. You can refuse the tempter in advance by saying no well before the moment of decision. In addition, you can think of yourself as having already passed the test. You can locate your temporal presence at some point beyond the gustatory battle and define yourself as already victorious, picturing yourself as attractively thin. The waitress cited in the Introduction does this in her reflection on her job. In effect, you can expand the felt present to include a successful engagement with your bad habits, thereby initiating a proud start to the New Year. In other words, the I-you-me conception of the self gives you a kind of time-traveling capacity such that you can self-regulate in psychological time even before your encounters in physical time. Peirce thought he had discovered this process, and he was quite proud of his discovery, but he did not know how to use Mead's insight into the I-me self.

Time as Pincer-like Movement

The I-you-me tripod of the self also tells us something about how the self is not only *in* time but also *is* time. The self has the power to grasp different size hunks of time, in a sort of pincer-like movement, by which I mean it can *be* different segments of time. Take the "life review" of elderly people, now often a written memoir. The examination of one's life, with an eye toward finding or giving it meaning, is with us our whole lives. We are constantly looking at different periods and stretches of our lives to make sense of them. This process is usually especially pronounced toward the end of life (Butler 1963). A common aspect of life review is to make peace with siblings and other relatives. You can call this a functional process, in the senses of Talcott Parsons and Robert Merton. Or you can view it as a symbolic interactionist and say it is part of the quest for meaning. Or you can look at it both ways at once.

All the unsolved problems of life are there for your review. When you are thinking about periods in your life, you are a bigger hunk of time. Ordinarily, the reflexive, I-you-me self is spread over at least a short period of time, such as a week or two. In this sense we *are* time because we are a week or two. But in longer life stretches we can become several decades. When I say we *are* time, it means we are stretches of felt or psychological time. The magnitude in which we are time can vary from a very short period to our whole lives. The lens through which we view the self-as-time is the I-you-me triad. That tripod can come in different sizes, each of which gives our durational quality a different temporal magnitude.

How the Self Is a Sign

For Peirce the I-you-me triad gives an interpretation of his somewhat cryptic idea that *the self is a sign*. I have already pointed out that this definition omits the body. Given that most racisms and inegalitarian theories are based on alleged differences in the body, this definition can be used to explain Thomas Jefferson's and Abraham Lincoln's idea that all human beings are equal.

But another implication of the triadic self is that the *structure* of the self is that of a sign. This is implied in Peirce, although he does not come right out and say it clearly. Peirce's sign has three parts: sign, referent, and interpretant. One must remember that Peirce uses the word "sign" both for the triad and also for the first of the three elements in the triad. This dual meaning is somewhat confusing, but Peirce is dead, and there is not much we can do to simplify this awkward terminology. Ordinarily the sign, in this specialized context, means the carrier of meaning (the sound of a word or its written designation), the referent is what the sign refers to, and the interpretant is the meaning of the sign. In the case of the triadic self, the "I" is the sign, the "me" is the referent, and the "you" is the interpretant. This interpretation clarifies the term "semiotic self" by showing exactly how the self is a sign. The self is a (macro) sign that contains and manipulates (micro) signs.

Both Peirce and Mead probably sensed that they wanted to poise the human dialogue as extending in both temporal directions, past and future. Mead's "me" includes aspects of Peirce's "you," and Peirce's "you" includes features of Mead's "me." But neither is sufficiently explicit about this. You have to bend their concepts to bring this about. In the following quotation, Mead shows he was trying to work in all three time periods—past, present, and future—at once.

> Now it is by these ideational processes that we get hold of the conditions of future conduct as these are found in the organized responses which we have formed, and so construct our paths in anticipation of that future. The individual who can thus get hold of them can further organize them through the selection of the stimulations which call them out and can thus build up his plan of action. (Mead 1932, 192, cited in Joas 1985, 192)

But Mead is stretching words to make his point. It is easier to say, with a Peirce-Mead synthesis, that the person is simultaneously working with the present, past, and future in an I-me-you triadic vision.

Exemplification

Finally, the I-me-you relationship can be mapped onto concrete examples of inner speech. The idea that we speak directly to the "you" and indirectly to the "me" is a reasonable description of how we think and engage in self-talk. When Husserl says, "You have gone wrong, you can't go on like that," he seems to be addressing both directions in the same sentence (Husserl [1913] 1982, 280). The me went wrong and the you has got to change. One can interpret Husserl's remark as suggesting his uncertainty about his research program after his *Philosophy of Arithmetic* got a distinctly negative and painful review from Gottlob Frege (1972). When Fodor, faced with a challenge, said, "You can do it, Jerry," he was saying, "You've done it in the past, and you can do it again" (Gopnik 2009, 157). What we say to ourselves is usually an attempt to interpret the past to the future, which is to use the I-you-me circle.

These thirteen points show the temporal insights of expanding the inner speech model into an I-you-me triad. They indicate how much more flexible and powerful the triadic approach is than either Mead's or Peirce's dyadic approaches. In particular, they describe a process that is much closer to the actual way we think and engage in inner speech. These points also show the advantages of an innovative approach to pragmatism, as over against a literalist approach. Both Mead's and Peirce's theories become alive and grow when they are combined into a single matrix.

To sum up this first theme of the chapter, Mead and Peirce rediscovered the ancient and launched the modern, philosophical study of inner speech. This was a profound advance, and it became, with the additional ideas of James and Dewey, one of the central notions of classical pragmatism. Mead and Peirce remain, however, rather formal and generic in their analysis. They visualize inner speech as characterized by purposefulness and propriety, but they do not make much creative use of it.

When they talk about the content or topics of inner speech, they tend to favor such useful functions as self-regulation and problem solving. The self-regulation is typified by Peirce's idea that we can substitute good habits for bad and the problem solving by Mead's examples of everyday physical difficulties. They pay little attention to the random passivity of much inner speech or to self-aggrandizing daydreams or to the uncontrolled imagery we have before falling asleep or for that matter to the widespread if secretive sexual fantasies. They did, however, create the foundations and guidelines for the study of this topic. But the Russians pushed these insights, without officially knowing about them, in completely new directions.

Vygotsky and Bakhtin

In the absence of examples, neither Peirce nor Mead found what Vygotsky would later find: that the linguistics of inner speech, both in semantics and syntax, is distinctly different from that of outer speech. Vygotsky, too, does not explicitly use examples or quotations. Instead, he draws loosely and generically on the "private" speech of children. This is the "thinking out loud" that children do around ages two to seven. This vocalization is abbreviated and is in the child's own linguistic style, both syntactic and semantic. But it is clear that Vygotsky is also observing his own thought processes and analyzing examples of his own inner speech when he shows the unique qualities of this internal linguistics.

Using his own inner speech and not just the private speech of children for his examples is the only way Vygotsky (1987b, 281) could have arrived at some of his insights. I say this because some of his comments are too subjective to have been discovered by listening to children talk aloud. For example, his saying that we initially get the meaning of our inner speech utterance all at once, and then a bit later string it out into sentential form, could not have been obtained from listening to children. Or his comment that we sometimes just touch on the initial sounds in an inner speech statement and do not even pronounce whole words in their entirety is also something one could find only by self-observation.

Bakhtin also gives no examples from his own mental processes, but he uses examples from novels, particularly those of Dostoyevsky. Bakhtin, then, is the first to use explicit instances of inner speech. Vygotsky uses inner speech texts, but without quotation and only as background materials. Bakhtin is more explicit and actually states his examples. These examples allow us to use Bakhtin to build on Vygotsky.

Vygotsky and Bakhtin both started writing after the Bolshevik revolution. Artistic freedom ebbed and flowed during the decades of the revolution. Marxism has no clear implications for art and aesthetics, in other words, there is no Marxist aesthetic, so the party line had no anchor. During the Stalinist period the party position sometimes changed rapidly, making it difficult to write the same book from beginning to end. Bakhtin had trouble staying in the good graces of the party, and he spent several of his early years in political disgrace—internal exile in Kazakhstan (1919–1936). Vygotsky's writings were actually condemned by the party in 1936 after he had been dead for two years, and scholars subsequently avoided his ideas. Nevertheless, he gradually became influential in the rest of the scholarly world.

One problem that political censorship created for Bakhtin scholarship is the authorship of three disputed manuscripts. Two of these reflect Freudianism: *A Marxist Critique* (1927) and *Marxism and the Philosophy of Language* (1929). Both of these are usually attributed to V. N. Voloshinov, although some scholars think they were written by Bakhtin. The third is *The Formal Method in Literary Scholarship* (1938), which is attributed to the joint authorship of Bakhtin and P. N. Medvedev, although some scholars think Bakhtin was the sole author. A further problem is that without knowing the authorship of these books, we do not fully know what Bakhtin's ideas were. These are preliminary concerns, and I now turn to the actual theories of Vygotsky and Bakhtin.

As noted earlier, it is not clear whether these two authors, Vygotsky and Bakhtin, were influenced by each other. They were both writing in the 1920s, and they could have read things by each other, but they do not cite each other or obviously use each other's ideas. Vygotsky died in 1934 of tuberculosis, at thirty-eight years of age, and Bakhtin died in 1975 at eighty years of age. This means Vygotsky did not get to write as much as we might have expected of him, and he was no longer alive when Bakhtin wrote his later works. So their dates affected their relation to each other.

In addition, Vygotsky had a somewhat specialized interest in child development. Although this topic does introduce all the philosophical questions of human nature, it does not broach the larger issues of history and society. In other words, it is micro rather than macro. In contrast, Bakhtin was interested in broader social questions. This includes those encountered in the novel, especially those by Dostoyevsky.

If we pay special attention to inner speech, both Russians are dissimilar to Peirce and Mead. In addition, they are dissimilar to each other. They differ from the pragmatists in not being so confined to generic formality or to moral propriety. They take inner speech as it is, without looking solely for functionality or for social refinement. In addition, the Russians are less concerned with constructing a formal theory of the self, or with the related question of which aspect of the self is talking to which other aspect. They leave this latter question implicit and unaddressed.

As I said, Vygotsky uses private speech for his empirical base—that is, the language in which children speak aloud to themselves, from about ages two to seven. This is not actually inner speech, although it does have many similarities with it. This language is highly abbreviated and salted with the child's slang vocabulary. It may be functional—aimed at achieving goals—but it also has a random, chitchat quality at times. In other words, it is less formal than the pragmatist's model.

Private speech is also uncensored and earthy at times, expressing the child's unrefined consciousness. This source of data, which Vygotsky may have chosen as a genuflection to behaviorism, ensured that he would use data that were fairly close to inner speech itself. As Vygotsky puts it, "The study of egocentric speech [talking out loud] is the method of choice for the study of inner speech" (1987b, 258). Many of his ideas are actually anti-behavioristic, but he seems to want to keep up the pretense, possibly to seem to be following the party line, of following broadly behavioristic assumption. As I said, Vygotsky seems to have smuggled in texts from his own inner speech at times, but this cannot be proved. In any case, he uses data that make him depart from the pragmatists' formality and propriety.

Bakhtin, too, uses relatively natural sources for his examples. He does not (at least not openly) use examples from his own inner life. Instead, he uses characters from several novels, especially those of Dostoyevsky. His favorite example is Raskolnikov, the nihilist killer of an elderly woman pawnbroker in *Crime and Punishment*. Raskolnikov is raw in the intensity of his emotion, the psychopathology of his inner speech, and the blurred line between his inner and outer speech. In contrast to the pragmatist model, Raskolnikov's inner speech is informal, dysfunctional, and amoral.

The contrast between the Russians and the pragmatists that I want to emphasize is in the way they independently come closer to real inner speech. Vygotsky and Bakhtin each move in a direction different from the pragmatists, but they do so by going down somewhat different paths from each other. Vygotsky regarded his discovery as one concerned primarily with the syntax of inner speech—that is, the way it is organized grammatically and linguistically. Internal sentences, or rather utterances, are put together differently from those of ordinary person-to-person language. Some of Vygotsky's discoveries concern issues of semantics, but these, at least in his opinion, derive from syntactical peculiarities. He is showing that inner speech is a language of its own, and a private one at that.

Bakhtin, in contrast, innovated in how he presented the meanings of inner speech. Vygotsky had been interested in certain universal peculiarities of inner speech. He derived these from the study of child development and from children's tendency to talk out loud. He showed that inner speech has quite different qualities from outer speech. Bakhtin confined his studies to adult inner speech, and he found qualities of a completely different, though complementary, nature than those of Vygotsky. These were not universal but embedded in his examples, taken mainly from modern novels.

Now let me elaborate on Vygotsky's and Bakhtin's contributions. Vygotsky's main syntactical idea concerning inner speech is his notion of predicativity. He thinks inner speech tends to be confined to the predicate and to abbreviate or eliminate the subject. The usual meaning of predicativity is to speak telegraphically, as in "coming home soon," "ran into trouble," and so on. The subject, being the subject of the telegram, is already known, so the word "I" can be eliminated. This is efficient, and it saves money by producing a shorter telegram. Some people also write ordinary letters, as well as e-mails and text messages, in this way.

But Vygosky uses "predicate" in another sense. He refers to this as psychological as opposed to the more common grammatical notion of the term. Here the predicate, which can be any grammatical element, is the new thing in a sentence. If someone asks me, "When are you going?" and I say, "Nine," this is an abbreviated way of saying, "I am going at nine o'clock." If someone says, "Can I have a drink of water?" and I say, "Yes," this is shortened way of saying "Yes, you can have a glass of water." In contrast, the psychological subject is the part of the sentence that is already known. In my previous two examples, the shortened responses eliminate the unnecessary or known part of the sentence.

Given this notion of predication, Vygotsky points out that inner speech tends toward psychological predication. Interpersonal dialogue also has this quality, but inner speech has it more so, because the speaker already knows the context of the answer. All the speaker wants is the new element.

A second feature of Vygotsky's inner speech, using a distinction Frege had made, is the predominance of sense over meaning (Frege 1972). Meaning is the core semantic feature of a word, and sense is its whole range of peripheral meanings, facets, and situational understandings. In our inner speech it is economical to use the same word in as many ways as possible. This means we twist it, shrink it, and stretch it to make it work for us. In contrast, when talking to someone else we tend to use a word in its stable, core meaning. We also vary our words to achieve style. But in talking to ourselves we forget style and maximize utility. Using a word in its many senses is smart. We can get by with fewer words, and the ones we use have a more plastic and variable semanticity than when used in outer speech. This inner vocabulary is more like a carpenter's kit with a moderate number of well-used tools than a dictionary with a huge number of rarely used verbal instruments.

A third feature that Vygotsky sees in inner speech is condensation, an infusing of many meanings into a word. Words are already jammed with meanings if we are using their sense in contrast to their meaning. But they can be even more condensed if we place new, possibly idiosyncratic meanings into them. Vygotsky thinks book titles often give a condensed indication of the entire book, Nikolai Gogol's *Dead Souls* (1842) being his favorite example (1987b, 278). Our own personal vocabulary also can contain words that take on meanings idiosyncratic to our biographies. These can be ritual words, personal slang, terms that suggest elaborate memories, or words that stand for complicated narratives. Because of this condensation Vygotsky suggests that our inner speech may be inexplicable to others, even if they have full access to it. It would be too connected to the details of our minds and lives. He suggests that this makes inner speech a private language (1987b, 204).

Finally, Vygotsky suggests that these inner words may become quite egocentric in the sense of having our selves stitched into their meanings. These terms have been used for us and by us for a long time. This makes us (i.e., our selves) seep into the words. These words, then, all say something about us—that is, we are in some way the subject of the entire inner vocabulary, and these words also have inflections and tones that are peculiar to us.

Vygotsky discusses several other attributes of inner speech, but they are all interrelated, and the ones already mentioned are representative of his approach. Actually, most of these qualities seem as much semantic as syntactical, but since he regards predication as the key to all the other qualities, I suggest that, as he thinks, his analysis is primarily syntactical.

Vygotsky does not say much about the purposes or functions of inner speech. His examples are from the "private speech" of little children, so the topics would have been confined to their concerns with problem solving and self-regulation. These children also seem to be practicing their linguistic skills. If Vygotsky was also paying attention to his own inner speech, as I think he was, he is simply silent about whatever issues or problems he was thinking about. In contrast, Bakhtin has all the problems in Dostoevsky's novels to rummage through. In particular, I show which of Raskolnikov's issues he singles out.

Bakhtin's Contribution

I present Bakhtin's approach by touching on several of his key ideas: voice, dialogue (including addressivity and responsivity), and the personalizing of the nonpersonal. I discuss some of Bakhtin's concepts in Chapter 1, so I do not repeat them here. Bakhtin is quite insightful in describing the structure or "working parts" of a dialogue. But he does not always distinguish interpersonal from internal or intrapersonal dialogue, and he seems clearest when working with the interpersonal. His insights into inner speech are largely drawn from Raskolnikov. This Dostoevsky character is emotionally disturbed and, although not quite psychotic, rather close. He is haunted by guilt from murdering the elderly female pawnbroker and her sister. He had committed the first murder to test the "nihilistic" idea that morality is a tool of the landed elite. He wants to see if he can transcend guilt.

Dostoevsky himself, at the time of writing *Crime and Punishment*, had abandoned his revolutionary ideas and was a political conservative. So his portrait of Raskolnikov is, seemingly, an attempt to make the nihilistic revolutionaries look bad. I think it is a good idea to try to ignore politics—that of Raskolnikov, of Dostoevsky, and of Bakhtin and that of the Bolsheviks—when analyzing Bakhtin's views on inner speech. Otherwise, the causal mixture is just too complicated.

One point Bakhtin makes is that an internal utterance has not only the voice of the speaker but also draws on the anticipated voice of the listener as well as the voices that influenced the formation of the utterance in the first place. In addition, the voice of the speaker might be multi-vocal—that is, composed of two or more, often conflicting, voices. These voices might be from those who influenced the speaker, such as close family members. They might also be those of distinct facets or "sub-selves" of the speaker. The speaker might not be conscious of this multi-vocality, but Bakhtin finds it in his literary examples. These voices, with their distinct inflections and messages, are melded into the voice of the person engaging in inner speech. In other words, Bakhtin decomposes what appears to be one voice into several.

This approach seems especially apt for capturing social conflict. In the period before the Bolshevik revolution, which is the period of *Crime and Punishment*, there was plenty of conflict in Russia. Not only was there class conflict, both in factories and between landowners and peasants; the intellectual class—of which Lenin, Trotsky, and Stalin were members—was also often in conflict with the landowners. In addition, there was ethnic and religious conflict as well as conflict between Russia and its neighboring countries.

It is common in social science to look for attitude conflict as a component of social conflict. If two ethnic groups, for example, are at odds with each other, this will usually be manifested in their social attitudes. Also conflicting behaviors, such as engaging in physical harm, are a frequent indicator of conflict. But linguistic conflict is not usually looked for as an aspect of social conflict. Hostile semantics, such as name-calling, may be present, but not the kind of subtle and pervasive linguistic conflict that Bakhtin speaks about. In other words, Bakhtin has discovered a powerful symptom of social conflict, showing how linguistic practice, what Saussure calls parole and Chomsky calls performance, is a manifestation of conflict.

Bahktin here reminds me of Weber's genius, because Weber, too, is good at spotting subtle conflicts in lifestyles, modes of language being one aspect of lifestyle. More generally, Bakhtin, like Weber, lived in an intellectual atmosphere where Marxist theory was quite powerful. But both Bakhtin and Weber kept their distance from, and added powerful insights to, a Marxist social context.

In addition, the dialogical process itself influences the meaning or semantics of inner speech. For Bakhtin dialogue, which he contrasts with the more rigid and inflexible monologue, has the qualities of openness and welcoming. His concept of dialogue also applies to outer language and person-to-person interaction. But it applies just as much to internal conversation and inner speech.

In dialogue the speaker extends "addressivity" to the listener. This addressivity greets or names the listener, but it also welcomes and embraces this person. The listener or "other," in turn, responds with what Bakhtin calls "responsivity." This is the obverse of addressivity. Taken together, addressivity and responsivity create a kind of existential circuit. Dialogue entails a certain amount of emotion and an attempt to create a meeting of minds.

Bakhtin's notion of addressivity is close to Mead's taking the role of the other, and when this attitude is mutual, the relationship is one of reflexivity. Since Mead defines the self as reflexivity or being self-aware, Bakhtin's dialogue seems to be about the same as Mead's definition of the self (Perinbanayagam 1991a, 6).

Another feature of Bakhtin's addressivity is its contrast with the French theorist Louis Althusser. Althusser (1971) had the idea that addressing, which he also calls "hailing," not only initiates communication with another. It also creates the other. Here Althusser suggests Sartre's refrigerator-light theory of the self, mentioned in Chapter 3. Hailing not only calls the other into an interactional relationship. It also calls it from nonexistence into existence. For Althusser the idea that there is a self justifies capitalism's ideas of property and contract. But these arguments carry the point too far from inner speech, so I stop by just pointing out how Bakhtin's addressivity differs from Althusser's hailing.

There are three different positions on addressivity and how it treats the self being addressed. For Mead addressing another evokes his social self, interrupts his internal conversation, and gets him into the role-taking "set," which orients him to conversation. It moves him from intra-subjectivity to intersubjectivity. Bakhtin's addressivity does everything that Mead's does, but it goes a step further. It alerts and vivifies the self, causing it to gather up and ready its energies. It also gives the self the form of receptivity that corresponds to the particular kind of address being used. If the address is respectful, the evoked self is confident and poised. If the address is commanding and threatening, the self is on guard and prepared for trouble. If the addressivity is patronizing and superior, the self may immediately anticipate and insulate itself from insult. For Bakhtin there are many modes of addressivity and therefore many ways in which the self might respond to this address.

Althusser's addressivity goes well beyond both that of Mead and that of Bakhtin. His mirror self or "I" is, in his view, an error or delusion, and it tends to weaken if it is not continuously fed with self-evidence. Repeated looks into a mirror do this feeding. But more commonly, the recognition that others give to it in the addressing process brings it back to life. The hailing process is like the mirror process, for it strengthens our identification with the mirror image.

To summarize this point, Mead's addressivity evokes the social self, switching us from internal dialogue to interactional dialogue. Bakhtin's addressivity gives a particular, interactional form to the self and configures the relationship. Althusser's addressivity goes still further by evoking the (allegedly) disappearing "I" into existence. Just as sleep makes us dream and have a dream self, being addressed or hailed "centers" us and restores the "I" that organizes us as unified persons.

Bakhtin also suggests, but does not develop, the idea that we can communicate with and even have inner speech with nonpersonal objects, perhaps especially the built environment. I develop this idea in Chapter 9. Physical objects send semiotic messages to the people around them. If these messages are self-confirming or flattering, one might not even notice them. If they are self-denigrating, one might be made quite uncomfortable by them.

Another interesting idea of Bakhtin's is the "superaddressee." He thinks that utterances, both interpersonal and intrapersonal, are addressed to the second person, which resembles Peirce's tuism. But he also thinks utterances are simultaneously aimed at a generic third person, what might be called a "they." This idea resembles Mead's notion that we often speak to the community, understood as a "generalized other." Bakhtin thinks the superaddressee would understand one in "just the right way" (Morson and Emerson 1989, 135–136). Bakhtin's notion of the addressee invites more research, but it is a striking convergence with Mead.

A final point about Bakhtin is his analysis of Raskolnikov. Raskolnikov's problem is that he has been harboring two conflicting moralities, although Bakhtin would refer to these as voices. The morality Raskolnikov is aware of is the nihilistic platform he encountered among radical students in college. This position is that established morality is a conspiracy of the landed elite, or what Marx would call the ruling class. Traditional morality, including the prohibition against murder, protects property. If the peasants were to seize property, they might have to kill the owners. The rule against murder protects the wealth of the landed elite. Of course, all revolutionaries face the moral problem of attacking and possibly harming or killing the elite. Historically, this is not an unusual dilemma. This killing is usually justified as "politics" or "war," and sometimes even as self-defense. The nihilistic position was that once people began to break these laws on a widespread and principled basis, the psychological and moral weight of these prohibitions would gradually disappear.

The opposite morality or voice is the traditional one that forbids murder. Raskolnikov thinks he has abandoned this morality, but as the novel proceeds, it becomes obvious that he still, down deep, believes murder is wrong. So the novel is about the clash of the two voices, the two moralities, the two Raskolnikovs. And the dialogue is between these two moral voices. This is true of Raskolnikov's interpersonal dialogue, but it is also true of his internal or intra-psychic dialogue.

One revealing peculiarity of Raskolnikov's problem is that he is socially isolated. He is not an active member of a political party or a revolutionary cell. The nihilist intellectuals were not socially organized into political groupings, and this made it harder for them to maintain and act on their political attitudes. Raskolnikov needs allies to give him social support and help him alleviate his anxieties. Being a lone wolf and taking on the psychological pressures of a political murder subject him to more anxiety than he can handle. The novel is largely about how he slowly collapses and then gradually redeems himself from his guilt, largely with the help of a sympathetic woman.

These pressures affect Raskolnikov's dialogical style and inner speech. When he is talking to others, he sometimes seems to be talking to himself. In particular, he reveals details about his crime, seemingly not realizing that the other person is listening. Presumably, it is Raskolnikov's agitation that lets him think he is talking to himself when he is talking to others. It is also possible that Raskolnikov thinks others, perhaps everyone, knows about his crime. Intense guilt can produce a paranoid delusion of this kind—thinking others know your secret, that your mind is transparent, that your psychological privacy has let you down.

Comparing the Americans and the Russians

I have now discussed the contributions of the two Americans, Mead and Peirce, and the two Russians, Vygotsky and Bakhtin. I have also made some comments concerning the differences between the two pairs. Now I make that comparison more systematic.

The Americans give a somewhat distant analysis of inner speech. They emphasize the overall communication structure and the aspects of the self that are involved in the communication. I have synthesized their structural views into the I-you-me model, which shows how the two views can be put together. The two Americans give no examples of inner speech; nor do they show in any detail how this process works.

When they speak about the content or meanings of inner speech, they both emphasize functional and socially approved meanings. Mead says inner speech is thought and, in particular, problem solving. He ignores more serious (e.g., sociocultural) problems or interpersonal conflict. Mead also alludes, quite laconically, to how we "pat ourselves upon the back and in blind fury attack ourselves" (1964, 288). Peirce emphasizes self-regulation, especially attaining good habits. Neither talk about trivial or morally awkward uses of inner speech—for example, ordinary daydreaming or sexual fantasies or thoughts about how to harm someone.

Mead emphasizes how a blocked or frustrated action, such as an attempt to cross a river, might be resolved. This unattained goal causes us to think about how to solve the problem, and this thinking is in the form of inner speech. There is a prettified aspect to Mead's thoughts here. Some researchers have found that most inner speech is reflexive and about the self, not about external problems (Morin and Uttl 2013, 1). Moreover, we grapple with ourselves; we use all of Freud's defenses and we are constantly protecting the self from disintegration and harm. Mead tends to "normalize" inner speech, meaning he softens the edges and makes it look highly respectable.

Peirce, in contrast, emphasizes the self-regulation or self-steering process in inner speech. In other words, his blockage is not "out there" but "in here." In particular, he discusses how we can eliminate a bad habit and replace it with a good one by modeling this action in our inner speech. He was also struck by how his younger brother anticipated saving a woman whose dress was on fire. In both the habit change and the preparation for a fire emergency, Peirce thinks of how we can model our future actions by rehearsing them in our inner theater.

But Peirce is prettified here, too, because he was dismally unsuccessful in changing his bad, personal habits. If he had been more honest and attempted to figure out other ways of harnessing inner speech, he might have produced far more interesting examples. It would have been nice if he had come right out and named his bad habits—for example, problems with illegal drugs or impulsivity in his relations with others. Then he could have told us how he tried to change these habits with self-talk and why, in his opinion, this did not work. He also might have generated a lot more theory in this manner. He is being too evasive to be really useful. Still, his analysis of the overall context of inner speech is a major contribution. His discovery that we constantly talk to our you, to our "becoming," and how we embrace this mode of existence is a spectacular and highly consequential insight.

To just take these two theorists as they are, Mead's problem-solving function and Peirce's modeling function are not very far apart. In both cases we are finding a way through our environment by engaging in a mental experiment. Still, the striking thing about both thinkers is that they do not talk about the inner speech process itself. In particular, they do not make any reference to possible texts or utterances that might be used in these mental experiments. The two thinkers remain at a distance and confine themselves to the perimeters or overall communication structure.

In particular, they also do not talk about how inner speech can help one understand and care for one's self. A lot of inner speech is aimed at what might be called auto therapy or making one's personality more healthy (or less unhealthy). The most obvious path is to think positive thoughts about one's self, thereby lifting one's mood. But there are also questions about how to work on one's defense mechanisms or minor psychopathologies. A lot of our self-care is done by way of inner speech, but there has not yet been much writing on this topic. I predict that the inner speech of self-care will be of increasing interest in the future.

Returning to the Russians, Vygotsky, in contrast to the Americans, ignores the overall communication and psychological structure and concentrates on inner speech itself, emphasizing syntax and semantics. Bakhtin does attend to dialogical structure but he pays most attention to the interpersonal one, not the intrapersonal one. Concerning the latter, which is inner speech itself, Bakhtin does not analyze the two communicating poles the way Mead does with his I-me analysis. What Bakhtin does is to concentrate on Dostoevsky's characters and their minds.

One could say, allowing for some oversimplification, the Americans concentrate on the "container," or the I-you-me circle within which inner speech goes on. The Russians pay most attention to the "contained"—that is, the inner speech itself. Another way of stating this distinction is to use the syntax-semantics distinction for the whole inner speech apparatus, not just for the linguistic content. If we do this, the Americans concentrate on the syntax or outer forms. The Russians concentrate on, given the special way I define this word, the semantics.

Finally, the Russians use data and the Americans do not. Vygotsky tells us about his experiments with children's private speech, their talking out loud. These materials, Vygotsky tells us, give him insights into the way the syntax and semantics of inner speech are abbreviated and personalized. I have a hunch that Vygotsky also used his own self observation here. Some of the things he says about inner speech could not have been observed from children's private speech. I see nothing wrong with self-observation, but Vygotsky might have understood his findings better if he acknowledged this source of information.

Bakhtin uses novels for his data. The use of literature as a source of inner speech has its limits, but Bakhtin manages to transcend these limits. If you just comment on Joyce or Woolf, you are stuck with their materials. But if you treat characters as though they were real people, which is what Bakhtin does with Dostoevsky's creations, you can use literature to get at reality. Bakhtin treats these characters the same way one might treat real people— the same way, for example, a psychotherapist might treat a literary figure. It helps that Dostoevsky is good at liberating his characters and letting them live their own lives, so to speak.

So both Vygotsky and Bakhtin, in contrast to Mead and Peirce, use inner speech data. Vygotsky uses children's private speech, and Bakhtin uses materials from novels. They both make such powerful and intense use of their materials that they are unusually successful in squeezing real information from their examples.

Conclusion

In this chapter I review two spurts of inner speech theory: that of the pragmatists, especially Peirce and Mead, and that of the Russian theorists Vygotsky and Bakhtin. Both pairs are extremely creative, and the current condition of inner speech theory is largely what people are making of these four intellectual leaders. At this point, the pragmatists and the Russians have not been seriously compared, let alone combined or integrated. My purpose is to begin a framework within which all four of these thinkers can be located. I realize that this is just an approach and not an arrival, but the project seems worthwhile, and I am sure others will gradually do more to achieve that arrival.

CONCLUSION

Perhaps the major finding is that inner speech is such an important and unrecognized aspect of how the human animal works. As Noam Chomsky (2012, 11) says, the great majority (99.9 percent, he suggests) of human language is in the form of inner speech. The overriding presence of this inner discourse is often obscured by its near invisibility. We are usually more oriented to our outer environment than to our interior lives. So we barely notice the inner dialogue. Nevertheless, inner speech has a constant and pervasive influence on how we live. Not only is our outer or interpersonal speech an expression of our inner speech; our actions are planned and guided by inner speech. In particular, major life decisions, including our important transitions and rites of passage, are formed by inner speech. As Oliver Sacks puts it, "Our real identity lies in inner speech" (1989, 59).

Another important finding is that Peirce and Mead fit together smoothly and make a creative mix. They combine into an I-you-me dialogical triad, a model that seems better than Mead's I-me and Peirce's I-you dyads. This triad improves not only the theory of inner speech but also the sociology of the self, especially when viewed dialogically. In particular, the triad illuminates the temporal structure of the self, a facet of theory that seems both neglected and quite promising (Flaherty 2010). Temporality and dialogue illuminate each other, in addition to providing two windows on the self. The field of sociology might also do well to add Peirce, particularly in his semiotics, as a founding father (Wiley 2006b).

Pragmatism, too, as a vibrant school of philosophy, could pay more attention to the Peirce-Mead relation. This combination gives pragmatism more explanatory power as well as new directions for analysis. In addition, the pragmatists' interest in inner speech—including James and Dewey as well as Peirce and Mead—seems like a central idea in their field. Pragmatism's emphasis on the "pragma" or practical feature of meaning is certainly a signature idea, but inner speech is a second distinguishing idea. It also combines well with the theory of meaning.

Another important feature of pragmatism is that all selves are equal in value. This is the Jefferson-Lincoln idea, but pragmatism shows how and why it works. I show how this is an implication of Peirce's thought. In other words, pragmatism explains how the underlying moral community is the basis for democracy. Not only do laws and institutions create democracy; the egalitarian charisma of human beings shows that humans have a natural democracy. To put it another way, Hobbes's war of all against all is a mistake. We are all sacred entities, and the healthiest response to this situation is mutual respect.

Another interesting finding is that inner speech is a language of its own. It cannot be explained by either Saussurean or Chomskyan linguistics, the two leading theories, except by stretching their concepts beyond recognition. Inner speech has several unique structural features, such as inherent dialogue, a condensed syntax, and a personalized semantics. The vocabulary is also small, compared to outer language. We use a modest number of words and repeat them over and over again. Aesthetics is always a consideration in interpersonal language—for example, having an engaging conversational style. But internal language drops all such considerations. Minimalism itself becomes the aesthetic. And a vocabulary with our personality and feelings stitched into it—a highly tailor-made semantics—rules in this discourse. This language is also private, both by being a one-person language and by being so idiosyncratic that it is meaningful and usable only to that person. Using Wittgenstein's criterion, it is the only private language in existence.

This semantics also contains a lot of nonverbal but meaningful elements, as stated earlier, inserted into the appropriate syntactic slots. These include visual images, sounds, touches, smells, and even tastes. In addition, there are emotions, kinesthetic states, desires, and psychological nuances. If, for example, you are daydreaming about the person you love, the particular aspect of this love can come in an indefinite number of varieties. For this reason the verbal vocabulary of inner speech is quite small but the nonverbal "vocabulary" is indefinitely large. Chomsky is right about inner speech when he says we could construct an infinite number of sentences, but this is true only of the imagery, not of the words. He had the wrong semantics in mind when he made this statement.

In other words, the field of linguistics cannot explain this form of language, even though Chomsky admits that almost all of our use of language is for inner speech. It is possible to say inner speech is based on the rules of the underlying language—that is, on what amounts to the ordinary Chomskyan formal grammar—but to do this you have to deny the unique linguistic structure, grammar, and rules of inner speech. Also, all languages tend toward the same specialized linguistic peculiarities when they shift to the inner speech mode. The demands of this form of language override the Chomskyan theory of grammar. Perhaps still another linguistic theory is needed to explain language that is both intra-subjective and dialogical. Vygotsky seems like a good start for this new linguistics.

Another finding is that inner speech probably starts, at least in crude form, around age one or two. Vygotsky places this start around age seven, following the period of private or "thinking out loud" language. But there are a number of suggestions that children are in some way communicating with themselves well before age seven. They may not have the full use of language, but inner speech does not use all the elements of language anyway. Both syntax and semantics are simplified. That makes these structures closer to the early stages of language learning.

In addition, it seems a major requirement of inner speech is to have inner duality, such as Mead's I and me or Piece's I and you or the I-me-you synthesis. This duality seems to be a condition for the dialectical relation, the back-and-forth, of internal conversation. This duality is based on the child's early discovery of the self. Once in place, this duality becomes the avenue along which internal communication can go through its own developmental stages. Just a there is an early stage of ordinary language learning, such that not all linguistic powers are initially present, there are early stages of inner speech, several of which are discussed in Chapter 2. Given that inner speech may start a lot earlier than Vygotsky had thought, it is also true that early inner speech, as Sacks suggests, is involved in the cultivation of the early self.

In Chapter 10 I show that the classical sources include two Americans, Peirce and Mead, and two Russians, Vygotsky and Bakhtin. These thinkers were not familiar with, or at times ignored, each other. The Americans fit together fairly well and, when merged, constitute a well-thought-out foundation for inner speech.

In contrast, the two Russians not only do not fit together very well; they do not connect easily to American thought. As a result, the field of inner speech is still in the process of building a coherent classical foundation. Usually a field, including a relatively new one, uses its past ideas to explain its present insights. Contemporary inner speech studies are the opposite. We need to use present findings and ideas to explain the starting points and foundations. This is because this field has four relatively independent "founders": Peirce, Mead, Vygotsky, and Bakhtin.

It is possible to let these four sets of ideas remain as they are and constitute separate tools in one's tool kit. Then you would use each theorist as he applies to whatever problem you are working on. Perinbanayagam has exploited the four classics brilliantly in his highly original books on the self. But if this field is to coalesce and became a critical mass (i.e., a field that has a fairly clear identity and the "bulk" to give it some disciplinary authority), it might well work on a more coherent and stable set of starting points. One suggestion, then, for future research is a beefing up of the foundations.

Perhaps this will automatically come about once scholars see the need for it. Bakhtin is so original that, at present, he is the one hardest to integrate with the other classics. He has an extremely rich and complex set of concepts. At times his ideas are similar to those of Mead, and a Bakhtin-Mead comparison is obviously a worthwhile objective in integrating the classics.

Bakhtin also uses emotional ideas more than the other three inner speech founders. One suggestion is that James's concept of self-feeling might be a useful bridge between the pragmatist thinkers and Bakhtin.

I also pay attention to how inner speech concepts connect to those of self and identity.

Concept of the Self

The concept of self is widely criticized in contemporary philosophy, particularly in those varieties of materialism that entail positivist methodology. For example, the self is often defined as a reflexive relation, but there is no truly or total reflexive relation in materialism (Hanson 1986, 66–76). For this reason it is widely believed that the idea of a self is inconsistent with the premises of contemporary philosophy—in other words, that there is no self.

In confronting this position, I distinguish fifteen arguments that there is no self and show how each entails the fallacy of reductionism. Taken as an integrated wave, these fifteen arguments have what appears to be overwhelming power. But if you look at each individually, these positions are both weak and repetitive. In other words, if your taken-for-granted premise is that only material things exist, obviously the self is disallowed. But if you allow non-materialistic properties, which seem to characterize the world in which we live, the self can easily be explained.

The existence of the self turns on an epistemological issue. If you believe that meaning and truth must be embedded in physical properties, such as size and shape, truth must be anchored in the external, material world, outside of our subjective experience. This is a "third person" epistemology. If, in contrast, you believe that our personal experience and direct consciousness also gives us access to meaning and truth, you are working with a "first person" epistemology. From this point of view, the world of nonphysical meaning exists. The German thinkers call the first the physical sciences and the second the sociocultural sciences. Reading, thought, decision making, self-regulation, action, memory, and conversation all (Windelband 1980) depend on inner speech.

In our everyday, practical lives we live in both worlds, the physical and the sociocultural. History, social institutions, and our psychological lives are based on the sociocultural subjective world. Without these semiotic phenomenon we would be back to our pre-linguistic, chimpanzee state.

The position I argue against suggests a "double truth" epistemology, similar to the one espoused by some medieval Islamic scholars (Russell 1945, 453, 542). For them there were two truths, philosophy and revealed religion. Reason and faith could contradict, but the doctrine of double truth legitimized them both.

The contemporary double truth position is, for some materialists, between the physical and sociocultural worlds. For these thinkers, the physical sciences argue that there is no self or even consciousness, at least not in a scientific sense. Their subjective beliefs, however, are based on the institutional system, which is a second form of truth and meaning. These positivistic scholars spend their working days in the world of physical meanings and then go home to the institutional world of their families. In their homes and neighborhoods, they live a second life that contradicts their materialistic work lives. Their back-and-forth epistemological shifts is the modern version of the double truth.

But this split between the material and sociocultural worlds is an inefficient way of organizing a life or a society. This split also contradicts Aristotle's principle of identity, that a thing either is or is not and cannot be both (at the same time in the same respect). The positivists want it to be both. Their selves exist in the subjective world but do not exist in their scientific world.

The positivists also re-create Descartes's mind-body split, although they do so in a de facto rather than a de jure manner. The positivists accept the material world in their philosophy, but they also accept the nonmaterialistic or sociocultural world by continuing to live in and rely on it. This "living in and relying on" fits Peirce's pragmatist definition of meaning (as practical consequences). And like Descartes, the positivists have no clear link or avenue between the two. Descartes at least had the pineal gland as his connection.

Identity

Inner speech is also closely attached to identity, and it appears that to a significant extent we create our identity with inner speech. To clarify this I distinguish three parts of the self. There is the generic self, which includes those properties, especially thinking and acting, which all selves have. At the other extreme are those relatively transient and superficial traits, which I term the quotidian self. In between the generic and quotidian selves there are the traits that characterize and define us as individuals but are not present in all individuals. These identity traits are both social and psychological.

The identity processes, which we spend our entire lifetimes on, involve the fitting together of our social and psychological traits—like a picture puzzle. This is one of those dualities we juggle to give us a satisfying self. Inner speech is a major process in forming an identity *that seems like the real us*. When our social and psychological sides work together like two blades of a scissors, we know we are at home. We have found ourselves, and we have a workable instrument for achieving our goals. Your identity is the best person you can be, the coherent and attractive you.

In conclusion, inner speech is a psychological capacity that we use as a multipurpose tool. Almost everything we do with the mind we do with inner speech. Reading, thought, decision making, self-regulation, action, memory, and conversation all draw on this process. People who lack this capacity or cannot use it effectively are usually saddled with some kind of psychopathology, schizophrenia being the most graphic example (Waters et al. 2012).

But inner speech, being hard to spot in our consciousness, is as yet poorly understood. There is a steady stream of research but not enough. The theory of inner speech is also still in the process of being worked out. In other words, this capacity is something of an unexplored continent. This book is an attempt to map out this subject in broad strokes. It is hoped that this work will accelerate research and nudge the field toward becoming a more widely recognized discipline.

REFERENCES

Abramson, Marianne, and Stephen D. Goldinger. 1997. "What the Reader's Eye Tells the Mind's Ear: Silent Reading Activates Inner Speech." *Perception and Psychophysics* 59 (7): 1059–1068.
Allen, Amy. 2000. "The Anti-subjective Hypothesis: Michel Foucault and the Death of the Subject." *Philosophical Forum* 31:113–130.
Althusser, Louis. 1971. "Freud and Lacan." In *Lenin and Philosophy and Other Essays*, 195–219. New York: Monthly Review Press.
Archer, Margaret S. 2003. *Structure, Agency and the Internal Conversation*. Cambridge: Cambridge University Press.
———. 2007. *Making Our Way through the World*. Cambridge: Cambridge University Press.
———. 2012. *The Reflexive Imperative*. Cambridge: Cambridge University Press.
Aristotle. 1984. *Physics*. In *The Complete Works of Aristotle*, vol. 1, edited by Jonathan Barnes, 315–446. Princeton, NJ: Princeton University Press.
Arkin, Arthur M. 1981. *Sleep-Talking: Psychology and Psychophysiology*. Hillsdale, NJ: Lawrence Erlbaum.
Athens, Lonnie. 1993. "Blumer's Advanced Course on Social Psychology." *Studies in Symbolic Interaction* 14:163–193.
———. 1994. "The Self as a Soliloquy." *Sociological Quarterly* 35 (3): 521–532.
Augustine. (417) 2002. *Augustine: On the Trinity*. Bks. 8–15. Edited by Gareth B. Matthews. Cambridge: Cambridge University Press.
Austin, J. L. 1970. "Performative Utterances." In *Philosophical Papers*, 233–252. London: Oxford University Press.
Bakhtin, Mikhail M. 1981. *The Dialogic Imagination*. Austin: University of Texas Press.
———. 1984. *Problems of Dostoevsky's Poetics*. Minneapolis: University of Minnesota Press.

———. 1986. *Speech Genres and Other Late Essays*. Austin: University of Texas Press.
Bakhtin, Mikhail M., and Pavel N. Medvedev. 1978. *The Formal Method in Literary Scholarship*. Baltimore: Johns Hopkins University Press.
Barkley, Russell A. 1997. *ADHD and the Nature of Self-Control*. New York: Guilford Press.
Bellah, Robert. 1970. "Civil Religion in America." In *Beyond Belief*, 168–189. New York: Harper and Row.
Bernstein, Basil. 1971. *Class, Codes and Control*. Vol. 1. London: Routledge and Kegan Paul.
Best, Joel. 2004. *Deviance: The Career of a Concept*. Belmont, CA: Wadsworth.
Bickerton, Derek. 1990. *Language and Species*. Chicago: University of Chicago Press.
———. 1995. *Language and Human Behavior*. Seattle: University of Washington Press.
Blauner, Robert. 1969. *Internal Colonialism and Ghetto Revolts*. Indianapolis, IN: Bobbs-Merrill.
Blumer, Herbert. 1969. *Symbolic Interactionism: Perspective and Method*. Englewood Cliffs, NJ: Prentice-Hall.
Boas, Franz. 1911. *The Mind of Primitive Man*. New York: Macmillan.
Buber, Martin. 2000. *I and Thou*. New York: Scribner.
Butler, Robert N. 1963. "The Life Review: An Interpretation of Reminiscence in the Aged." *Psychiatry* 26:65–76.
Carruthers, Peter. 1996. *Language, Thought and Consciousness*. Cambridge: Cambridge University Press.
Caughey, John L. 1984. *Imaginary Social Worlds*. Lincoln: University of Nebraska Press.
Chodorow, Nancy. 1978. *The Reproduction of Mothering*. Berkeley: University of California Press.
Chomsky, Noam. 2002. *On Nature and Language*. Cambridge: Cambridge University Press.
———. 2012. *The Science of Language*. Cambridge: Cambridge University Press.
Churchland, Paul M. 1981. "Eliminative Materialism and the Propositional Attitudes." *Journal of Philosophy* 78 (2): 67–90.
Colapietro, Vincent. 1989. *Peirce's Approach to the Self*. Albany, NY: SUNY Press.
———. 1999. "Subject Positions and Positional Subjectivity: A Pragmatic Approach." *Semiotische Berichte* 1 (4): 13–28.
Collins, Randall. 1982. *Sociological Insight*. New York: Oxford University Press.
———. 1989. "Toward a Neo-Meadian Sociology of Mind." *Symbolic Interaction* 12:1–32.
———. 2004a. *Interaction Ritual Chains*. Princeton, NJ: Princeton University Press.
———. 2004b. "Internalized Symbols and the Social Process of Thinking." In *Interaction Ritual Chains*, 183–220. Princeton, NJ: Princeton University Press.
Cook, Gary. 1993. *George Herbert Mead: The Making of a Social Pragmatist*. Urbana: University of Illinois Press.
Cooley, Charles Horton. (1902) 1983. *Human Nature and the Social Order*. New Brunswick, NJ: Transaction.
———. 1908. "A Study of the Early Use of Self-Words by a Child." *Psychological Review* 15 (6): 339–357.
Cooper, Mick. 2004. "Encountering Self-Otherness: 'I-I' and 'I-Me' Modes of Self-Relating." In *The Dialogical Self in Psychotherapy*, edited by Hubert J. M. Hermans and Giancarlo Dimaggio, 60–73. New York: Brunner-Routledge.

Davies, Bronwyn, and Rom Harré. 1990. "Positioning: The Discursive Production of Selves." *Journal for the Theory of Social Behavior* 20:43–63.
Descartes, René. 1987. "Discourse on the Method of Rightly Conducting the Reason." In *The Philosophical Works of Descartes*, vol. 1, 79–130. Cambridge: Cambridge University Press.
Dewey, John. (1910) 1991. *How We Think*. Buffalo, NY: Prometheus Books.
———. (1929) 1958. *Experience and Nature*. New York: Dover.
———. 1930. *Human Nature and Conduct*. Rev. ed. New York: Modern Library.
———. 1972. "The Reflex Arc Concept in Psychology." In *The Early Works, 1882–1898*, vol. 5, *Early Essays*, edited by Jo Ann Boydston, 96–109. Carbondale: Southern Illinois University Press.
———. 2008. "George Herbert Mead as I Knew Him." In *The Later Works, 1925–1953*, vol. 6, *1931–1932: Essays, Reviews, and Miscellany*, edited by Jo Ann Boydston, 22–28. Carbondale: Southern Illinois University Press.
Diaz, Rafael M., and Laura E. Berk. 1992. *Private Speech: From Social Interaction to Self-Regulation*. Hillsdale, NJ: Lawrence Erlbaum.
Dodds, Agnes E., Jeanette A. Lawrence, and Jaan Valsiner. 1997. "The Personal and the Social: Mead's Theory of the 'Generalized Other.'" *Theory and Psychology* 7 (4): 483–503.
Du Bois, W. E. B. (1903) 1994. *The Souls of Black Folk*. New York: Gramercy Books.
Durkheim, Émile. (1912) 1995. *The Elementary Forms of Religious Life*. New York: Free Press.
———. 1973. "Individualism and the Intellectuals." In *Émile Durkheim: On Morality and Society*, edited by Robert N. Bellah, 43–57. Chicago: University of Chicago Press.
Eddington, Arthur. 1928. *The Nature of the Physical World*. New York: Macmillan.
Eikhenbaum, Boris. (1927) 1974. "Problems of Film Stylistics." *Screen* 15:7–32.
Ericsson, K. Anders. 2001. "Protocol Analysis in Psychology." In *International Encyclopedia of the Social and Behavioral Sciences*, edited by Neil Smelser and Paul Baltes, 12256–12262. Oxford, UK: Elsevier.
Ewing, A. C. (1934) 1961. *Idealism: A Critical Survey*. London: Methuen.
Fields, Chris A. 2002. "Why Do We Talk to Ourselves?" *Journal of Experimental and Theoretical Artificial Intelligence* 14:255–272.
Firestone, Robert W. 1986. "The 'Inner Voice' and Suicide." *Psychotherapy* 23:439–447.
Fisch, Max. 1982. "Introduction." In *Writings of Charles S. Peirce: A Chronological Edition*, vol. 1, *1857–1966*, xv–xxxv. Bloomington: Indiana University Press.
Flaherty, Michael G. 2000. *A Watched Pot*. New York: New York University Press.
———. 2010. *The Textures of Time: Agency and Temporal Experience*. Philadelphia: Temple University Press.
Flavell, John H., Frances L. Green, Eleanor R. Flavell, and James B. Grossman. 1997. "The Development of Children's Knowledge about Inner Speech." *Child Development* 68 (1): 39–47.
Fligstein, Neil, and Doug McAdam. 2012. *A Theory of Fields*. New York: Oxford University Press.
Fodor, Jerry. 1975. *The Language of Thought*. Cambridge, MA: Harvard University Press.
Fontinell, Eugene. 2000. *Self, God, and Immortality: A Jamesian Investigation*. New York: Fordham University Press.

Foucault, Michel. 1973. *The Order of Things*. New York: Vintage Books.
Frege, Gottlob. 1972. "Review of Dr. E. Husserl's *Philosophy of Arithmetic*." *Mind* 81 (323): 321–337.
Freud, Sigmund. (1920) 1961. *Beyond the Pleasure Principle*. New York: W. W. Norton.
Gale, Richard M. 1999. *The Divided Self of William James*. Cambridge: Cambridge University Press.
Gallie, Walter Bryce. 1956. "Essentially Contested Concepts." *Proceedings of the Aristotelian Society* 56:167–198.
Garfinkel, Harold. 1956. "Conditions of Successful Degradation Ceremonies." *American Journal of Sociology* 61 (5): 420–424.
Gecas, Viktor, and Michael L. Schwalbe. 1983. "Beyond the Looking-Glass Self: Social Structure and Efficacy-Based Self-Esteem." *Social Psychology Quarterly* 46 (2): 77–88.
Goethe, Johann Wolfgang von. 1974. *The Autobiography of Johann Wolfgang von Goethe*. Vol. 2. Translated by John Oxenford. Chicago: University of Chicago Press.
Goffman, Erving. 1959. *The Presentation of Self in Everyday Life*. Garden City, NY: Doubleday.
———. 1967. *Interaction Ritual*. Garden City, NY: Doubleday.
Gopnik, Alison. 2009. *The Philosophical Baby*. New York: Farrar, Straus and Giroux.
Hanson, Karen. 1986. *The Self Imagined*. New York: Routledge and Kegan Paul.
Hardwick, Charles A., ed. 1977. *Semiotics and Significs: The Correspondence between Charles S. Peirce and Lady Welby*. Bloomington: Indiana University Press.
Hardy, James. 2006. "Speaking Clearly: A Critical Review of the Self-Talk Literature." *Psychology of Sports and Exercise* 7:81–97.
Harrison, G. B., ed. 1948. "Shakespeare's *Measure for Measure*." In *Shakespeare: Major Plays and the Sonnets*, 747–779. New York: Harcourt, Brace and World.
Hassin, Ran R., James S. Uleman, and John A. Bargh. 2005. *The New Unconscious*. Oxford: Oxford University Press.
Hazlett-Stevens, Holly. 2005. *Women Who Worry Too Much: How to Stop Worry and Anxiety from Ruining Relationships, Work and Fun*. Oakland, CA: New Harbinger.
Heil, John. 2013. *Philosophy of Mind: A Contemporary Introduction*. New York: Routledge.
Hermans, Hubert J. M., and Harry J. G. Kempen. 1993. *The Dialogical Self: Meaning as Movement*. San Diego: Academic Press.
Higham, John. 1988. *Strangers in the Land: Patterns of American Nativism, 1860–1925*. 2nd ed. New Brunswick, NJ: Rutgers University Press.
Holmes Paul, and Claire Calmels. 2008. "A Neuroscientific Review of Imagery and Observation Use in Sport." *Journal of Motor Behavior* 40:433–445.
Hoopes, James. 1989. *Consciousness in New England: From Puritanism and Ideas to Psychoanalysis and Semiotic*. Baltimore: Johns Hopkins University Press.
Hume, David. 1978. *A Treatise on Human Nature*. 2nd ed. Oxford: Oxford University Press.
Humphrey, Robert. 1962. *Stream of Consciousness in the Modern Novel*. Berkeley: University of California Press.
Husserl, Edmund. (1913) 1982. *Logical Investigations*. Vol. 1. London: Routledge and Kegan Paul.
Hymes, Dell. 1964. "Directions in (Ethno-)Linguistic Theory." *American Anthropologist* 66 (3): 6–56.

References

Jacobs, Glenn. 2006. *Charles Horton Cooley: Imagining Social Reality*. Amherst: University of Massachusetts Press.
James, William. 1950a. *The Principles of Psychology*. Vol. 1. New York: Dover.
———. 1950b. *The Principles of Psychology*. Vol 2. New York: Dover.
———. 1970. *The Varieties of Religious Experience*. New York: Collier Books.
Joas, Hans. 1985. *G. H. Mead: A Contemporary Re-examination of His Thought*. Chicago: University of Chicago Press.
———. 1993. *Pragmatism and Social Theory*. Chicago: University of Chicago Press.
Johnson, John R. 1994. "Intrapersonal Spoken Language: An Attribute of Extrapersonal Competency." In *Intrapersonal Communication: Different Voices, Different Minds*, edited by Donna R. Vocate, 169–192. Hillsdale, NJ: Lawrence Erlbaum.
Kant, Immanuel. (1781) 1965. *Critique of Pure Reason*. New York: St. Martin's Press.
———. (1800) 1978. *Anthropology from a Pragmatic Point of View*. Carbondale: Southern Illinois University Press.
———. (1804) 1983. *What Real Progress Has Metaphysics Made in Germany since the Time of Leibniz and Wolff?* New York: Abaris Books.
Kaplan, Abraham. 1964. *The Conduct of Inquiry: Methodology for Behavioral Science*. San Francisco: Chandler.
Klinger, Eric. 1990. *Daydreaming: Using Waking Fantasy and Imagery for Self-Knowledge and Creativity*. Los Angeles: Jeremy P. Tarcher.
Korba, Rodney J. 1986. "The Rate of Inner Speech." Ph.D. diss., University of Denver, Denver, CO.
———. 1990. "The Rate of Inner Speech." *Perceptual and Motor Skills* 71:1043–1052.
Kosslyn, Stephen M. 1994. *Imagery and Brain*. Cambridge, MA: MIT Press.
Lacan, Jacques. 1949. "Cure psychanalytique à l'aide de la poupée fleur" [A psychoanalytic treatment by means of a flower doll]. *Revue Française de la Psychanalyse* [French Journal of Psychoanalysis] 4 (October–December): 567.
———. (1966) 1977. *Ecrits* [Writings]. New York: Norton.
———. 2006. "The Mirror Stage as Formative of the *I* Function as Revealed in Psychoanalytic Experience." In *Ecrits* [Writings], translated by Bruce Fink, 75–81. New York. Norton.
Laqueur, Thomas. 1990. *Making Sex: Body and Gender from the Greeks to Freud*. Cambridge, MA: Harvard University Press.
Locke, John. (1689) 1979. *An Essay Concerning Human Understanding*. London: Clarendon Press.
Luhrmann, T. M. 2012. *When God Talks Back*. New York: Vintage Books.
Marske, Charles E. 1987. "Durkheim's 'Cult of the Individual' and the Moral Reconstitution of Society." *Sociological Theory* 5:1–14.
Martin, John Levi. 2003. "What Is Field Theory?" *American Journal of Sociology* 109:1–49.
Marx, Karl. 1983. *The Portable Karl Marx*. New York: Penguin Books.
McFarland, Philip. 2004. *Hawthorne in Concord*. New York: Grove Press.
McKay, Matthew, Martha Davis, and Patrick Fanning. 2011. *Thoughts and Feelings: Taking Control of Your Moods and Your Life*. Oakland, CA: New Harbinger.
Mead, George Herbert. (1913) 1964. "The Social Self." In *Selected Writings: George Herbert Mead*, edited by Andrew J. Reck, 142–149. Indianapolis, IN: Bobbs-Merrill.
———. 1930. "Cooley's Contribution to American Social Thought." *American Journal of Sociology* 35:693–706.

———. (1932) 1964. *The Philosophy of the Present*. Chicago: University of Chicago Press.
———. 1934. *Mind, Self and Society*. Chicago: University of Chicago Press.
———. 1936. *Movements of Thought in the Twentieth Century*. Chicago: University of Chicago Press.
———. 1964. *Selected Writings: George Herbert Mead*, edited by Andrew J. Reck. Indianapolis, IN: Bobbs-Merrill.
Meichenbaum, Donald. 1977. *Cognitive-Behavior Modification*. New York: Plenum Press.
Merleau-Ponty, Maurice. 1964. *The Primacy of Perception*. Evanston, IL: Northwestern University Press.
Morin, Alain. 1993. "Self-Talk and Self-Awareness: On the Nature of the Relation." *Journal of Mind and Behavior* 14:223–234.
Morin, Alain, and Bob Uttl. 2013. "Inner Speech: A Window into Consciousness." *The Neuropsychotherapist*, April 13. Available at http://www.neuropsychotherapist.com/inner-speech.
Morson, Gary Saul, and Carl Emerson. 1989. *Rethinking Bakhtin*. Evanston, IL: Northwestern University Press.
Myrdal, Gunnar. 1944. *An American Dilemma: The Negro Problem and American Democracy*. New York: Harper.
Nietzsche, Friedrich. 2001. *The Gay Science*. Cambridge: Cambridge University Press.
Normore, Calvin. 2009. "Concepts and Ideas: The Decline of Mental Language." In *Le langage mental du Moyen Âge à l'Âge Classique* [The mental language of the Middle Ages to the Classical Age], edited by J. Biard, 293–306. Leuven, Belgium: Peeters.
Onians, R. B. (1951) 1988. *The Origins of European Thought about the Body, the Mind, the Soul, the World, Time, and Fate*. Cambridge: Cambridge University Press.
Peirce, Charles Sanders. 1910. Unpublished manuscript 645. Houghton Library, Harvard University, Cambridge, MA.
———. 1934. *Collected Papers of Charles Sanders Peirce*. Vol. 5, *Pragmatism and Pragmaticism*, and vol. 6, *Scientific Metaphysics*, edited by Charles Hartshorne and Paul Weiss. Cambridge, MA: Harvard University Press.
———. 1979. *Charles Sanders Peirce: Contributions to "The Nation."* Vol. 3, *1901–1908*. Edited by Kenneth Laine Ketner and James Edward Cook. Lubbock: Texas Tech University Press.
———. 1982. *Writings of Charles S. Peirce: A Chronological Edition*. Vol. 1, *1857–1866*. Bloomington: Indiana University Press.
———. 1984. *Writings of Charles S. Peirce: A Chronological Edition*. Vol. 2, *1867–1871*. Bloomington: Indiana University Press.
———. 1986. "How to Make Our Ideas Clear." In *Writings of Charles S. Peirce*, vol. 3, *1872–1878*, 257–276. Bloomington: Indiana University Press.
Pencak, William. 2007. "The Peirce Brothers, John Addington Symonds, Horatio Brown, and the Boundaries of Defending Homosexuality in Late-Nineteenth-Century Anglo-America." *Journal of the History of Sexuality* 16:153–168.
Perinbanayagam, Robert. 1985. *Signifying Acts*. Carbondale: Southern Illinois University Press.
———. 1991a. "The Dialogical Self." In *Discursive Acts*, 5–25. Hawthorne, NY: Aldine de Gruyter.
———. 1991b. *Discursive Acts*. Hawthorne, NY: Aldine de Gruyter.

———. 2000. *The Presence of Self*. Lanham: Rowman and Littlefield.
———. 2006. *Games and Sport in Everyday Life*. Boulder, CO: Paradigm.
———. 2012. *Identity's Moments*. New York: Lexington Books.
Perry, Ralph Barton. 1935. *The Thought and Character of William James*. Vol. 1. Boston: Little Brown.
Plato. 1961. *The Collected Dialogues*. Edited by E. Hamilton and H. Cairns. New York: Pantheon.
Ponzio, Augusto. 1984. "Semiotics between Peirce and Bakhtin." *Recherches Semiotiques/Semiotic Inquiry* 4:273–291.
Rankin, Jenny. 2003. "What Is Narrative? Ricoeur, Bakhtin, and Process Approaches." *Concrescence: The Australasian Journal of Process Thought* 3:1–9.
Rawls, Anne. 1987. "The Interaction Order Sui Generis: Goffman's Contribution to Social Theory." *Sociological Theory* 5:136–149.
Reitzes, Donald C. 1980. "Beyond the Looking-Glass Self: Cooley's Social Self and Its Treatment in Introductory Textbooks." *Contemporary Sociology* 9:631–640.
Rochberg-Halton, E. 1986. *Meaning and Modernity: Social Theory in the Pragmatic Attitude*. Chicago: University of Chicago Press.
Rohrer, Jonathan D., William D. Knight, Jane E. Warren, Nick C. Fox, Martin N. Rosser, and Jason D. Warren. 2008. "Word-Finding Difficulty: A Clinical Analysis of the Progressive Aphasias." *Brain* 131:8–38.
Rose, Jacqueline. 1982. "Introduction." In *Feminine Sexuality: Jacques Lacan and the École Freudienne*, by Jacques Lacan, edited by Juliet Mitchell and Jacqueline Rose, 1–57. New York: Norton.
Rosenthal, S. 1986. *Speculative Pragmatism*. Amherst: University of Massachusetts Press.
Russell, Bertrand. 1945. *A History of Western Philosophy*. New York: Simon and Schuster.
Ryle, Gilbert. 2009. *The Concept of Mind*. New York: Routledge.
Sacks, Oliver. 1989. *Seeing Voices*. Berkeley: University of California Press.
Sartre, Jean-Paul. 1957a. *Being and Nothingness*. London: Methuen.
———. 1957b. *The Transcendence of the Ego*. New York: Noonday Press.
Saussure, Ferdinand de. 1959. *Course in General Linguistics*. New York: McGraw-Hill.
Scheff, Thomas J. 2005. "Looking-Glass Self: Goffman as a Symbolic Interactionist." *Symbolic Interaction* 28:147–166.
Schiller, Friedrich. (1795) 1967. *On the Aesthetic Education of Man*. Oxford, UK: Clarendon Press.
Schütz, Alfred. 1962. *Collected Papers*. Vol. 1, *The Problem of Social Reality*, edited by Maurice Natanson. The Hague: Martinus Nijhoff.
Shalin, Dmitri. 1984. "The Romantic Antecedents of Meadian Social Psychology." *Symbolic Interaction* 7:43–65.
Singer, Jerome L. 1966. *Daydreaming*. New York: Random House.
Snell, Bruno. (1953) 1982. *The Discovery of the Mind*. New York: Dover.
Solovey, Mark, and Hamilton Cravens, eds. 2012. *Cold War Social Science: Knowledge Production, Liberal Democracy, and Human Nature*. New York: Palgrave Macmillan.
Stone, Gregory P. 1981. "Appearance and the Self: A Slightly Revised Version." In *Social Psychology Through Symbolic Interaction*, by Gregory P. Stone and Harvey A. Farberman, 187–202. New York: Macmillan.
Tate, Loren. 1992. Untitled article. *Champaign-Urbana News-Gazette*, December 14.

Taylor, Marjorie. 1999. *Imaginary Companions and the Children Who Create Them*. New York: Oxford University Press.
Thomas, W. I., and Dorothy Swaine Thomas. 1928. *The Child in America*. New York: Alfred A. Knopf.
Tomlinson, Brian. 2000. "Talking to Yourself: The Role of the Inner Voice in Language Learning." *Applied Language Learning* 11:123-154.
Tye, Michael. 1991. *The Imagery Debate*. Cambridge, MA: MIT Press.
Vocate, Donna R., ed. 1994. *Intrapersonal Communication: Different Voices, Different Minds*. Hillsdale, NJ: Lawrence Erlbaum.
Voloshinov, V. N. 1973. *Marxism and the Philosophy of Language*. Cambridge, MA: Harvard University Press.
Vygotsky, L. S. 1987a. *The Collected Works of L. S. Vygotsky*. Vol. 1, *Problems of General Psychology*, edited by Robert W. Rieber and Aaron S. Carton. New York: Plenum Press.
———. 1987b. *Thinking and Speech*. In *The Collected Works of L. S. Vygotsky*, vol. 1, *Problems of General Psychology*, edited by Robert W. Rieber and Aaron S. Carton, 37-286. New York: Plenum Press.
Wagenknecht, Edward, ed. 1956. *Mrs. Longfellow*. New York: Longmans, Green.
Waters, Flavie, Paul Allen, André Aleman, Charles Fernyhough, Todd S. Woodward, Johanna C. Badcock, Emma Barkus, Louise Johns, Filippo Varese, Mahesh Menon, Ans Vercammen, and Frank Larøi. 2012. "Auditory Hallucinations in Schizophrenia and Nonschizophrenia Populations: A Review and Integrated Model of Cognitive Mechanisms." *Schizophrenia Bulletin* 38:683-693.
Weber, Max. 1946. *From Max Weber: Essays in Sociology*. Translated and edited by H. H. Gerth and C. Wright Mills. New York: Oxford University Press.
Weir, Morton. 1992. Letter to the editor. *Champaign-Urbana News-Gazette*, December 30.
Wertsch, James V. 1985. *Vygotsky and the Social Formation of Mind*. Cambridge, MA: Harvard University Press.
Whitehouse, Andrew J. O., Murray T. Maybery, and Kevin Durkin. 2006. "Inner Speech Impairments in Autism." *Journal of Child Psychology and Psychiatry* 47:857-865.
Wiley, Norbert. 1994. *The Semiotic Self*. Chicago: University of Chicago Press.
———. 2003. "The Self as a Self-Fulfilling Prophecy." *Symbolic Interaction* 26:501-513.
———. 2005. "Review of Margaret Archer's *Structure, Agency and the Internal Conversation*." *American Sociological Review* 110:1528-1529.
———. 2006a. "Inner Speech as a Language: A Saussurean Inquiry." *Journal for the Theory of Social Behavior* 36:319-341.
———. 2006b. "Peirce and the Founding of American Sociology." *Journal of Classical Sociology* 6:23-50.
———. 2006c. "Pragmatism and the Dialogical Self." *International Journal for Dialogical Science* 1:5-21.
———. 2008. "Combining Mead and Peirce with Vygotsky and Bakhtin on Inner Speech." Paper presented for invited address at California State University, Hayward.
———. 2011a. "The Chicago School: A Political Interpretation." *Studies in Symbolic Interaction* 36:39-74.
———. 2011b. "Mead and Cooley: A Merger." *American Sociologist* 42:168-186.

References

———. 2013. "Theory of Mind: A Pragmatist Approach." Paper presented at the annual meeting of the American Sociological Association, New York, August.

———. 2014. "Chomsky's Anomaly: Inner Speech." *International Journal for Dialogical Science* 8 (1): 1–11.

———. Forthcoming. "Mead's Field Theory and Its Macro Implications." In *Studies in Symbolic Interaction*, edited by Norman K. Denzin. Bingley, UK: Emerald Group.

Williamson, Joy Ann. 2003. *Black Power on Campus: The University of Illinois, 1965–1975*. Urbana: University of Illinois Press.

Wilson, William Julius. 1980. *The Declining Significance of Race*. Chicago: University of Chicago Press.

Windelband, Wilhelm. 1980. "Rectorial Address, Strasbourg, 1894." *History and Theory* 19 (2): 169–185.

Wittgenstein, Ludwig. 1958. *Philosophical Investigations*. London: Blackwell.

Yeung, King-To, and John Levi Martin. 2003. "The Looking Glass Self: An Empirical Test and Elaboration." *Social Forces* 81 (3): 843–879.

INDEX

Page numbers in italics refer to material in tables or figures.

abbreviated syntax, 5, 15
aborigines, 20
abstraction, 5
abuse, 143
act, the, 97
action, 101–102; of others toward self, 143
addressivity, 139, 169–170
aesthetic, 94–95, 155, 164, 176
agency, 18–19, 62, 126, 152; Blumer and, 101–103; choosing, 80–83; cultural and physical, 82; defining, 79–80; emotion and, 77–79; enacting, 83–84; and establishing habits, 84–89; frustration and, 77–78; link with inner speech, 75–90; process of, 76–77; reflex arc and, 111; stages of, 79–84; structure and, 155–156; voice and, 140–141
agentic self, 62, 119
Althusser, Louis, 37, 169
American Creed, 145
Americanization movement, 122–123, 127–128
answerability, 139, 169
anthropology, 18, 45, 122
anti-self concepts, 34–35, 47–48
appearance, 18
Archer, Margaret, 6, 89, 92, 96
Aristotle, 18
Asian religions, 36, 41
atheism, 52, 97–98
Athens, Lonnie, 100
Augustine, 5, 151
autonomy, 37

Bakhtin, Mikhail, 7, 9, 31–32, 89, 97; on addressivity, 139, 169–170; inner speech theory and, 150, 158, 163–167, 168–171; internal dialogical polarity and, 32; labeling theory and, 148–149; Marxist party line and, 32, 97–98; on self as dialogue, 42; on voice, 134, 138–141, *144*, 148–149, 168
behavioral routines, 23–24
behaviorism, 101–102, 165
Bellah, Robert, 50–51
Berkeley, George, 68
Bernstein, Basil, 59–60
Blumer, Herbert, 92, 101–103
Boas, Franz, 37, 45, 86, 121–122
body, 7, 120–121, 124, 161

Bolshevik revolution, 164, 168
born-again process, 135
Bourdieu, Pierre, 156
Buber, Martin, 32, *32,* 91
bureaucracies, 52

capitalism, 36, 63, 89, 169
category error, 36
Catholic philosophers, 151
Caughey, John L., 3
charisma, 52, 55, 61, 127, 130, 176
childhood: discovery of self in, 23; inaudible inner speech in, 19; interpersonal relation in, 114–117; Oedipus and Electra complexes in, 115–116; origination of inner speech, 22–33; private speech in, 3–6, 13, 22–26, 63, 163; thinking-out-loud stage of, 5–6, 19
Chodorow, Nancy, 115–116
choice, 6, 27, 102, 126; agency and, 80–83; in felt time, 160; voluntarism, 130
Chomsky, Noam, 2, 5, 13, 15, 175, 176–177; on grammatical theory, 56–57; inability of, to explain inner speech, 73–74
circular structure of inner speech, 10–15
citizenship, 50
Civil War, 128
code words, 4, 13
"cogito, ergo sum," 26, 27, 36, 38, 120
cognitive dissonance, 89
cognitive science, 41–42
cognitive therapy, 142
cognitive unconscious, 143
Colapietro, Vincent, 6, 91, 93–94, 154
Cold War, 41–42
collective consciousness, 144, 156
Collins, Randall, 3–4, 13, 20, 92, 97, 154
communalism, 49
community, 98; self as, 12, 62
competence, 15, 74
complex activity, talking through, 19
comprehensive dialogicality, 157–158
computer, self as, 38, 39–41, 114, 151–152
Comte, Auguste, 52
condensation, 4, 8, 13, 74; key words and, 60–61; and relation to mother, 116
conflict, 139
conscience, 98, 116–117
consciousness, 7–8; collective, 144, 156; split, 71–72

consequences, 104–106, 122
controversy, 145
conversational style, 12, 18
Cooley, Charles Horton, 21, 30–31, 32; on imaginary companion, 99–101, 103; limitations of looking-glass self, 141–145; on looking-glass self, 30–31, 50, 127, 134–138, *144*; on self-feeling, 48, 61
creativity, 21
Crime and Punishment (Dostoyevsky), 31, 141, 158, 165, 168
critical self, 94, 98, 155
cultural consequences, 104–105
cultural self, 131
cultural sphere, 82
cultural studies, 56
culture, 18, 37, 86, 121–122, 131

daydreaming, 20–21, 78; in childhood, 24
Dead Souls (Gogol), 167
death: of God, 48; of man, 48; of the subject, 48–49, 52, 66
decentered self, 106, 129–130
Declaration of Independence, 145
decoding practice, 143, 145
deconstruction, 110
definition, 80
degradation ceremony, 137
deliberation, 99, 102, *103*, 107, 112–113
democracy, 80–81, 106, 128, 133
depression, 31, 136, 142
Derrida, Jacques, 106, 110
Descartes, René, 6, 26, 27, 36, 38, 120, 121, 179
determinism, 80–83, 102
deviance, 67
Dewey, John, 77, 86, 91–92, 101; and free will and determinism, 81; and mental experiment, 99, *103*, 107–108, 112; pragmatist theory of self and, 111–114
dialogical pair, 23, 24
dialogical polarity, 29–33
dialogical self, 42, 64, *103*, 124, 129; pragmatism and, 91–108; rediscovery of, 93–95
dialogical speech, 9
dialogue, 7, 139–140
differential theories of meaning, 57, 65–70; parole and langue, 70–73

disabilities, 100–101, 140, 149
disapproving visitors, 31
disenchantment gap, 52
Dostoyevsky, Fyodor, 31, 138, 141, 158, 165, 168
double consciousness, 50
double truth epistemology, 179
dreams, 21, 53, 71, 84–85, 170
dualism, 39, 68
duality, inner, 26–29, 33, 37
Du Bois, W.E.B., 50
Durkheim, Émile, 20, 51–53, 121, 128, 143

economic inequality, 51
ecstasies, 155
Eddington, Arthur, 39, 40
efficiency, 16
egalitarianism, 36, 106, 128, 133, 161, 176
egalitarian self, 130
ego-alter dialogue, 32
egocentricity, 14, 57, 61, 165
Eikhenbaum, Boris, 8, 72
elaborated code, 59–60
elective affinity, 122
electronic gadgets, 37
ellipsis, 57, 59, 60, 67
emotional process, 12
emotions, 16, 18, 21, 61; agency and, 77–79; "linguifying," 78; pragmatist views on, 97; self-awareness and, 159; self-regulation of, 68–69. *See also* self-feeling
empirical person, 92–93
empirical speech (parole), 57, 67, 70–73
enactment, 83–84, 111–113
enhancing self, 53–55
environmental voice, 140
epistemology, 49, 178–179
error, 15, 27, 63
European thought, 38
evolution, 99
exact analysis, 110
exemplification, 162
external world, 68

family members and friends in inner speech, 30–31
family resemblance, 132–133
field of control, 16
Fields, Chris, 10–11, 12, 17
field theory, 131

figurative devices, 4
Fisch, Max, 30
Fodor, Jerry, 5
foresight, 79
formal language (langue), 57, 67, 70–73
The Formal Method in Literary Scholarship (Bakhtin and Medvedev), 164
form versus content, 132
Foucault, Michel, 35, 48–49, 52
four causes, 18
free will, 80–83
Frege, Gottlob, 162, 166
Freud, Sigmund, 21, 24, 115, 143
frightened speech, 87
frustration, 77–78, 111
functions of inner speech, 17–21; daydreaming, 20–21; ordinary thinking, 17–18; self-control/self-regulation, 18–20

Garfinkel, Harold, 137
gays and lesbians, 140, 146–147
genders, 116
generalized other, 83, 89–90, 96–100, 152, 155, *156*, 170; development of, 114–117
generic level of self, *44*, 44–47, 49, 180
German thinkers, 82, 128, 179. *See also* Kant, Immanuel; Weber, Max
Gettysburg Address, 145
Giddens, Anthony, 89
glassy essence, 123
Gödel, Kurt, 110
God of prayer, 30, 31
Goethe, Johann Wolfgang von, 159
Goffman, Erving, 18, 20, 44, 47–48, 127, 137
Gogol, Nikolai, 167
Gopnik, Alison, 24
grammatical personhood, 160
grammatical theory, 56–57
group social attribution, 144

habit, 19, 44, 76, 152; establishing, via inner speech, 84–89; as unit of culture, 86, 113
habitus, 156
Heil, John, 39
Hobbes, Thomas, 6
Homer, 62
homunculus, 37
Hoopes, James, 91
hormonal secretions, 31
humanism, 133

human nature, inner speech as defining feature of, 6, 22, 91
Human Nature and Conduct (Dewey), 113
Human Nature and the Social Order (Cooley), 137, 149
Hume, David, 12
Husserl, Edmund, 10, 12, 17, 36, 40, 159, 162
Hymes, Dell, 66

"I," rise of, 62–63
I and me (present and past self), 9–10, *10*, 27, 30, 32, 65, 72–73, 92–93, 98–99
I and you (present and future self), 9–10, *10*, 30, 54, 72, 77–78, 95, 130, 175; and emotionally enhanced self-awareness, 159; in inner speech theory, 152–153, 155, 158–160
idealism, 38, 104–105
idealistic metaphysics, 68
ideal types, 70
identity, 35, 43–55, 179–180; as enhancing self, 53–55; as level of self, *44*, 44–46; review of issues regarding, 47–51; as sacred object, 43, 51–53; self versus, 47–48; singular and plural, 46; social and individual, 45–47, 49–51
I–generalized other conversation, 98–99
imagery, 58–59, 64, 69, 73; habit and, 84; as nonlinguistic language, 65
imaginary companion, 99–101, *103*
imaginative play, 3
imagistic semantics, 13
imagistic thinking, 14–15
I-me dialogical self, 9–10, 27, 30, 89, 90, 93, 95–99, 125, 152
I-me distinction, 92–93, 107, 126–127
I-me reflexivity approach, 126
individual, 144
individual identity, 45–47, 49–51
individualism, 49
"Individualism and the Intellectuals" (Durkheim), 51–53
individuation, 46
Industrial Revolution, 116
infinite regress, 37
inner speech: condensed quality of, 4; examples of, 3–8; internal dialogical polarity, 29–33, *33*; as language, 56–64; nature of, 2; not language, 74; peripheral forms of, 84–85

inner speech theory, 150–174; comparing Russians and Americans, 171–174; implications of Peirce-Mead approach, 154–163; I-you-me triad, 153–155, 158–162, 172–173, 175, 176; Peirce and Mead on, 151–154, *156*
inquiry, 17
institutional voices, 140, 142–143, 145, 149
intellectual synthesis, 110
intentionality, 40
interaction order, 70
interactive/conversational speech, 9
internal conversation, 102, *103*
internal dialogical polarity, 29–33, *33*
internalization, 22, 28–29, 31, 68–69, 90, 134, 143, 149; in inner speech theory, 152; movie example, 71–72; in pragmatist theory of self, 114–119
internal relations, 68–69
interpersonal dialogue, 7, 31–32, 78, 139
interpersonal relation, 114–115
interpersonal speech, 5
interpretation, 8, 72, 120, 161
interrogation/questioning, 28
intrapersonal dialogue, 7, 18, 31–32, 139, 159
introspection, 153–154
intuition, 11, 26, 104, 120–121
irreducible self, 129
"I-thou" (Buber), 32
I-you-me triad, 9–10, *10*, 12, 36, 54, 70–71, 83, 95, 130, 152; and comprehensive dialogicality, 157–158; in inner speech theory, 153–155, 158–162, 172–173, 175, 176; and network theory, 154–155

James, William, 8, 30, 61, 91; and free will and determinism, 81, 83; on habit, 85; on I-me distinction, 92–93, 107, 126; and internal dialogical polarity, 32; pragmatist theory of self and, 124–128; preliminary concepts of, 92–93; and self as internal dialogue, 91, 92; on self-feeling, 45, 48, 61, 92, 97, 110–111, 126–129; and stream of consciousness, 85, 92–93, 102–103, *103*, 107, 124–126, 157; on "worlds," 38, 53, 125
Jefferson, Thomas, 161, 176
Johnson, John, 4, 13, 57
Johnson, Samuel, 80
Joyce, James, 84, 141

Kant, Immanuel, 26–27, 35, 36, 48, 123
Kantian episteme, 35
Kaplan, Abraham, 17
Keynes, John Maynard, 89
key words, 60–61
King, Martin Luther, Jr., 146
knife-edge present, 119, 152, 157
Kuhnian paradigm, 49

labeling theory, 148–149
Lacan, Jacques, 16, 28, 29, 36, 63
language: as analytical device, 56; and differential theories of meaning, 57, 65–70; extralinguistic elements, 57, 61–62; history versus systematics of, 62–65; inner speech as, 56–64; as self-enclosed system, 66; two axes of, 57, 58–62, 66
langue (formal language), 57, 67, 70–73
law, 51, 142
Lincoln, Abraham, 161, 176
linearity of self, 37
linguistic conflict, 168–169
linguistic innovations, 15
linguistic rules, 4, 70
linguistics, 56, 151–152; Chomsky's, 56–57; Saussurian, 57–58, 66, 68, 73–74
linguistic self, 93, 105, 116
linguistic strings, 24
listening skills, 63
Locke, John, 43, 122
logic in use, 17–18
logic/reason, 17–18, 45; self-awareness as matter of, 27–28
Longfellow, Fanny, 112, 128
looking-glass self, 30–31, 50, 127, 134–138, *144*; group, 140; integrating Bakhtin and Cooley with, 145–148; limitations of, 141–145; minority status and, 140, 142, 143–144
love, 135
lovers' language, 8, 31
lucid dreams, 85

main world, 38
Marx, Karl, 82, 140
Marxism and the Philosophy of Language (Voloshinov), 164
A Marxist Critique (Voloshinov), 164
Marxist party line, 32, 97–98, 164
mass society, 37
materialism, 7–8, 35, 38–39, 125, 178

"maxisign," 41
"me," 62–63
Mead, George Herbert, 6, 14, 26, 28, 32, 41–42, 45, 72; Cooley's work and, 101; and free will and determinism, 81; and I-me dialogical self, 9–10, 27, 30, 89, 90, 93, 95–99, 126, 152; inner speech theory and, 150–163; pragmatist theory of self and, 113–120; on reflexivity, 92, 114, 126, 136–137; on role-taking, 29, 97, 116, 123; and self as internal dialogue, 91–92
meaning, 14, 24, 40; personal, 105–106; public, 103–105; theory of, 103–106, 108. *See also* semantics
mechanical reflexivity devices, 114
meditation, 17, 85
Medvedev, P. N., 164
Meichenbaum, Donald, 86–89
memory, 11, 43, 156; in childhood, 23
mentalese, 5
mental health, 46
mental illness, 73, 81, 180
mental language, 5, 6, 151
Merleau-Ponty, Maurice, 29, 36
Merton, Robert, 122, 161
metaphor, 4
metonymy, 4
mind as property bundle, 39
mind-body problem, 38–39, 179
mini-selves, 12
minority status, 50, 140, 142, 143–144; confrontation and, 145–146
mirror analogy, 123–124
mirror insight, 28–29, 36, 63
monological speech, 9
monologue, 10, 139–140
mood control, 19–20
mood disorders, 31
morality, 49, 94–98, 164–165, 168, 170–171; and generalized other, 116–117
mother/caretaker, 24, 63, 115–117, 135, 152
movies, 71–72
multiple realities, 53
Myrdal, Gunnar, 145

narrative, 141
nature, sphere of, 82
near-sleep experiences, 84–85
network theory, 154–155
neutralizing negative comments, 142
Nguyen, Michael, 5

Nietzsche, Friedrich, 48
nihilism, 168, 170–171
nominalism, 6
noncognitive discourse, 15
nondetermination, 80–83
nonmaterialistic concepts, 39
nonverbal thought, 11
nothingness, 122

object, 104, 170; and duality of self, 26–27, 29
obscurities within self, 11
Occam, 6
Occam's razor, 37
Oedipus and Electra complexes, 115–116
On the Aesthetic Education of Man (Schiller), 94–95
ontogenesis, 45, 62–65, 78, 99, 135
ontology, 80–81
oppression, 149
ordinary language, 57; inner speech as different from, 4, 5
origination of inner speech, 22–33; childhood syntax, 23–24; dialogical polarity, 29–33; inner duality, 26–29
outer experiences, 71–73
outer language, 15, 57–58, 62, 67, 70–71, 72, 169, 176
over-socialized view, 96, 101–102, 136

paradigmatic axis, 57, 58–62
paranoid fantasies, 85
Parisian intellectuals, 35
parole (empirical speech), 57, 67, 70–73
Parsons, Talcott, 102, 161
particular other, 117
passion, 97
Peirce, Charles Sanders, 6, 8, 9–10, 17, 42, 90; and dialogical self, 93–95, 124; and free will and determinism, 81; on habit, 85–86; on human nature, 6, 22, 91; inner speech theory and, 150–163; and internal dialogical polarity, 32; and I-you dyad, 9–10, 30, 54, 72, 78, 95, 130, 152, 155, 158–160, 175; and mirror analogy, 123–124; politics of, 121; pragmatist theory of self and, 120–124; and rediscovery of dialogical self, 93–95; and reflexivity, 92, 118, 126; and self as internal dialogue, 91–92, 102–103, *103*; on self-awareness as matter of reasoning, 27–28; on semiotic self, 120–123; on tuism, 30, 72, 158, 159; unpublished papers of, 6, 86, 94, 109, 154
Peirce, Herbert, 85, 112–113, 128
Peirce, James Mills, 121
Peirce's Approach to the Self (Colapietro), 6, 154
performative dialogue/practice, 11, 12
Perinbanayagam, Robert, 36, 41–42, 91, 109, 178
Ph.D. thesis process, 76–77
phenomenological awareness, 124
philosophical baby, 24
philosophy, 34, 38
Philosophy of Arithmetic (Husserl), 162
phobias, 86–89, 142
phonetic aspect of inner speech, 15
phylogenetic origins of self, 62, 78, 99, 117–118
physical appearance, 18
physical consequences, 104–105
physicalism, nonreductionist, 39
Piaget, Jean, 24–26
pidgin, 13, 58, 59
Pike, Kenneth, 66
Plato, 5
politics, 121, 164; of the self, 127–128
populist refutation of self, 36
positioning, 149
positivism, 104, 105, 178–179
postmodernism, 37, 106
post-structuralism, 35
practice, 11, 19; habits and, 85–86, 152; by imagining results, 19; and reflex arc, 111; rehearsal and enactment, 83–84, 111–113
pragmatism, 6, 77–78, 91–108, 176; Blumer and agency, 101–103; Cooley and imaginary companion, 99–101; Dewey and mental experiment, 99; James and preliminary concepts, 92–93; Meads and I-me dialogical self, 95–99; Peirce and rediscovery of dialogical self, 93–95; theory of meaning, 103–106
pragmatist theory of self, 109–133; Dewey and, 111–114; family resemblance in, 132–133; form versus content in, 132; general properties of, 129–131; James and, 124–128; Mead and, 113–120; Peirce and, 120–124; use of pronouns in, 119–120. *See also* self

Index

prayer, 30
predication, 13, 15, 58, 166
preexisting language, inborn, 5
present: and I-me distinction, 9–10, 27, 30, 32, 65, 72–73, 92–93, 98–99; knife-edge and saddle-back, 119, 152, 157
presentation of self, 18, 47–48, 137
The Presentation of Self in Everyday Life (Goffman), 47–48
pride, 137
primates, 99, 117–118
primitives, 45
private language, 2, 25, 57, 167, 176
private speech (thinking aloud), 3, 5–6, 13, 22–26, 63, 165, 176; Vygotsky-Piaget debate, 24–26
problem solving, 99–100, 111
Project 500 program, 146–147
pronouns, 29, 32, 96–97, 119–120; and parole and langue, 70–72
property: metaphor of, 126–127, 129; morality centered on, 170–171
property dualism, 7, 39
proto-emotion, 48
psychological construction, 80
psychology, 40, 93, 107, 113
public meanings, 103–105
purposive human action, 76

qualia, 125
quotidian level of self, *44*, 44–47, 180

racism, 7, 50, 86, 107, 115, 121, 122–123, 128, 145, 161
rationality, 121
rationalization, 52
reading, 24
reality construction, 20
reconstructed logic, 17
referent, 161
referential theories of meaning, 57, 65–70; parole and langue, 70–73
reflex arc, 111
reflexivity, 29, 35, 36, 37, 92, 114, 116, 118, 126; mechanical/partial, 40–41
refrigerator-light theory of self, 37, 169
rehearsal, 11, 111–113
relation, 37, 66
relational self, 130
religion, 51–52, 104
Religion of Humanity, 52

religious rituals, 20
re-minoritization, 51
researcher bias, 143–144
responsivity, 139, 169
restricted code, 59–60
results, imagining, 19
ritual, inner, 12, 19–20, 167
Rochberg-Halton, Eugene, 91
role, 149
role-taking, 29, 97, 116, 123, 136, 169
Russian theorists, 138; comparing Russians and Americans, 171–174; in Stalin era, 164. *See also* Bakhtin, Mikhail; Vygotsky, Lev
Ryle, Gilbert, 36, 38

Sacks, Oliver, 1–2, 23, 175
sacred self, 51–53, 127, 128, 130
saddle-back present, 119, 152, 157
sameness, 43
Sartre, Jean-Paul, 36, 118, 169
Saussure, Ferdinand de, 56–58; on history versus systematics, 62–65; on internal relations, 68–69; on the signifier, 58; on two axes of language, 57, 58–62, 66
Scheff, Thomas, 135, 137
Schiller, Friedrich, 94–95
Scholastics, 5, 6, 93, 121
Schütz, Alfred, 159
science, 39, 52
secrecy, 67
self, 34–42, 178–179; as capitalist trick, 36; as computer, 38, 39–41, 114, 151–152; constituents of self as, 36; as elitist concept, 35; as identity, 35; identity as level of, *44*, 44–46; identity versus, 47–48; as illusion, 36; as immortal soul, 38; as internal dialogue, 6, 22, 42, 64, 91; as language effect, 35; as legal entity, 36; multiple meanings of, 34; as nothingness, 37; sacred, 51–53, 127, 128, 130; as sign, 89, 120–123, 161–162; as story about "itself," 38; as time, 41; tripartite, *44*, 44–47. *See also* pragmatist theory of self
self-acceptance, 159
"self" and "other" pair, 31–32
self-awareness, 46, 79, 158–159; computers' lack of, 40–41
self-body problem, 39
self-compliments, 142
self-concept, 46, 156

self-control/self-regulation, 6, 18–20, 65, 68–69; childhood private speech and, 22, 25
self-deceit, 118–119
self-definition, 46
self-esteem, 142
self-evidence, 170
self-feeling, 45, 48, 61, 92, 97, 110–111, 126–129, 156; I-me distinction and, 126–127; as reflexivity, 136–137. *See also* emotions
self-interaction., 101–102, *103*
self-love, 159
self-other dialogue, 32
self-recognition, 28–29
self-refutation process, 110
self-work, 136
semantic embeddedness, 14, 40
semantics, 5, 12–14, 24, 38; differential versus referential word meaning, 65–70. *See also* meaning: theory of
semiotic nature of self, 41, 93–94, 120–123, 161
semiotics, 86, 93–94, 104–105, 107, 121–122, 131, 151, 176
semiotic self, 120–123
sexual adventure daydream, 21
Shakespeare, William, 6, 123
shame, 135, 137
shortcuts, 8, 57
sign, self as, 89, 120–123, 161–162
significant symbol, 97
signifier, 58
sign language, 64
silence, 57, 58, 85, 149
silent movies, 8
Singer, Jerome, 3, 4, 13, 21
skills improvement, 19
sleep, 53
sleep talk, 16–17
social class, 35
social conflict, 168–169
social construction, 20, 80, 82, 149
social-demographic traits, 45, 47
social facts, 121, 143
social identity, 45–47, 49–51
social justice, 107
social movements, 149
social sciences, 6, 40, 74, 75, 105, 131, 179
socioeconomic class, 49–51
Socrates, 12, 18, 44, 151

soliloquies, 6, 10
soothing effects, 104
soul, 38, 118
Soviet Union, 42
special worlds, 38, 53
speed of inner speech, 60
split consciousness, 71–72
Stalin era, 135, 164
stream of consciousness, 5, 7–8, 25, 85, 92–93, 102–103, *103*, 107, 124–126, 157
structural features of inner speech, 5, 9–17, 155–156; circular, 10–15; dialogicality, 12–13; phonetic, 15; possible objection to, 15–17; semantics and syntax, 12–14
structuralism, 66–67
structure, 140–141
subjectivity, 48–49, 159
substantive rationality, 52
superaddressee, 170
syntagmatic axis, 57, 58–62, 66
syntax, 12–14, 30, 38, 40; childhood, 23–24; predicated, 13, 15, 58, 166
systematics, 62–65

tabula rasa, 122
Tate, Loren, 147
Taylor, Marjorie, 100
temporality/time, 8, 30, 41, 96, 118, 156–157, 175; diachronic versus synchronic, 57; as pincer-like movement, 160–161
themes of inner speech, 4
theory of mind, 133
thinking aloud. *See* private speech (thinking aloud)
third-person epistemology, 178–179
Thomas, W. I., 80, 102
traits, 134–135
traumas, 143
triadic self, 9–10, 12, 36, 54, 83, 130
trial and error, 12
tuism, 30, 72, 158, 159
two tables, 39

Ulysses (Joyce), 84, 105, 141
unanticipated consequences, 122
unconscious, 143; emotional, 16; and sleep talk, 16–17
unconscious stream of thought, 5
understanding, 40
unfinished business, daydreams as, 21

United States, 42
University of Chicago, 101, 128, 151
University of Illinois at Champaign-Urbana, 140, 146–147
University of Michigan, 101
urban industrial model, 63
U.S. Constitution, 50

Valli, Frankie, 18
Varieties of Religious Experience (James), 92
verbalizing thoughts, 18
vocabulary, 14, 73, 167, 176
vocalizations, 6
voice, 134, 138–141, 148–149, 168
Voloshinov, V. N., 164
voluntarism, 130
Vygotsky, Lev, 12–15; and debate with Piaget, 24–26; and implicit self-other dialogue, 31–32; inner speech theory and, 150, 158, 163–167; and internal dialogical polarity, 32; on internalization of outer speech, 22, 24; Marxist party line and, 32, 97–98; on predicated syntax, 13, 15, 58, 166; and private speech theory, 5, 19, 22–26, 163, 176

"Walk Like a Man" (Valli), 18
"Walter Mitty" routines, 20, 31
Weber, Max, 49, 51, 70, 82, 117, 122, 127–128, 130, 132, 140, 169; on ideal types, 70; on rationalization, 52
Weir, Morton, 148
Wiley, Katie, 4, 13
will to believe, 104
wish fulfillment, 21
Wittgenstein, Ludwig, 57
word selection, 57, 58
"worlds," 38, 53, 61, 125
worry, 20, 136
writers, 59

Norbert Wiley is Emeritus Professor of Sociology at the University of Illinois, Urbana, and the author of *The Semiotic Self*.